The author of four critically acclaimed books, *Mississippi Solo, Native Stranger, South of Haunted Dreams,* and *Still Life in Harlem,* EDDY L. HARRIS has generated the kind of notice and praise that attends the rise of only the finest talents. As America's premier African-American memoirist and travel writer, he has written with emotional depth and courage about the Mississippi River, Africa, the South, and Harlem respectively in these books. A graduate of Stanford University, he has also studied in London and has been a screenwriter and journalist. He lives in St. Louis, Missouri.

MISSISSIPPI SOLO

A RIVER QUEST

EDDY L. HARRIS

A Holt Paperback
Henry Holt and Company
New York

Holt Paperbacks
Henry Holt and Company, LLC
Publishers since 1866
175 Fifth Avenue
New York, New York 10010
www.henryholt.com

Library of Congress Cataloging-in-Publication Data

Harris, Eddy L.
Mississippi solo: a river quest / Eddy L. Harris.—1st Holt paperbacks ed.
p. cm.
Originally published: New York, N.Y.: N. Lyons Books, c 1988
ISBN-13: 978-0-8050-5903-8
ISBN-10: 0-8050-5903-2
1. Mississippi River—Description and travel. 2. Canoes and canoeing—Mississippi River. 3. Harris, Eddy L.—Journeys—Mississippi River. 4. Afro-Americans—Travel—Mississippi River.
I. Title.

F355.H37 1998 98-24706
917.704'33—dc21 CIP

Henry Holt books are available for special promotions
and premiums. For details contact: Director, Special Markets.

Originally published in hardcover in 1988 by Nick Lyons Books

First Holt Paperbacks Edition 1998

Printed in the United States of America

D 20 19 18 17 16 15 14 13 12 11

To my Uncle Robert

How can I get away without a word of thanks to the many people who brought me here, who helped make possible the dream and the dreaming and the reality? Some of them are old friends, some new, some strangers in passing. All are important; most know who they are. A few I am compelled to mention: Ralph and Robin and Roxy. Walter and Harry and Joe. Peter and Nick. Doris and Lee and Brian and Beckie and CooChung. And of course, my family: Sam and Georgia, Tommy and Camilla, without whom . . . .

And since determination is fueled as much by doubters as by supporters, let me also thank those who said it couldn't be done.

I do not know much about gods; but I think that the river
Is a strong brown god—sullen, untamed and intractable . . .
Unhonoured, unpropitiated
By worshippers of the machine, but waiting, watching and waiting . . .
The river is within us.

—T. S. Eliot
The Dry Salvages

1

THE MISSISSIPPI RIVER is laden with the burdens of a nation. Wide at St. Louis where I grew up, the river in my memory flows brown and heavy and slow, seemingly lazy but always busy with barges and tugs, always working—like my father—always traveling, always awesome and intimidating. I have watched this river since I was small, too young to realize that the burdens the Mississippi carries are more than barges loaded with grain and coal, that the river carries as well sins and salvation, dreams and adventure and destiny. As a child I feared this river and respected it more than I feared God. As an adult now I fear it even more.

I used to have nightmares filled with screams whenever I knew my family planned some excursion across the river and I'd have to go along. That old Veteran's Bridge seemed so weak and rickety. My imagination constructed a dilapidated and shaky span of old wooden slats, rotted and narrow and weak with no concrete support anywhere. The iron girders that held the poor thing up were ancient and rusty, orange and bumpy with oxidation where they should have been shiny and black. The bridge wavered in the wind and was ready to collapse as the car with my family in it approached, and then we would plunge through the air after crashing the brittle wooden guardrail and we'd dive toward the river. Everyone screamed but me. I held my ears every time and waited for the splash. It never came. I always awoke, always lived to dream the dream again and again, not only when asleep but even as we crossed the river.

The river was full of giant catfish and alligators, ice floes and trees that an often enraged and monster-like river had ripped from the shores along its path.

The Mississippi. Mighty, muddy, dangerous, rebellious, and yet a strong, fathering kind of river. The river captured my imagination when I was young and has never let go. Since I can remember I have wanted to be somehow a part of the river as much as I wanted to be a hero, strong and brave and relentless like the river, looming so large in the life and world around me that I could not be ignored or forgotten. I used to sit on the levee and watch the murkiness lumber down to the sea and I'd dream of the cities and towns the river had passed, the farms and fields and bridges, the magic in the debris picked up here, deposited there, and the other rivers along the way: Ohio, Illinois, Arkansas, taking all on a beautiful voyage to the Gulf of Mexico and beyond. I wanted to go too. I wanted to dip first my toes in the water to test, then all of me, hanging onto whatever and floating along with it, letting the river drop me off wherever and pick me up later and take me on again. I didn't care where, I just wanted to go. But my parents wouldn't let me.

But now I am a man and my parents can't stop me. I stand at that magical age, thirty, when a man stops to take stock of his life and he reflects on all the young-man's dreams that won't come true. No climbs up Everest, no try-out with the Yankees, no great American novel. Instead, reality: wives and babies and mortgages, pensions, security and the far-away future. No great risks. No more falling down. No more skinned knees. No great failures. I wondered: is all this inevitable?

I've never minded looking stupid and I have no fear of failure. I decided to canoe down the Mississippi River and to find out what I was made of.

2

ONCE THEY HAVE REACHED a certain age, dreamers are no longer held in high esteem. They are ridiculed instead, called loony and lazy, even by their friends. Especially by their friends!

Dreams are delicate and made of gossamer. They hang lightly on breezes and suspend as if from nothing. The slightest wind can tear them apart. My dream was buffeted by my friends. What the hell for? they asked me. What are you trying to prove? Why don't you just go over Niagara Falls in a barrel?

And this was from my friends. God, how that hurt. One friend even told me to take a bus, for God's sake. Instead of helping me fly, my friends were pulling me down, and laughing at me.

Putting a canoe into the headwaters of the Mississippi and aiming it for New Orleans is not something a man is supposed to do. It is not considered normal or sane. Perhaps it is the danger involved, or perhaps it is too much an act of desire and determination, an act of passion and volition, or simply too out of the ordinary.

For whatever reasons, my idea met with disapproval, and instead of childish jubilation I approached canoeing the river with doubt and sorrow—sorrow because the glory with which I first came upon this adventure was dashed by friends. Like Galileo before the Church, I was ready to relinquish my radical approaches and be normal.

But this dream of mine, still suspended on the breeze and delicate as ever, was just as real as those flimsy summer spider webs hanging in the air, and just as clinging. Once the webs attach themselves to you they are hard to get rid of. And so it was with my desire to ride the river.

3

A MAN BLESSED with a flood of ideas has the luxury to squander them, to sift through his wealth until he finds the right idea for the right occasion. He may lose a great many of them, but he can afford it.

When a man has only one great notion, it becomes all the more valuable, a jewel, a prized and noble possession. He cherishes it like a kid with his last stick of candy. He guards it, he secretes it away, taking it out every night at bedtime just to look at it, to hold it up to the light and ponder it and wonder just when to taste it at last, all the while being haunted by its existence and his burning desire to hurry up with it. An obsession.

For weeks I ached with the thought of doing the river. But I had no canoe. I had no camping gear. I had no money. The initial reaction from my friends had left me secretive and without allies to support even spiritually my idiotic plan. And pretty soon it would be too late to go. Already it was the first week of October and Minnesota, where I would start, had seen its first snowfall.

One friend came to mind and I turned to him not because he could help give birth to this dream I had, but because of all the people I knew, Robert would at least listen to me and not tell me I was crazy. He would not tell me to give it up.

He was an old man, and every time I went to see him I was sure it would be the last I'd see him alive. He's been my special friend since long before I can remember, more like an uncle than just some old man I knew and liked, the kind of friend who will always understand. He is always your last resort, when he should be your first. An old man from a long time ago when every problem could be solved with a couple of drinks and a couple of hours of talking—with him mostly listening. When you need good advice, the one to turn to is the one who listens well; the best talk, the best advice comes from yourself.

Robert and I used to drink sodas together, back when he tried to teach me music. About the time I was heading off for college, I graduated to beer. Tonight I would be doing advanced studies. Tonight, he did most of the talking.

A skinny black man with a head shaped like a peanut, Robert had very little hair and what hair he did have he wore cut so close to his scalp it looked more like razor stubble. He always wore a fedora, either grey or brown, even indoors.

Normally I would come to him and he'd be working on the transmission of his car or taking his stereo apart and putting it back together. He was always tinkering with something and there was junk lying all around. I'd come over and watch him and hint in roundabout fashion that something was bothering me and he'd tinker patiently with me and we'd take our time until we'd squeezed the problem out. Then we'd have a look at it and a drink.

But not today. Today he wanted to get right to it, as if he were in a hurry. Not that he had someplace to get to, but a different kind of hurry, as if he hadn't much time to waste anymore.

"Well, let's get to it," he said. And I knew this session was going to be different from all the others. If there was any advice or wisdom to offer, he was going to give it out straight and not have me scratch around until I found it.

"I haven't seen you in a long time," he said. "Something must be bothering you. What is it?"

I felt like a worm of a man who only calls his friends when he needs some favor. But more than that, I felt all the frustration that surged through Robert and made the squiggly vein in his temple twitch, frustration I was noticing for the first time.

I told him my plans, that I was going to do the river. I told him the obstacles that blocked me, that I still had no canoe, no gear, no money, and that everyone I knew had said it was impossible and stupid. And he said:

"Don't you listen to them. They got no imagination. They got no vision. And it makes them jealous because you do, and they'll try to stop you, try to change you. But don't you let them."

It was not advice. It was a command.

Robert had at one time been a wonderful tap dancer. His apartment was littered with photos and newspaper clippings and momentos of when he and his partner used to tear up the boards on the circuit. Their special routine: standing back to front, only inches apart and dancing in unison, so swiftly as to be a blur, their timing so exquisite that from head on you could see the movements of only one man. The big time called, movies, New York, but he never went. He never said why, but now I had a glimpse.

He turned instead to music, taught himself the trombone, played in local jazz bands and learned music so well that he did most of the arrangements for the bands he played in. Again there was a chance for the big time. Again he stayed in St. Louis.

He got married, had children, and settled into a normal job. The closest he got to music any more was teaching it to me. He used to give me trumpet lessons. The jobs he settled for were all a black man in those days could expect: shining shoes, being a custodian in office buildings and schools, mopping and polishing floors, cleaning desks and mending broken things.

He reached across the table and grabbed me. His fingers were long and bony, his hands strong from building things. He held me by the wrists and squeezed me hard.

"I know you can do it," he said. "I have confidence in you. Always have."

Canoeing? Writing?

His eyes gathered in the soft light around us and sparkled with a thousand secrets.

"And maybe there ain't nobody else who does," he whispered, "but we don't much care what they think about us no how. Do we?"

The old man licked his lips, his dry-looking tongue flicking out past his dentures, feeling the air and smacking his lips lightly as if he were tasting something. He wore an expression I took to be sadness, but maybe it was just fatigue or longing. Maybe it was the inevitable expression of commingled jealousy and exhortation an old man finds when he knows his time has come and gone and all he can do is pass the baton.

He pulls down a bottle of whiskey from the shelf and one glass. Before he comes to sit again he pauses and looking down at me he shifts the false teeth in his mouth and nods to himself with a satisfied smile. He grabs a second glass from the shelf and slides it across to me. Without a word, Robert was telling me plenty.

He leaned in close. His eyes squinted, studying me.

We sat quietly just like that for a moment. I squirmed in my seat until we drank. Our drinking is clean, without ceremony. No clinking of glasses, no toasts. Just eyes locked, his on mine, and the simultaneous raising of glasses to lips.

The whiskey burns. I emit a noise you might hear in a cartoon. Robert screws up his face as though suffering with each swallow. He clears his throat with a guttural, teeth-clenched "Aaah!"

When he finally speaks, he whispers.

"Are you afraid?"

"Well," I reply. "I'm no expert canoeist. I swim okay, but—"

"That's not what I mean."

"What else is there to be afraid of? Drowning? Freezing to death? Wild animals? Or just not being able to take it?"

"Well," he says. "If you get out and you can't take it, that sure is going to mess with your mind. How you deal with failure is just as important as the failure itself, but that's not what I'm talking about neither."

He reaches slowly for the bottle and he pours. This time, before we drink, he tilts his glass toward me.

"You're black too, you know," he says. His smile is cunning. "Or have you forgotten?"

"I haven't forgotten, but so what? What's that got to do with anything?"

He takes a long slow sip and sneaks a peek at me from over the rim of his glass.

"What is it you're wanting to do?"

"Canoe the Mississippi."

"From where?"

"From the beginning."

"And where's that?"

"In Minnesota."

"In Minnesota," he repeats. "Do you know how many black people there are in Minnesota? About six."

He takes another sip.

"And how far you planning to go?"

"New Orleans."

"Through the South," he said. He sips again. "From where there ain't no black folks to where they still don't like us much. I don't know about you, but I might be a little concerned about that."

Then I see the river. First as a blue line on a map. Then, as Robert talks on and I see myself out there, a black man alone and exposed and vulnerable, the blue line blurs and fragments until there is more than one Mississippi River. There is the river of legend, the Father of Waters. The river of steamboats and gamblers. The river flowing with the tears and sweat of slaves. I can hear the beating of Indian drums and the singing of slaves resting in the shade of plantation willows on the banks of the old man river. The river has come alive in my mind, the sights, sounds and smells of the river in my imagination.

But I know the river won't be like that, fur trappers in buckskin shirts, paddlewheelers piled high with bales of cotton, Indian canoes sliding silently. I know it won't be like that, but I don't know what to expect. If I had any idea before of how it might be, I don't now.

Robert says to me: "Did you ever stop to think that your friends might not want you to do this because it might be dangerous?"

"No, I never did. They just made fun of me."

"You know how friends are. Maybe it's their way of saying they don't want you to get hurt."

I hesitate. "Maybe." I'm not convinced.

"Maybe they don't want you to get shot by some redneck in the woods. Maybe they don't want you to fall in and drown. Or maybe they're trying to protect you from something else."

"What's that?"

"You see, everybody thinks his way is the right way. The Bible-bangers think God is the answer. A man with a wife and kids and a house and a good job, if he's happy with them all, he thinks that's where satisfaction comes from. Everybody thinks he knows what's best so when a friend comes by with a different way, especially a risky way, you want to save him. You see?"

"I see," I say, but I'm really confused. "But what about imagination and vision? What about jealousy?"

"Oh, I'm not saying they're not jealous. Envy is what fuels their convictions. When a man secretly wants what you have and maybe he's ashamed of it and maybe he knows he can never have it, that's when he goes out of his way most to make it seem worthless. Just like some men are reassured by other people's failure. That's where vision and imagination come in."

"Without vision and imagination," Robert says softly, "you never look for your own path to glory. And glory can mean Mount Everest or Nobel Prizes or a wife and kids and security. It can even be canoeing down the Mississippi. But it takes vision to see what shoes fit you and what shoes fit the other guy. And the thing to remember is: don't take it all so serious. Failure is horrible, but it's not the worst thing there is."

4

ROBERT, A WEAK OLD MAN with absolutely no power over me—with my bare hands I could snap him in two like a pencil between my fingers—and yet it was he who had the power to set me free. Old people and children, frailty and innocence: they seem so innocuous that we battle them laughing and unarmed, like David and Goliath. Then they beat us with magic.

I toppled from my perch of indignation and admitted to myself that maybe I was being foolish in wanting to do the river, maybe I was wrong. I still wanted to do it, but I was trying at least to see the objections.

I hadn't thought before of any genuine concern. When my friend Walter suggested I tow along behind me a second canoe—like a spare tire in case of emergency—I thought he was making fun of me. (The suggestion was a little crazy.) But now I could see Barbara's fear for my safety when she wanted me to pack a walkie-talkie—just in case.

And never before had I considered jealousy. I had figured any opposition was pettiness and spite. Now there existed the possibility that they'd love to dream such dreams, to take such journeys but could not and resented me because I could. Until I opened my mind to their motives I could never admit that there lurked within the darker corners of my soul my own jealousies and simpler longings, like when I hug a friend's wife or carry their baby or lie on the floor in the warmth and coziness of their home. Only then could I see the merits of their chosen style and admit that my style was part rebellion but also in part reassurance that my choices, risky and exciting and unconventional, were the right ones.

Because of an old man, I could approach my less-traveled roads more securely, less troubled and without the feeling that I am in some sort of competition. Without that extra burden, I opened up. I could admit my desires and acknowledge my deficiencies and fears. And suddenly friends came to the rescue, just as friends are supposed to do.

Enthusiasm becomes contagion. When Brian says, "Tremendous idea. Do it!" the feeling is one of jubilation; there is approval at last, the butressing of those tender spots.

When Bobby C. reaches out in that quiet and soft voice that's almost a whisper and says, "You're going to make it. It just takes time, but I know you're going to make out," there is sadness at not having much to show for all the years of dreaming, the struggling and the failing, and there is pressure to perform, to pull back up and try again and make people proud. And there is, of course, determination. *Damn right, I'll make it!*

And when Robinovich catches fire with my fever, it's as if I had known all the time that I'd make this journey. She gets so caught up in the excitement that she wants me to go as much as I want to go myself. She wants to go too, but can't. She can, however, drive me up to Minnesota when the time comes and, wonder of wonders, she knows where I can borrow a canoe. If not for Robinovich. . . .

Late on a Friday night in mid-October, ten days after the first snow has fallen on Minneapolis, Robinovich and I left St. Louis and headed north for Lake Itasca, the river's source.

Armed with a purple rabbit's foot and a plastic Jesus, a St. Christopher and some miracle dirt from a shrine in Sanctuario de Chimayó in New Mexico, and for warmth a bottle of tequila, we were far too excited to be scared.

5

AND THERE—Oh my God!—it is. Lake Itasca in all its pristine glory.

The air is as pure as the kiss from a child at bedtime and very cold and very clear, its sharp edges stinging my nose with every deep breath I take, but so sweet in its purity that I take breath after painful breath until my face hurts and my eyes water.

The sun hangs low in the southwest sky about to set behind ranges of trees stretching endlessly in every direction. As the sky sheds one layer of light and color for another hue, a darker hue edging toward purple, the air cools off even more. Any other time, any other day, I might be hopping around frowning and shouting and hating the cold. But not this day, for too much has gone into my getting here and far too much emanates *from* here, and cold though I am anu chilled right through, I am as giddy as a child on champagne and just as excitedly foolish. I dance and jig and flit from here to there wearing no coat nor sweater. My flannel shirt is plenty warm for I am finally and emphatically here. Lake Itasca. And it is truly splendor and beauty.

Robinovich watches me, laughing at me. She is bundled up and ready for winter. She probably thinks I'm crazy, but she knows me well so it's all right. She knows I'm crazy. For the past few hours since we entered this land of green pine, blue skies and lakes, she has suffered through my oohs and aahs and other exclamations of delight as I absorbed the beauty of northern Minnesota.

"One," I'd shout, then, "there's one, and two and three . . ." as I tried to count the lakes we passed to see if really there are ten thousand in this state as the motto claims.

Ten thousand lakes, I don't know. But there are plenty and the land around all covered with tall timber, pine and birch trees white and speckled like dalmatians, and lakes everywhere that remind me of the north of Sweden. Winters here must be equally severe so it's no wonder this land was settled by Swedes. Nothing in this world could remind them so much of the beauty and harshness of their home.

Robinovich is still laughing. I laugh too just thinking about how funny I must appear. And what a sight we must have looked driving up here. Sporty red car with an eighteen-foot green canoe on top, in late autumn, in the cold and in the wind. Being shoved about on the highway by that wind and having to stop every so often to readjust the ropes that lashed canoe to car. Long after the season for recreational boats of size and strength. And here we were out with a canoe? No wonder we took our share of stares.

"Lake Itasca? In that thing?"

At Avon, a stone's throw of a town in either direction, the man pumping gas for us frowned in a most peculiar way at the very notion of it. He held his laughter very well, however, and spoke with a straight face, but I'm glad I didn't tell him the whole plan.

"It's a beautiful spot up there all right, but I don't know if I'd want to be out on the lake today. Why in the world did you pick this time of year to go canoeing?"

"Took me this long to round up the canoe. But it's not too cold, do you think?"

I was shivering in the wind while we talked. He looked at me like I was crazy.

"Better wait til tomorrow just the same," he advised. "Gonna get colder, but this wind should die down some by then."

He was right. The next day did turn colder. But it was cold enough right then and I went and huddled inside his little gas station and waited for him to finish pumping the gas. He didn't need my help out there.

It was a little station, one set of pumps. The whole set-up came straight out of old photos of the South. Small station big enough for maybe three cars at a time. Any more than that and they'd spill out into the street, which wouldn't have been any major crime, in this little town.

Inside there was little warmth, only a break from the wind. These Minnesotans must be tough, I figured, and when he came back in, I told him so. He smiled.

"Yeah, well," he said. "I guess you get used to anything."

He brushed off my comment casually, but I could see he took it as a compliment, with pride.

"You think this is cold," he said. "Wait til winter sets in. Freezing winds, snow up to your elbows and nothing but grey all around. Those who can't take it get on out. But it's like anything else; all depends on what you're used to."

Then he took down one of the maps he had for sale and unfolded it among the clutter of tools and tires and grime, and he showed me the route to the lake.

A small kindness, and at the time I thought nothing of it. He showed me the route, and I let him. I already knew the way, of course, but if he wanted to be helpful, who was I to spit on his generosity. Goodness takes two: giver and receiver. Besides, he might have known a short-cut. But he didn't.

On leaving Avon, my mind turned back to Robert and what he'd said about going from "where there ain't no black folks to where they still don't like us much." And I thought about being black.

For me, being black has never been such a big deal, more a physical characteristic rather like being tall: an identifier for the police and such. Part of my identity, but not who I am.

I do not intend to imply that I would be exactly the same person if I were not black—any more than if I were not tall—but I'll leave it to the existentialists to debate how I might have turned out if I'd been Chinese and short, or what other preoccupations I might have if I weren't losing my hair. As far as I have always been concerned, I'm who I am from the inside to the out, not the other way around. I never gave great importance to how people reacted to my being black or tall or bald. What mattered most was how I reacted—to all my assets and deficiencies.

But suddenly being black, as well as being tall, took on new meaning. Being tall because of the long journey ahead with me sitting cross-legged in a canoe. Being black because of how I would perceive and be perceived.

The gas station man in Avon had treated me just as I would have expected him to: with courtesy, kindness and respect. Was this how I was going to be treated all the way down the river, with kindness? If so, I wouldn't mind. But I'd be less than thrilled if I were looked on kindly because there were no other blacks around to set the tone, just as I'd be disappointed if people mistreated me because of their exposure to blacks. I would most like to witness some general goodness in the human soul pouring out to strangers, and barring that, I'd want people to give me a chance to make my own imprint on them—for good or for bad—and then their behavior toward me would be based on me. Too selfish? Too simplistic? Well maybe. But I hoped that's what the gas station man's behavior was a reflection of: my being a thoroughly charming and friendly fellow, and he was only reciprocating.

But still the haunting question: where are all the black folks?

I had seen one little black kid playing in front of a house along the road we traveled, but that was way back in Iowa. There must be some in Minnesota, but where were they?

And a better question: why weren't they?

It is perhaps startling to realize that there are places blacks don't much go to.

For obvious reasons, blacks don't lie on the beach much or hang out by the pool.

Blacks aren't often found cruising the bazaars in Bankok, or sliding down the ski slopes. Finances could be a problem, but the travel magazines seem not to want blacks to travel, or think that blacks don't travel, or maybe just don't care. The advertisement photos rarely—extremely rarely—show blacks enjoying exotic holiday destinations. Why?

And why aren't there very many blacks in Minnesota? Too cold in winter? Safety in numbers? Small town conservatism and bigotry? More jobs in the major industrialized urban centers? Or are there some more subtle rules being worked?

I went to a wonderful bluegrass music festival in Park City, Utah, high up in the Uinta Mountains. Sunshine, spectacular scenery, fabulous musicians. I was the only black face there. Why? Because blacks don't want to listen to certain kinds of music? Because blacks don't like the mountains and crisp clear air? Or because blacks feel there are certain places where they don't belong, certain things they can and cannot do? Is the exclusion self-imposed or by hints both subtle and overt?

You don't find many blacks canoeing solo down the Mississippi River and camping out every night. Why not? Are there evils out there to greet them if they do?

I never thought the things I did were so remarkable. My getting to travel and see so much of the world I pinned on restlessness and good fortune. Good fortune, yes, but maybe more. Maybe a quiet statement that this world has too much to offer for me not to want to reach out with arms wide, that there is too much good music and good food and scenic beauty and I want to sample it all, that there is no place on earth where I can't go, where I don't belong, and nothing I can't do. Forget about taboos and accepted patterns and fears—even common sense. The only restrictions are the ones I (we all) put in place.

But for all my boldness and my reaching out to embrace the world, what would be waiting for me out there on the river?

Kindness or evil? Beauty or savagery? Whatever, I didn't want to miss a thing. The up days would make up for the down, I knew; the beauty is worth the pain.

Itasca is worth every agony of getting here. For here, quite possibly, is the most beautiful place on earth.

The beauty surrounding Lake Itasca is so quiet. Other sites of sheer beauty—the Alps, the Himalayas, expansive seas and deserts—blare their splendor and overwhelm the beholder. But so pristene and serene in its beauty is this place, it can hardly be called majestic or imposing, overpowering or breathtaking. Instead, it whispers at you. It calls and sings sweetly, bathing you in melody that you finally notice and eventually feel and see, misting around you like a warm morning fog in spring, bathing you in delight and soothing you until you are at the same time both silent and on the edge of shouting with joy. It's not a Gothic cathedral, but a lovely little chapel whose absolute artistry you do not expect, and you're awestricken.

Itasca. From the Latin *verITAS CAput,* the true head, the real as opposed to any spurious source of the great river. The birth of a river, the calm before the rage.

Robinovich and I have stopped the car near the park ranger's office. We need to register and pick out a campsite before dark. I don't want to. I'm too anxious to get around to the outlet of the lake where the river begins, but Robinovich, the voice of reason, insists.

So okay. We'll go register, but the campsite can wait. I want to find the river. I'm like a kid who just can't deal with the vegetables for the nagging thoughts of dessert.

We manage to conclude the business quickly and rush back to the little road winding around the lake another mile or so to the north. After a few quick steps down the path and through the trees, there it is. Gurgling, cooing gently, the great river is just a baby.

Around here the lake is a still sheet of blue. As blue as the sky. (Minisota: a Dakota Indian word which means water painted blue like the sky.) Tall trees border the water and shield it from the wind. The trees rise up high but also lie upside down across the water. The lake is a mirror. I see everything twice.

A cloud of loons skirts low over the surface of the lake then lifts high and banks around the bend out of sight. Their cries are loud and wild.

The sun is going down, shadows are long, everything is swathed in hues of yellow and gold. Along the edge where the lake is shallow, marsh grass grows the color of ripening wheat and creates a fake shoreline extending out ten yards or so. It looks solid and thick enough to walk on, but it's not.

And just south of those golden reeds, the bank of the lake turns in, receding like an old man's hairline. Big rocks stretch across the opening almost as if to stop the flow, but there is no stopping this spill. The little flow of water which babbles playfully over these rocks is the start of something. Like a snowball down a mountain. Like the storming of the Bastille. Like a great upheaval whose time has come.

My God! The greatest river in the world. The Ojibway Indians call this river Mesipi: the great river. Other tribes call it Father of Waters. The Volga has been called the Russian Mississippi, the Murray-Darling has been called the Mississippi of Australia. But the Mississippi is compared to none. It is the yardstick, the standard for greatness. And here, it's just a creek. I stand on the rocks and feel mighty. My shoes don't even get wet. A child could walk safely across here.

Maybe ten feet wide, about twelve inches deep, clear and clean enough to be drinkable. The creek bed is pebbly. The river is not at all the muddy monster that rolls by St. Louis. It hardly seems even a distant relative.

I leave the river with a casual wave. "See you tomorrow."

It's nearly dark now and time to make camp.

6

PITCHING CAMP is a breeze. Modern tents are so simple, especially the one I've brought, I could set it up in five minutes in the dark. And in fact I was so quick getting it up and done with,

Robinovich and I had time for a leisurely stroll in the woods before dark.

The shimmering reflections darkening on the lake faded into the dusk. The wind fell to a breeze. The evening stilled to the quiet time that's perfect for strolls hand in hand and for silent thinking.

Suddenly, a pounding. The earth trembled. It sounded like a heavy fist slamming quickly against a punching bag, then stopped. It startled us. I looked but saw nothing. Then the pounding came again and a huge buck bounded out of nowhere, emerging from the trees to stop and eye us. His antlers stuck up from his head like a TV antenna. He lowered them and charged straight at us, his hooves thumping the cold hard ground and creating that frightening sound of thunder. Neither Robinovich nor I budged a muscle. Threatening as he was, he was still too wonderful to take our eyes from. Better to be gored to death by a TV antenna than to miss such effortless athletics.

His running turned to leaping and just at the very last second, he sprang to his left and darted out of sight. Triumphant.

The pounding came from inside my chest now. I was breathing hard. *Life in the woods,* I thought.

Lying in the tent later on, reality and its questions grab hold. *What the hell am I doing?* Sure, the thing that awaits me is a creek. In three days journey, though, it turns into a series of lakes, one of which stretches more than ten miles across. After that I'm facing a real river, with current, wind and waves, and traffic. And animals and no phones and no easy way out.

I was very nearly ready to call it quits.

It's gotten very cold out by now. I've put on my long underwear, tops and bottoms, and tried to get a good blaze going for warmth, but it's been raining up here lately and the wood is all wet. I'd always heard that birch makes such wonderful firewood. The bark does burn easily, but when the wood itself gets wet, it turns into soggy pulp. And the pine needles and cones lying around which would usually make good kindling are wet as well. It's a miracle that we can get any fire started at all, and even then it's only enough to cook by, not a blaze that throws off heat.

And to think, the ranger's office had bundles of wood for

sale. They're closed by now and anyway, I had said to Robinovich:

"That's too easy, not like really roughing it. And if I can't find wood enough and can't get a fire started, I'm going to be in a world of trouble."

After a quick dinner of soup and cheese and crackers, the cold opened to us like a freezer door and we hurried to get inside the tent and stay there for the night. Anything we'd left out could just stay there until morning.

We broke out the tequila and made funny noises after every sip. It's strong and burning, just the way it's supposed to be.

Deep in the night I was awakened by growling and snorting. I couldn't tell where it was coming from. I looked over at Robinovich. I couldn't really see her but, by her stillness and by the deep heavy breathing I knew she was sleeping soundly.

I sat up straight in the darkness to listen. Each time I would try to hear, the sounds died away. When I lay back down, they came again. Animal sniffing noises. Spooky sounds in the night.

Soon I heard clankings of pots and cans, tearings of paper and plastic and cardboard. What did we leave out for it to get into? I wonder what kind of beast it is and hope it doesn't decide to slash its way inside for more treats.

Later on, after the sounds have once again moved around to the rear of the tent and I've unzipped the back flap for the nth time, I catch a glimpse of the beast by the soft white light of the risen moon. It's a bear. A small one, rising up on its hind legs stretching up against a tree. I know bears, even these small ones, can be lethal, but my fears go away and the vacuum fills with amazement.

I poke at Robinovich, but she is too far into sleep and dreams. And quickly the bear is gone anyway.

I settle back in my sleeping bag and I'm excited. I'm wishing I could see the bear again, more clearly, and the moon and stars too. I can hardly sleep, but I do. In the morning I'm raring to go.

A quick scan of the area just at sunrise reveals the bear's activity. The metal pots and plates and cups have been investigated and discarded. The empty soup cans have also been tossed aside; too hard for a bear to get into. But there had been a box of crackers and it's clear the bear enjoyed them. The plastic has been ripped to pieces and the cardboard box torn apart and dragged to the edge of the woods. There was nothing else for the bear to get its paws on and I'm glad. Feeding the wild animals is as bad a habit as it is for the animals to eat man's garbage. So I vow never to leave food out for the animals to get into, and to leave no trash behind. Whatever I bring in comes out with me and no one will know by such trashy signs that I've ever been along this river. It's a promise I end up breaking only twice.

I am ready then for what turns out to be a beautiful morning and a glorious afternoon and, until a few weeks later, the roughest night of my life.

7

We were up before the sun. The air was soft and fine, but cold. The morning seemed brittle. When the sun finally rose it looked like it would have taken any excuse at all and gone back to bed. The same for me, so it was quickly tea and soup, break camp and head on down to the lake.

Without much ado we unloosed the canoe from its perch atop the car and set it in the water. I tied an extra paddle to one of the cross struts in the canoe, slipped a line through the stern, and I was ready.

Nothing else needed to be stowed in the canoe because Robinovich had agreed to stay on for the day and meet me periodically along this early portion of the river. Just to make sure I got the hang of it and to put both our minds at ease.

I took a long hug and a kiss, donned my yellow life jacket, and I was away.

The lake invites me with its stillness. Any turbulence might have discouraged me, but the water is so calm and pretty and the morning so quiet and finally beginning to take on some color that I shove off easily and paddle straight out to where the water is deep and cold and scariest. I suddenly have no fear of falling in and if not for the river calling me I could easily stay here and paddle up and down this lake all day.

But the river does call. I turn my canoe north and glide toward it.

Right away I discover that canoeing is an art, one which I will eventually have to learn. On the quiet lake my zigzagging poses no problem, but I will need to learn to control this thing or I might find trouble later on. I don't want that.

I settle in quickly amid the cushioning quiet of this near-wilderness. The lake reflects the dark green trees and the sky striped white and blue. The trail I lay behind me in the water is a soft S-curve of bubbles and swirls. I make so little noise. Only the light swishing of my paddle, the drips of water tapping the lake when I cross the paddle from my left side to my right, a little plop when each time I dig the paddle into the water, and a slight suction sound when I pull it out for the next stroke. And all about me is fine and silent until a handful of ducks skims across the water. Their noise is the flapping of heavy wings and the dragging of duck feet across the lake.

I lengthen my stroking. I'm coming faster and faster across the water now. It's almost effortless, a feeling much like gliding across calm seas in a sail boat. I feel the spirit of this water rising up from the morning's mist and I hear it whispering to me that I have nothing to worry about.

As I carve my path across the water, I see ahead the river falling away as though spilling into a drain. I'm caught in the current. Still paddling, of course; the current isn't *that* strong. It must be a psychological pull that makes me feel I could stop paddling and still not keep from aiming for those rocks and that river.

A father and mother are showing the baby river to their two children. They wave and call to me as I slow to negotiate the rocks that cross the river.

"Where are you headed?"

"New Orleans." I feel like an expert now, an old pro at this. I try to look cool, like I know what I'm doing, but I add, "I hope." They laugh and wish me luck.

It's a transaction I will undergo a hundred times before I reach the end, each one very much like this one. Some will wish they could go along, others will think I'm a little on the loony side, but each one will encourage me and no one will wish me bad luck or ill. Well, almost no one.

When the river finally falls into the gulf, it will have reached a depth of about two hundred feet, but just beyond these big rocks the Mississippi's bottom lies only inches below the surface. My canoe and its 185-pound paddler have a draft of about six inches and when the creek bed rises to its shallowest point, the canoe touches bottom and I'm stuck. Not ten yards from the beginning and I'm stuck. I hope no one is looking. Is this an omen?

There! I dig my paddle hard into the pebbly bottom and lean against it and just shove until the canoe slides free, dragging bottom at first but finally getting loose and afloat again. This will happen many more times before the river has found a few more inches to accommodate me, but a little strength is all I need. I manage.

Shortly on I come to a little bridge. Lying flat in the canoe I slide under the bridge, scraping bottom again and having to shove my way free while almost lying down. With higher water I could have floated under more easily but my head would have been taken off by the low bridge.

The creek bends left, it bends right. Another footbridge lies across my path and blocks my way. No way can I get under this one, not even if I lie flat and try to slide by again. Easy solution. Get out, set the canoe adrift and let it float under the bridge by itself, then grab it as it comes through the other side. Good idea, but when I get out of the canoe and take the weight of my body with me, the canoe rises in the water and sits too high to squeeze under. The bow of the canoe knocks into the bottom of the bridge. I can stand in the canoe until the front end is under the bridge, climb up onto the bridge myself and then push the canoe through, but the canoe still won't go. It gets stuck in the rafters that support the bridge. I pull it back out and think again.

The bridge is just too low. The embankments are too high to drag the canoe up, but I've no choice. Unless I want to go back and go home. That remains a possible solution to every difficulty I encounter along the way, but I don't take the consideration seriously here. I'm simply forced to get out of the canoe and try to drag this thing up the embankment and across the bridge to the other side.

The canoe is not mine. It's on loan to me from a youth organization in St. Louis, run by a friend of Robinovich's. I hope I don't bend it or break it or put holes in it, but it feels like all of these will happen. In the meantime I'm pulling this boat inch by inch, slipping into the mud and getting my feet wet. At times I go to the back end and lift and shove and finally I get the cursed canoe up and over and back down into the water. No damage to the canoe, only to me and my already weak back.

But soon I'm on my way again along the sparkling waters. I'm in a canyon of trees, two hundred-year-old pines. The river cuts left, it cuts right.

Up ahead another bridge. This time the river has been funneled through what looks like a huge metal sewer pipe and the water builds up there and shoots through to the other side with a rushing noise that sounds like Niagara Falls. I can only go through if I lie down. I do and I'm at the mercy of the river. I hold my breath and go for it. Gathering speed I shoot through the tunnel and out the other side and I feel like I've shot the rapids or done a ride at Disneyland.

For a few minutes I sit in a large, quiet pool at the other end of the tunnel. The river is coming hard and noisily at me. But here it widens and quickly quiets once more and becomes clear and slow again. I move on.

A beaver dam blocks my way. The beavers will create many problems for me before this day is done, and this first dam is the least of them. It stops up the river and a tree has been thrown across half the creek to make getting around it difficult. I wonder if these dams serve a purpose, if beavers really live in them, or if beavers are just great big jokers who like to slow down people in small boats. I'm certainly slowed down. I'm not an expert yet and I struggle to get the canoe going sideways at the right times. Too often I get going backwards. I hit a branch. I'm caught in a snarl of limbs. I get stuck.

The river here is so gentle. A heron rises up out of nowhere. It squawks: follow me. I do. It drifts downstream to hide, be flushed again, and hide again. It's playing games with me. Eagles in the sky above soar over me and probably laugh at me. Critters scurry through the brush on the banks and never let me see them. The air is crisp and cool but sunny enough and I'm paddling enough to stay warm. Further on I find baby fishes flickering as they dart for cover when I disturb their water. I feel I've got a continuum here, that fish will be with me unlike any other creature all the way to the end and I'll not be so alone. When the river deepens and I encounter the bigger fish loitering in the shade, I know it for certain. But I'm wrong. At the highway bridge just this side of the marsh the river deepens considerably and a school of fish lives here, but they are the last fish I see. The river shallows very quickly again and the fish are gone.

I'm totally alone. This is wilderness.

Now the river really meanders. Soft curves become zigzags and I must cover a lot of ground to gain such a short crow-fly distance. I find myself enmeshed in a maze of meanderings and marsh. The trees stand a long way off now but are still all around, and I'm floating in a plain of rice grass. Tall blades of dense pale yellow, the color of ripened wheat, surround me and the river branches infinitely through. I do not know which branch to take.

Advice from an old man in Wallace, Idaho: When you come to a fork in the road, always take the right road.

The route left looks just as good. The right might be the wrong. Maybe they all come out at the same place. Maybe this way is shorter than that. If I only had a helicopter. Or if I had a motor boat and could just plow through the rice fields. Or a pole instead of a paddle.

The sun is behind me and to my left, high in the sky. I'm okay for time, and the branch to the right seems to go the most north. I take it.

Ducks quack up around me, breaking the quiet. A hawk hovers overhead. The rifle shots of deer hunters echo way off in the distance. Other than that I am so totally alone and the day is so serene and noiseless, I can hear the whooshing of the wind through the tall grass. I feel like singing. Even if I take the wrong way and have to double back, I'm doing fine. The weather is fine, I've got my Nature Valley granola bars to eat, and a canteen filled with tasty spring water. As long as I don't get lost in this maze, I'm okay.

These three miles—by park ranger estimation—take forever. Later in the journey I will expect to do three miles in no time, but these three take so long that by the time I reach Wanagan Landing to stop for lunch, I'm actually considering staying here for the night.

Already my legs are stiff, my hands are sore and my back is tense and tired. I pull the canoe up and lie in the grass. I drink from my canteen.

In a moment, Robinovich arrives. She's been out admiring the area on her own, driving dozens of miles in the time it's taken me to make three. And she's laughing at how tired I am.

We get a small fire going and have a simple lunch. I get warm. Robinovich opens up the treats sent along to me by friends. Trail mix, peanuts, cashews, cookies, and a mountain of granola bars, which I never liked before but which by the time this trip ends will be among my favorite snacks.

Never before could I understand why bicycle racers are surrounded by cars carrying extra bikes, food, and drink. I always thought a racer should be out there doing his job, on his own, and if he has a breakdown he just pulls out. I look at Robinovich, my support team—preparing lunch, encouraging me, prodding me with her presence so I'd be too ashamed to quit—and I understand.

I'm back on my way and we've agreed to meet twelve miles further on at the campsite called Coffee Pot. The Minnesota Parks and Recreation Department has carved into the wilderness along this first sixty-mile stretch of river a series of landings and campsites. They are beautifully done and clean. Some have fire rings and pit toilets and water pumps, others picnic tables. Others are primitive. But they all blend in well with the green surroundings and don't intrude much.

Three miles took forever. Twelve more should take four times as long. But no! The next twelve will take much longer. But how can this be? I was rested. The sun was still high. I had just eaten. And the river straightened. On top of that I was gaining experience as a canoeist with every stroke. How could I not make the next twelve miles in a hurry?

I'm feeling really fine. The river deepens and the rice marsh lines only one bank. The other bank is woodsy for now.

Too quickly the marsh and the meanderings are back, but only for a short time. Still, the going is not swift. Soon the sun is slipping down beyond the pines. When the sun goes, the cold comes. And now I'm deeper in the woods where the air is naturally fresher and cooler. I put on my gloves and don a sweatshirt with a hood. Robinovich has my warm jacket. I was thinking she would need it more than I. After all, all this paddling so far has kept me warm. In the sun.

I come to a low wooden dam that threatens to force me out of the canoe. But I'm feeling expert. I can ride this. I do, but the riding is tricky and I get wet. The wet makes me colder. The beaver dams take time. Time takes away my light. There is another obstruction and I'm forced out of my canoe to portage around it. More time. More effort. More cold coming fast into the valley. Whose idea *was* this?

Rapids. They are loud and swift and the rocks are boulders and I'm scared. I may be expert, but I'm not *that* expert. But what choice have I? I've got to shoot them, and shoot them I do. A long series of rapids after rapids—probably because of the shallow water in autumn—and with each one I gain more and more confidence. After each one I shout with triumph and glee. But with each one I get wetter. And as the darkness descends, each one gets more difficult to see and thus trickier to negotiate.

One time the river spins me into a rock and I nearly fly from my seat. The rock spins me around sideways and soon I'm going swiftly downstream backwards. I can't turn around. The river narrows and the canoe won't fit. I'm stuck.

Another time I'm thrown into the side of the river. Low branches force me into the bank and I can't turn around. The water from the side is too fast and strong for me. I have to get out and push the boat around. My shoes get soaked and my feet get cold and my gloves get wet.

To dry the gloves I lay them on the struts. The next set of

rapids tosses up the front end of the canoe. Only a keen sense of balance—no canoeing skill—keeps me from falling into the icy water.

I look. My gloves are gone.

The river has become an adversary. I see deer munching leaves on the shore. They know better than to do what I'm doing and they feel safe from me. How can I get at them even if I want to? They watch me and I feel stupid.

Finally it's dark. Then it's night. I'm freezing right through to the bone and my hands and feet are numb. I'm worried about frostbite. I'm worried about being lost. I'm worried about how to find Robinovich out there in the night. I don't know how far I've come or how far I've got to go. I'm scared. So I sing. I worry about running across more rapids, falling in, freezing to death.

That rushing sound, the sound of rapids, terrifies me each time I hear it. The river has begun to meander again and the bank has hidden deep behind the marsh that has popped up again. I can't get out of the river because I can't get out of the canoe. I don't know if I'll find solid ground or if I'll sink to my waist. I'm forced on.

The sound of rapids is the same sound of water falling over those huge beaver dams that threaten my progress. I hate the dams but I fear the rapids even more. The dams I can go around—when I can see them. The ones that completely cross the river I can plow over. The ones that are too thick I can approach and step out on and slide the canoe over. I'm hoping beavers don't bite.

Finally the moon rises and throws down its light. I breath easier. I can see a bit. But it's still very dark and mostly what I must do is listen. Hearing, smelling: other senses take over when you can't see and right now (despite the moonlight) my eyesight is fairly useless. I rely on a sense I didn't even know I had and it somehow keeps me in the water, upright, away from the marsh and out of too much trouble. I carry on and I sing.

I'm wondering how long before the search party comes looking for me. Off in the distant night sky a signal flare shoots a bright arc and falls. Someone, I'm sure, is looking for me. Pretty soon a helicopter will thump through the air overhead and shine down an intense spotlight on the river. A voice in a loud speaker will ask me if I'm all right and will light my path on the water. I'm sure of it.

But no. I'm still all alone and still miserable. My toes are dead numb and my fingers are swollen. They're locked around the paddle and cannot unbend. Frostbite.

Off in the distance, high on a hill, a light. I aim straight for it and tell myself when I get close, I'll get out and hike. It's a good mile straight up a hill, but at least I know there's a house. I can phone from there or get a ride to Coffee Pot. But dogs are howling up there on the hillside. I keep going.

Beaver dams. Each time I step from the canoe to go over them my feet get wetter. I'm just freezing. In my pocket I do have a box of waterproof matches. If I could find a place to pull out I could at least build a fire and dry off and warm up a little.

Up on a rise, not far from the river, a shed. Old and rickety, but made of wood. I can burn that thing if I need to, burn it to the ground for warmth, and yes I need to. My life or the life of this old shack.

But then I smell smoke. Someone else has built a fire. Hunters maybe, or Robinovich. I keep going.

A big mistake. I find no fire, no hunters, no Robinovich. My spirit is sinking fast. I sing to keep from losing it completely. Between songs I call out to Robinovich. No reply. Just my own voice echoing hollowly back to me from the walls of the night.

I can give up, get out right now and just die. It'll be easier.

I find every scrap of energy that's in me and push on. I can't see any better now and I don't need too much speed to make me crash into something or send me into the weeds. I pick my way carefully.

And then I see the light from a fire. I smell smoke. I see the lights from a car. I'm yelling my head off but no sound comes back to me. How far away am I?

Finally I arrive. Coffee Pot. The fire, a big smoky blaze, is ours. Robinovich has built it. She's gone, though, when I pull out from the river, gone to search for me. Not knowing where or how to search she quickly returns. The car lights I saw were hers.

I'm by the fire trying to warm myself when she comes back over the hill. She runs down the hill from her car and throws herself at me. We hold onto each other, but that's not warming enough. I'm back at the fire shedding wet clothes for dry ones.

I pitch the tent. I open cans. Robinovich gets the dinner going. Pork and beans from a can with bits of chopped up Polish sausage mixed in. A little sugar on top and slices of bread. Cups of tea and swigs of tequila.

It's glorious. I moan with delight and satisfaction. I spoon the beans and sausage into me. It's hot and delicious and thick and sticky. I'm slopping food all over. Beans drip down my chin and hang from my beard. It's messy but it feels so nice. I can't get enough. I'm going faster and faster until my legs tremble and I'm shaking all over and finally I drop exhausted and satisfied to my knees. Breathing hard I moan pain and pleasure at the same time. This is the most passionate meal I've ever had.

Until now my best meal ever had been *Lapin à l'antillaise,* a rabbit dish I had one night in Montreal in a restaurant owned by a Cuban who thought I was Haitian and so brought out his best. My eyes lit up like rockets in the night when I took the first bite, just as they did tonight. I thought that no other food would sting me through and through with good flavor the way that dish had done, but that meal has been surpassed by beans and weenies in the wilds of Minnesota. Never have I been so happy to be living.

8

In the night the mind voices what was only a creepy suspicion during the day. *What in the world am I doing out here?*

I'm a city fellow, urbane and civilized. I always use the correct fork. I keep my napkin in my lap. And like a good little boy who does what his mommy tells him, I chew my food fifty-six times before swallowing. My idea of travel and good fun is shooting craps in Las Vegas or playing roulette in the Grand Casino at Monte Carlo, fishing for marlin off Bimini, scuba diving the reefs of the Caribbean, hiking the Swiss Alps and skiing the Austrian, dining and wining in Paris, bicycling through Scotland. I see myself wearing tuxedoes and drinking champagne, not eating beans and weenies and wearing the same smelly clothes for weeks.

And I'm no expert in a canoe. That much is evident now. I think I'd been in a canoe maybe five times before. Floating the Black River a couple of times—mostly just an easy stream but I still managed to tip over and fall in. One time canoeing leisurely in the summer sun on the Thames not far from London. Once on a lake just drifting lazily with a fishing rod in hand but not even a nibble to worry about, only the weeds and the marsh and the water lilies snagging the canoe and forcing me to work. And once on the Severån, a lazy little river in the north of Sweden. Not exactly training for the proving ground of the Mississippi.

Nor was I any more experienced as a camper. Not an outdoorsman at all. Cleaning fish is not one of my favorite things. I don't like snakes, can't stand mosquitoes, and creatures that growl in the night scare me.

And yet. . . .

I'm haunted by the ghost of Ernest Hemingway. All writers—American male—probably are. His style of writing, sure, but mostly his zesty style of living—big-game hunter, deep-sea fisher, hard drinker. Lover of man and women and good times and travel to exotic locales. A courter of danger.

It was a different world then, though. Everything wasn't taken so much for granted. A punch in the nose risked a return punch in the nose, a few moments' sweat and adrenaline, not a lawsuit. Air travel was an adventure. Getting there—anywhere—was as thrilling as being there. Skiing was not chic, the thing to do, but rather hard work down the mountain, harder work back up, an exhilaration, an exotic adventure. Your tales had zing in those days because everyone you know hadn't already been to Europe. Living was an adventure. And Paris was really Paris.

It was a different world all right.

Now life is a media event. Well publicized, well sign-posted, the paths well worn and all the right things to do and places to go marked out. And absolutely everyone has a ticket to watch.

Is that what we've become? Mere spectators at a zoo? With real living removed from us and kept safely behind bars?

I hope to God I'm not out here because I miss the Good Old Days.

What good old days? Twenty years from now, these will be the good old days.

And not because I wanted to be Ernest Hemingway.

I want to be Eddy Harris. I want to live a life of my own adventures, my own tryings, triumphs—even failures.

I look at the Mississippi and I see a symbol of America, the spine of the nation, a symbol of strength and freedom and pride, wanderlust and history and imagination. The river is also a symbol of our times, for the river fights in a desperate battle against the US Army Corps of Engineers who refuse to let the river find its own way. The Corps of Engineers fights the river with technology and brute brain power to bend the river, make it conform to the needs of society in order to save homes that would otherwise be flooded, to aid shipping, to strip the river of its power and its will and its natural dignity. Nobody has asked the river. The river which yearns to be free, rages for it.

Alas! Time runs out—for the river, for me, for us all. The world around closes in.

Computerized, mechanized, itemized, formalized, and most dangerously, standardized. Laws hemming us in and fencing us out, stripping us down and standardizing behavior. Hotel chains and fast food joints standardize travel and eating. Dallas looks like Denver looks like Tacoma looks like Tallahasse. Traveling is truly home away from home. No surprises, no disasters at mealtime, no disappointments, no thrills. Just a steady heartbeat and a blank look.

Doesn't it make you mad enough to holler and spit?

Taking chances. Isn't that what life is all about? Sometimes you come up winners, sometimes you lose. But without the risk of defeat, where is the triumph? Without death hanging over the head, what value is life?

And *that* is why I wanted to do this foolish thing. If I were expert with canoe, fishing gear, bow and arrow and rifle, if I were the Daniel Boone type used to spending weeks at a time in the same clothes, in the woods, if I loved gutting rabbits and sleeping out in the rain, a trip down the big river would have been a simple thing. Fun, but little more than routine. Only half an adventure.

This voyage, on the other hand, was a true adventure. Looking back on all I had to go through just to get here to Lake Itasca, it was no wonder I said to Robinovich:

"I don't really have to go now. The climax was getting the canoe." (And canoeing out of Lake Itasca, of course.)

And in a way, it was. I had spent so much energy and emotion trying to put this expedition together that once it was done and everything had finally slipped into place, it felt as though I had already succeeded. I didn't need to go on. Much the same as the seducer who gets the one desired moves on once he's won. The thrill is in the hunt.

I had decided on August 18 that I would do this thing and would leave October 1. I thought a month and a half would be plenty of time to prepare. Even three weeks beyond the target date I barely had enough gear, and I did *not* have the canoe.

Canoes are very personal, like toothbrushes, and people who have them do not lend them out. I thought I would have to buy one. But I had no money. Not for the canoe, not for good warm clothing, not for a telephoto lens for the camera and a mountain of film. Not for lanterns and a sleeping bag, life jacket, knives, axes, cooking and eating equipment and all sorts of other junk I considered necessary if I was going to do this right: safely and as comfortably as possible.

It soon became clear that if I was going at all, I would not be going in style. I cut my list to the bone, to the barest essentials, and I borrowed most of those. I managed to buy a handgun for small game—rabbits and squirrels for Daniel Boone dinners—and for protection, as it turned out. But I took nothing fancy and nothing for comfort.

Just before it would have been too late, a friend of Robinovich's came up with the canoe. I was going, but not in grand style.

And by then, despite the lateness of the season and the advancing winter, despite the fear which mounted now that the dream had become as real as surgery, despite the drain and the strain and the low energy, I had to go.

This river trip would be different. So deep inside me would this thing reside that it would be a part of my soul, and yet with a spirit of its own that would leap to mind of its own accord, being such a part of me that it would enter my marrow and alter the way I think and feel and walk, leaving me with more than memories and smiles, leaving me changed in a deep and abiding way. Rather like love that defies explanation, deep and passionate and affecting even long after the object of that love has vanished. In the heart it remains.

The Mississippi offered this to me, promising that if I gave her a try she would be a part of me forever. It wouldn't matter if I finished, if I went for twenty-five miles or twenty-five hundred, six days or six weeks. The desire and the intention were what really mattered. (I learned this along the way.) A marriage. You enter it, if it's real, with every intention of seeing it through to the end, *till death do us part*. You plan to weather the storms and the cold nights, enjoy the sunshine and the warmth and have plenty to look back on when you're old and finished. But sometimes, try as you might, work hard as you can at it, fighting with all the strength that's in you, it just is not to be and you're forced out. Sad and painful but even after it's long over it remains a part of you.

An adventure, a challenge, no tuxedoes, no ties, no uniforms. Not civilized and no rules apply. Just very basic: hard work and dirty hands. You don't need a diploma. No experience is necessary. Just common sense and guts. Anyone can do it. *Just put in and see if you can handle it, see how far you can get*. That's what the river said to me in the night, daring me to succeed the same as my father used to bait me when I was a kid, daring me to try something new, pushing me to be strong and courageous, preparing me for life. I accepted his challenges; I accepted the river's.

But I was still scared.

9

I BUILT A FIRE early and let Robinovich sleep. I had slept like a dead man and awakened still feeling like one. Stiff and sore all over, my body didn't like the way I was treating it. All parts rebeled. They did nothing I asked without resisting and complaining violently. My hands ached and my fingers refused to bend. Just yesterday these had been the soft, sensitive hands of a concert violinist. Now they were the sore, puffy hands of a prizefighter. And they would get worse.

I heaped loads of wood on the fire but just could not get warm. Dampness still lingered in my bones.

Awakened by the smell of smoke, Robinovich finally came crawling from the tent. We ate and then plinked at empty cans with my revolver. I wanted to see if my hands remembered how to aim and my fingers how to shoot. They did. (I also wanted to show Robinovich I knew what I was doing and to prove it I showed her that for safety reasons I normally keep my revolver loaded with only four cartridges. I leave the hammer resting on an empty chamber in case I drop the gun and keep the next chamber empty too in case I inadvertently cock the thing and pull the trigger. I don't want any accidents.)

It was time to get going. The river, unfortunately, had not moved. It waited for me, beckoning me with its teasing gurgles and chuckles. I stopped to listen and to take a very long look.

By the time Robinovich left me for good—or for bad—I had been given a glimpse of what this journey was going to be, although in no way could I have articulated it at the time if anyone had asked me. Like answering why do you love somebody. No reason; a hundred and one reasons. You just do.

My thoughts turned strangely toward Disneyland.

This riding of the river is not unlike a ride at Disneyland. Breath-taking spectacle, scenery, excitement, magic, fun. Even that best of all Disneyland attributes, the ability to leave ourselves and our cares at home. The difference, however, is that while the spine tingles and the blood rushes through the body at a furious pace during the excitement of Disneyland, you know that you are never in any real danger. When the day is done you pack up the car and head back to the real world. Back to your cares and woes, the distractions that heap layer upon layer of enamel coating that keep us from getting at the sweetness—or the yuk—that is our warm and creamy center.

You can't see the teeth on a buzz-saw. If you can stay busy enough or distracted enough, you never have to venture into that dangerous territory of boredom, discontent, and fear. Too much diversion can keep us from knowing how miserable or how happy we are, what bores we are or what fun, how much we want, need or lack.

Each day on the river I shed more and more of my external self until I find eventually that I'm left totally alone with the core, facing myself as angry and aggressive, often afraid, no physical superman. Just a man and nothing special.

A vacation is external. A pilgrimage is internal. An adventure combines them.

10

THE MISSISSIPPI FROM COFFEE POT changes from one minute to the next. Now it's swift. Now it's swamp. There are rapids and rocks. Then the river is a stream again with overhanging branches with gnarled fingers to clutch and snag the canoeist. The water runs low, the canoe drags bottom. Paddling takes strength and skill, and what skill you lack, you learn.

Still the river teems with beauty and youthful charm. It meanders capriciously past landings with names that evoke images from a hundred years ago: Stumphges Rapids, Bear Den, Pine Point, Pine Lake. Pines do rise up and line the river like a corridor of sentries. Deer forage near the edge of the river. Foxes scamper along the banks. Other animals I know are here watching me—badgers, otters, wolves—but they are cautious creatures and they watch without revealing themselves. I know they are there. I hear them splashing to get out of the way and rustling the leaves on the shore as they survey my progress.

Waterfowl constantly shoot downstream away from me, and unseen songbirds decorate the air with music that hangs on the stillness like ornaments of sound.

When there are no rapids to fight, no branches to duck, no obstructions in the river to deal with, the time glides by and the river and its atmosphere soothe. It is so peaceful. So beautiful. But the river can change character rapidly, as capriciously as a kid, as cunningly as an old codger. And always you wonder why. What is this old mystery man trying to say to you, trying to teach?

And then, Rice Lake.

As the name suggests, Rice Lake holds beds of wild rice that Indians have harvested for maybe a thousand years. The history of the river shouts at you here beside this, the first of a series of lakes the river edges or spills into and out of.

Canoes made of birch bark silently paddled by Indians of flesh and steel, Indians who knew this land and loved it as I'm learning to. Oza Windib was one of them, who guided the Schoolcraft expedition to Itasca in 1832. A hundred years before, La Salle had reached the mouth of the Mississippi, but Schoolcraft and his men wanted to get to the actual source: Lac La Biche, as Itasca was known before the river was traced backwards to it. I sit in my canoe and wonder where I'd be if those earlier explorers had begun their treks at the gulf and rather than travel south on the river from Illinois had moved upstream instead and had turned left at St. Louis to go west along the Missouri River. That river would then become the main branch of the Mississippi and I'd be somewhere in Montana with *four* thousand miles ahead of me on the second longest river in the world. *Lucky me!*

The Missouri moves swifter than this thing. All of a sudden this river has fallen into a wide marsh that is more confusing and slower than the meandering marsh I first encountered. The river had relaxed its meandering just after Rice Lake, but now it zigzags again and the going is slow and boring.

From Iron Bridge Landing down to Lake Irving and on into Lake Bemidji, the river alters its face once more, twisting through a dense forest canopy of sweetly scented pine and finally straightening out as the river leaves its wildness and youth behind. Residences and farmland, houses and cabins, more bridges with more cars. People, campsites, and civilization.

The wind had come up blustery and cold, chopping a little sea of whitecaps on the lake. Kontiki crossing the Pacific had it easier than I would have if I had ventured out to cross Lake Bemidji, but at this stage it never even occurred to me to try.

Later on I would brave such insanities, but not yet. I was not so confident to be so foolish and daring and besides, I was scared.

I beach the canoe and stomp my foot in anger, not so much because I'm forced to stop, but because I'm so afraid. Nobody likes to be as scared as much of the time as I've been lately, and I wonder if the man I see inside is a coward. I shout my frustrations out loud: *God Almighty! Give me a break!*

Why can't I just have a simple day with no trouble at all, no calamities, no trepidations? Is it going to be like this every mile of the way? Because if it is, I'll quit and go home and put an end to this. This is supposed to be an adventure, yes, but fun. I don't like this fear gnawing at me and telling me to give up. I don't like fear at all. It paralyzes you and freezes your fun and restricts your do's with a lot of don'ts and can'ts and shouldn'ts. And I certainly do not want to look into a mirror and get the reflection of a coward smiling back at me. I hate the thought of it, and luckily when I look into the water, the lake is too rough to throw back any reflection at all.

Then the river god—or the river as God—answers me. A voice from within soothes me. I settle down.

Bear with me. There is still a long way to go and I know what I'm doing. When you get to the end, you'll be happy you gave me a chance.

Suddenly the sense of turbulence disappears. The air around me is calm. The wind has not died down and the waves on the lake have not smoothed out, but still it seems calm. I am calm.

The day is grey and the sky hangs with smoke-colored clouds. They shift around overhead like penned cattle, restless and angry. When they shove together in the right way, light appears between them and cuts a swath of blue. Bands of silver sunlight stream down to strike the lake, brightening its ominous grey.

All of a sudden I realize that I am no match for this river or any piece of nature. No match at all. Whatever anger or aggression or spite that boiled in my soul and made me think I *was* such a match has departed. Nature is a superheavyweight and I am but a flyweight. Don't for one second think you can enter into a competition with nature. The wind and the water and the earth will not lose. The river is telling me that.

Why this revelation should soothe me, I don't know. To realize that I'm not big and brave and strong and handsome, not a know-it-all or a do-it-all, should spur me from this trip. But it doesn't. It urges me on.

My eyes are open now and I can see. Knowing I absolutely cannot win does a strange thing to me. I'm a trouble maker, a hard-head, yet suddenly I want to submit to a power greater than myself, to let the river lead me and take me where I need to go, to obey and accept its will as my own. To struggle against the river is to drain my strength. Then I shall surely be powerless and lost. But to submit is to ride the wind like a leaf, to relax and become part of the river, part of the life around me. So I can be calm.

And yet at the same time I know I will not fail. I know I am strong. I look around at the ocean of water before me, deep and grey and cold. My determination swells. Just as deep, just as cold, just as steely grey. And all about me are signs of the splendor and the strength of nature and I respect and appreciate them. But I no longer fear them. I can forge these and other elements together to form a shield against fear and paralysis. Now I can go on.

"You may have to give in and stop, but you'll not quit. You'll never quit."

At first I'm sure it's the voice of the river. But as I listen I know the words are coming loud and clear from my own lips.

11

I WAS LOOKING for a liquor store. I wanted to get a bottle of brandy to swig from time to time and knock the chill off my bones. I still had the tequila, of course, but tequila is such a serious drink. Brandy sounds softer.

Bemidji the town looks like two towns, although it's actually only one, split in two where the river spills from Lake Irving into Lake Bemidji. The two lakes are not very far apart and if they ever flooded seriously they would probably make one slightly larger lake, swallowing up the narrow strip of the town that wisely isn't there. Instead, there is a part of town lining the west bank of the lake and a smaller stretch off the south shore. And I didn't know which half to search.

As I walked, as I was trying to contemplate the wind and the waves and the two thousand miles remaining, I found that I could not keep my mind on my search. My urban attitudes cloaked my thoughts, and I kept wondering if someone would steal my canoe and my gear. If my stuff was gone when I got back to the lake, the rest of the journey would be gone too.

Every few steps I turned to look over my shoulder, back to the canoe, until the lake was gone from sight. I wandered helter-skelter down the narrow streets past cute frame houses, in nervous haste until finally I had to get back to the lake. I felt as if I had dashed into the supermarket for only a moment and left the keys in the car and the motor running.

I hurried back, and the canoe was gone. *Damn!*

My heart pounds loud enough to be heard over the wind. I clench my fists and beat them against my thighs. I'm mad at myself, at my stupidity, hot and angered enough to spit.

At the same time I'm upset with myself for entertaining—however briefly—the creeping relief that comes from knowing I'm finished. If I don't find the canoe, I have an excuse for not succeeding. I can say I tried. I can go home, defeated but valiant.

I shoved the relief aside and let confusion take its place. There would be a solution only if there were a question. *What the heck do I do now?* And then, the redeeming question. *Where can I get another canoe?*

No doubt because I was sincere, the river god answered.

"Yo! Need some help?"

I must have looked like it. I imagined how I appeared: lost, pacing a few steps, searching the water and the road, shivering and wearing a life jacket with not a boat in sight.

A pick-up truck pulled off the road and a woman climbed down. She was wearing a heavy wool shirt, faded loose blue jeans and worn cowboy boots. Her sleeves were rolled partway up her arms and her arms were muscular and strong. She looked like a woman used to being and working outdoors, who could take care of herself in any situation and except for the huge diamond ring and wedding band on her finger she could easily have just come from the woods where she'd been chopping down trees all day.

And still, in a way, she was pretty. Her face was thin and lined, either from age—middle to late forties—or from Minnesota winter wind, or both.

She came down to the edge of the water and stood beside me.

"You're not from around here, are you?"

"No. St. Louis." I wasn't feeling particularly cordial and didn't have much to say. If my trip was really going to be over, what did it matter if I met anybody or what she had to say?

"You look like you're going to do some boating." She waited for some sort of response, and when I offered none, she said, "Not a good day for it though. Too windy. That water's too rough."

"It's not a good day for much of anything," I finally said. I turned away and added, "I lost my canoe."

"Canoe! What do you mean canoe?"

Then I told her I was canoeing the length of the Mississippi. Or at least I was until I lost the boat.

"What are you, some kind of expert, or just a nut? A canoe? This time of year? Look at that wind. That water would flood a canoe even if you are an expert, but if you're an expert how did you lose your canoe?"

"I'm not an expert, but that's not how I lost my canoe anyway. Somebody stole it."

And I told her how it happened. She disagreed.

"People in Minnesota," she said, "don't steal."

"Then where's my canoe?"

She pointed off somewhere to the east.

"That's the way the wind's blowing; that's the way the water goes. Your knot came loose, a wave came up and took your canoe, and now it's out there floating somewhere or it's washed up on the bank. That's what happened."

And I was thinking: *knot? What knot?*

There had been nothing to tie onto. I had pulled the canoe up out of the water and wedged it between a couple of the big rocks on the shore. I felt like an idiot.

The woman said she'd help me find the canoe. I followed her

dumbly to her pick-up truck and climbed in. She swung out into traffic and took the road that wound around the lake.

She told me her name was Emily. I told her mine. She didn't tell me her last name, and I didn't ask. Talking to strangers is funny. You want to get to know them, to hear what they have to say, but you don't want your conversations with strangers to turn into interviews. You don't want to pull out a tape recorder and shove a microphone under somebody's nose. (Besides, all that stuff was in the canoe.) The best you can hope for is a good memory and a feel for how the strangers talk. Cadence and word choice. You can jot down notes and recollections later.

Emily's voice did not match her appearance and manner. She seemed really tough. She looked like a lumberjack. Her handshake was meaningful, her grip strong and tight, almost competing. Yet, though her voice was low in pitch, it was not husky, but rather soft in tone and deep and strong. And the more she talked, the mellower her voice became. She got used to me quickly, relaxed and eased into longer and longer sentences the same way she eased her truck from gear to gear.

While she drove and kept her eye on traffic—as much as she could while talking to me and trying to make eye contact—I searched the shoreline of the lake for my canoe. I fully expected to find the thing, if I saw it at all, foundering in the middle of the lake with no way for me to get to it. Or worse, beached on the opposite shore and hard to get to. Or still worse, dashed against the rocks or tangled up in trees, bent out of shape, the hull ripped to shreds, my gear sunk somewhere at the bottom of the lake.

We found the canoe lying on a soft grassy patch of land that spread up in a shallow hill from the water. The wind had carried the canoe this far and obviously someone had found it and dragged it up on shore.

"That's the way people in Minnesota are," Emily informed me. "At least away from the city. We don't steal."

Next she showed me how to tie a clove hitch. I had a long rope with me but hadn't used it. Now however I ran the line through the holes in the stern of the canoe and learned how to tie a good knot. I would need one if ever I wanted to leave the canoe at the edge of the water.

All of a sudden she was dragging the canoe up the grassy mound toward the pick-up truck. I automatically went to help her and asked what we were doing.

"You aren't going anywhere the rest of the day because the wind is still too high and water is still too rough and if you try to be brave and daring on a day like today you can just kiss your trip and your life goodbye. So if we can get this thing up in the truck bed and tied down, we can go off and grab a bite to eat and talk."

It sounded sensible to me so we unloaded the gear from the canoe, hoisted the front end into the back of the truck and lifted and shoved the canoe into the bed. I let her secure it. A good portion of the canoe stuck out over the back of the truck, but that would be all right. We tossed in the duffle bags, the big plastic garbage sacks, and climbed into the truck.

"Aren't you glad I came along when I did?"

Emily beamed when I told her yes.

"Aren't you glad I drive a regular sized pick-up and not one of those little miniature Japanese jobs?"

I was happy for that too and she settled contentedly in her seat and drove away happy to be appreciated.

Our first stop was a little liquor store in Cass Lake, the next town over named for the next lake over. We whipped into the parking lot and stopped at the side of the little building. I waited for Emily to get out, but she wasn't going anywhere. She had stopped here for me. She remembered that I had been searching for a liquor store when I misplaced my canoe. So I went in, a little apprehensive because I wasn't convinced that Minnesotans don't steal, and maybe Emily was really from New York City. But I went in anyway.

The sign in the window said something about wild rice. I knew that ricing was restricted to Indians and to those granted special permission and that because of the restrictions the price was high. The woman behind the counter was an Indian, short and wide with a round face and a big grin, but when I asked her about ricing, she could tell me nothing. She only sold the stuff. She smiled warm and friendly, but she was saying without saying it: *Go away; don't bother me.*

I got a bottle of Benedictine and Brandy but not before stopping to notice the display case in the back of the store. It was eerie, filled with stuffed animals, presumably caught and killed in the region of the lakes. Squirrel, wolf, beaver, chipmunk, some with little trees for the critters to perch on and peep around. I didn't like it.

I left the Indian and her pets and went back to Emily. She was still there and after a brief stop at the tourist information office, which was closed for the season, we headed for lunch.

Little did I know, but lunch was going to be quite a ride away, in a little town called Walker, in an empty little restaurant and bar decorated in an ocean-going motif. On the walls, pictures of fish, although the fish were not from the sea but from the freshwater lakes nearby. Northern pike and muskellunge, hooked and flopping fiercely above the water, straining some poor guy's line and trying to break away. I found myself rooting for the fish. Alongside the fish, lifebuoys and pelicans and coils of rope. All sorts of junk to make you feel that you're somewhere on the ocean having your lunch.

Just outside lies a magnificent lake, Leech Lake. I hate to think how it got its name. Maybe seeing it while you eat rounds out the feeling of dining at the seashore, maybe this restaurant offered a view of the lake from the dining room at the rear, but we sat at the bar up front. We could see the street if we wanted, or the television which was what the other patron was looking at. The bartender and the waitress too. It must have been a slow time during a slow day.

For lunch, fried clams, French fries and a couple of cold beers.

I chatted with the waitress for a few minutes. She filled me in on the soap opera she was watching. During commercials she told me about life in Walker. Not much goes on but she liked it anyway. But then again, she hadn't been here very long. She had come up from the southwest corner of the state to be near her boyfriend. She wasn't sorry she had come; the people had been very nice to her so far.

"You see?" Emily said. "You should think about moving to Minnesota."

In a simple sort of way Walker, Minnesota is a beautiful little town. Beautiful because it is so typically American, if there is such a thing. When you close your eyes and try to imagine small town America, a place like Walker shimmers into view. One long expanse of a main street, the only street except for a few thin branches stemming off the artery. Where are the houses? I don't see where the people live. In these little towns, I guess, people live in outlying areas. A few might live in houses that dot the smaller streets, but you can't expect to find high-rise apartment buildings here. Small houses and mobile homes in trailer parks. Rural America and single family dwellings.

The buildings along the main street are made of brick. All of them. Not one over two stories tall. Which may account for the friendly feeling here and in most small towns. You have to be neighborly because your neighbors know where to find you. You can't hide on the eighty-second floor. You can't be anonymous because there are no crowds to get lost in. And if you're a stranger, everybody knows it.

I get a few stares as I stroll up the street and look in the shop windows. I'm not wearing my life preserver, so I know they're not staring at that. I think they can tell I'm from somewhere else. Either that or I'm the first black man this town has ever seen.

Being stared at is a spooky feeling. But it's not too bad; the street is nearly deserted. One man sits on the curb across the road and just watches. Three other men stand near the end of the block. They are deep in conversation—probably about the size of a fish caught, guessing from the way one of them holds his hands apart, the length of some super northern pike. They're joking among themselves. Maybe they don't believe what the one fellow is saying. They notice me and look me over, but the conversation never stops or slows. And when I wave at them, they wave back. Cordially.

Luckily the staring is not hostile. Only curious, which is natural. I don't feel, as you can while traveling to many foreign monochrome countries, like such an anomaly. These men are not staring at a freak, just a stranger, and if I wanted to I could go up to these men and add my own fish story, if I had one.

The sun has come out full time now. The street is awash in bright light and carved up with dark shadows. Already the sun has passed its zenith in the sky. The wind is still blowing and without the sun the day would be very cold.

The flag in front of the hardware store beats in the breeze, practically the only movement on the street. The street is lined both sides with parked cars, but pedestrians are few. A yellow tiller for sale sits solidly in the wind not far from the flag. If the day were more ominous, grey and gloomy, Walker would feel like a ghost town, deserted just hours ago, things and people not heavy enough simply blown away like tumbleweed by the stiff wind from the lake.

Walker sits on the edge of the lake. A short walk down a shady street takes you down past the tiny public library right to the water and a makeshift marina, a series of floating wooden piers for tying up fishing boats. There is an American flag flying on the waterfront too, the flagpole rising high and white against a background of pine trees in the distance. The flag hangs out almost straight in the wind, its rope clanking against the pole.

The waves on the lake have not diminished any. And I don't know if the Mississippi passes through Lake Leech. It's a beautiful lake, very wide and surrounded by trees. But it looks rough and I don't think I want to canoe across it. Certainly not if I'm not going to find the way out and into the river. I have no map.

When Emily beckons, I'm ready to climb back into the pickup and let her take me farther on down the road. Evening is spreading out across the sky in a golden glow that washes over the valley. I wouldn't make many more miles this day no matter how hard I canoed. Emily had an easy time convincing me that she should not take me back to Bemidji but downstream further instead.

I protested lightly. Emily responded with a hmph. She pressed the accelerator pedal harder and said: "Men!"

12

I HAD NEVER IMAGINED how difficult and yet at the same time how easy traveling this first part of the river would be. Before I knew it, the upper lakes were behind me. Thanks to Emily, because I had managed to circumvent the dangers of those lakes, I had left behind a lot of fears and was once again eager to get back into the river and continue the journey. The angel the river god had sent to me rescued my lost canoe, made dangerous waters disappear, salvaged the journey. She made it a thing of adventure again. And now she was dragging me through the heartland of Paul Bunyan country. The significance was not lost on me.

Paul Bunyan. A giant of a man, with a hearty laugh and a robust zest for living. He probably bathed in the lakes and used the Mississippi as his running tap water. How sweet it must have tasted then!

He was born not far from here. And his sweetheart Mary Hackensack—a giant sized statue of her—stands patiently waiting for Paul's return. Bright smile and rosy cheeks and a dress as blue as the Minnesota skies.

Thanks to Emily I was able to meet Miss Hackensack and pass through Brainerd, which *does* have an apartment building. Strange for a town so small, I thought, but still the building stood only a couple of stories tall. Paul could have stepped over the little building on his way to meet his sweetie and never notice it.

The legends of this country. Most of them hardly remembered except by children and tourists who are bombarded with reminders. Here, they remind you with the Paul Bunyan Amusement Center, but late autumn when the tourists have all gone home and the kids are back in school it is deserted. But who needs amusement centers anyway? Let your imagination fly. When you pass this close to the seats of the legends, you become a part of them and they don't seem so legendary after all. They are as real as the trees. You half expect to see Paul himself stepping through the trees, axe over his mountainous shoulder, Babe his blue ox in tow, taking his time with his thunderous miles-long earth-moving strides but still eager to get back to his ever-patient sweetheart.

I'm itching now to get on with my own voyage. At Fort Ripley, just through the trees behind the marker telling us about the old fort that once stood here, the river has finally become a real river. No more creek, no more lakes to pass through, just the real Mississippi. Not yet mighty. Still in its childhood, its skinny youth. And I long to be a part of it. I've driven far enough.

It comes to me somehow that Emily is not a lumberjack afterall, and I ask her.

"No. I look like one though, don't I? Strong and tough."

Minutes before I would have answered yes. I can tell that's what she wants to be, but right now she looks anything but tough.

The ghost of Hemingway rides along in the truck with us. I can hear him breathing but in the fading light of the late afternoon I cannot see him clearly. I wait for him to tap me on the shoulder. I wonder what he will say; I wonder what he would have done. Already I think I'm cheating a little, maybe too much and should be ashamed. The thought worries me.

Emily reads my mind again.

"You're probably thinking you've ridden far enough already and you want to get back to what you're doing and start thinking about the river again and a place to camp for the night."

Hemingway vanishes abruptly and I confess that I'm ready to go back. In a few minutes we are back at the river.

I pack the canoe, putting all the gear in the middle for stability and tying it down with short pieces of rope. I zip up the yellow life jacket and step in and push off.

But I can't get the damn thing to face downstream. It goes sideways a bit and then backwards and I simply cannot control it. I struggle and I give up and get back to shore.

Emily is looking pretty frantic. My heart thumps louder. The prospect of failure. The notion that there is success in effort is noble, but still it's failure. I don't want to fail.

I don't know what to do. The river—the real river now—is too rough, too tricky and swirly and maybe too angry at me for stopping and driving to let me continue. Too dangerous. I'm ready to climb out and give up. I don't know enough to deal with this. But I'll give it one more try and I say so to Emily. She looks worried, not wanting me to quit.

I rearrange the gear and stow it in the bow of the canoe, trying to balance the weight front to back and side to side. Then I shove off again. And now I'm right out here in it, out in the river. It flows under me, all around me. It's a river all right, wide and powerful. I can feel the power of this animal beneath me, right through the hull of the canoe.

The canoe heads the right way now, as if it wants to head downstream and get on with the journey and not go back upstream and do the parts I missed. The river is not too very mad at me. I want to lift my arms in triumph but I don't dare. I'm too busy and there's no triumph yet anyway. I do manage a cautious wave to Emily. I feel that at last I am truly on my way.

13

THIS IS WHAT I've brought along:

A small but comfortable two-man tent that isn't very long and I'm forced to sleep diagonally in it or curled up or else I won't fit. At night when I bring in food and things I don't want to be wet or disturbed by critters in the dark, the two-man tent has room enough for only one.

My sleeping bag is called Silver Cloud and it keeps me toasty and warm, even on the coldest nights. It's supposed to be useful even if the temperature drops down to five degrees, but I hope I never have to prove it.

The sleeping bag is not stuffed with goose down, but rather with some special kind of man-made fabric. Down bunches up when it gets wet and loses its loft and insulating quality. I don't plan on getting wet, but canoes have minds of their own. You never know. The sleeping bag packs almost as tightly as a down bag, and it was cheaper.

I have an air mattress that inflates by itself. It is an extra layer between me and the cold ground. It's not thick enough to provide great comfort, but without it even the Silver Cloud won't help on certain nights. It's easy to use: unscrew the valve, forget it until it has inflated, close the valve. In the morning it rolls up to the size of a small log.

I have food. Granola bars, trail mix and cashews, chocolate bars, Malt-o-meal for breakfast, apples, a lot of cans. Soups, beans, stews. Hot dogs, peanut butter, bread, cookies. I carry it all in large, black plastic trash bags.

In fact I carry everything in those plastic bags. My extra clothes are in a duffel bag lined with a plastic bag. Extra jeans. A bright yellow vinyl rain suit. My warm jacket that has an outer vest that unzips to be worn alone when the vest and inner shell are too hot. A sweatshirt with a hood. Extra thermal underwear. More socks. Cowboy boots. Canvas bicycling shoes, which I wear while I canoe. They make my feet look like kidney beans—the same shape—and they are soaked every day, all day, and I have to dry them every night by the fire.

I've got the kind of enameled metal cooking set that cowboys in the old West used. At least the cowboys in the movies use them. A pot for soups and stews, a skillet for frying, matching plates and coffee cups, and a coffee pot.

(I don't drink coffee unless I'm trying to feel like an adult. I drink tea. And that's the reason I didn't grow up to be a cowboy. Cowboys don't drink tea. They drink coffee. They ride into camp after herding the dogies and they settle around the campfire and drink coffee. When they're alone out on the trail and they meet up with a lonesome stranger, the stranger offers them coffee. All my life I've wanted to be a cowboy. Not liking the taste of coffee is what stopped me, though by the end of this trip I will have drunk enough coffee offered by strangers that I won't be able to use that excuse again.)

A canteen. A five-gallon plastic collapsible water bag. An axe. A fileting knife for the fish I catch. A sharp hunting knife for other things. A Swiss Army pocket knife. A stack of notebooks. A camera and film. A pocket-sized tape recorder for note taking and for conversations. A powerful lantern that throws a beam about a mile and that floats. Extra batteries. Waterproof matches. Ammunition. All carried in plastic. Some things are first locked away in plastic sandwich bags and then stowed in the big plastic garbage bags. Some things go straight into the garbage bags. Still others go in the little bags, placed in bigger bags, then stowed away in the second duffle bag I have with me.

The duffel bags are nylon and camouflaged. Those were the cheapest ones, and at that price I would have taken absolutely any color. In fact I would have preferred any color, even fire-engine red, to the camouflage. I hoped no one would think I was one of those trendy idiots who walk around in combat fatigues trying to be stylish. I also didn't want to be confused with those hard-boiled neo-nazi survivalists who lurk like commandoes in the woods waiting and hoping for Armageddon, looking for somebody to shoot.

I was well equipped, not equipped enough, and too equipped, all at the same time. They were the barest essentials if I used everything. I didn't, so they were extras. I always over-pack. Still it was not enough for luxury or real comfort, but it worked out fine.

And it was enough weight in the front of my canoe where I stowed everything to keep the canoe pointed in the right direction. Most of the time.

The river has grown. He's a different river now; he wears a new face. He's a young boy struggling with his youth, learning himself, getting used to his power and size and getting ready for the work ahead.

The river is still clean, or so it seems. The water is blue-grey and you can see into it. I have seen no commercial vessels yet, only pleasure craft—and not many of those; it's nearly winter, after all. But that will change as the river does, as it ages, and starts to work. As it does, it will become stronger and swifter and the barges will add a new dimension of danger.

But with the river's change comes a new security. For as I glide south I know where I am. At last I am on the navigation maps issued by the Army Corps of Engineers. Those Army engineers have a usefulness after all.

The Corps of Engineers, along with the Coast Guard, maintains the river. They make sure the river is navigable for commercial traffic and, by a series of locks and dams, dikes and canals and dredgings, they keep the river at least nine feet deep in the channel. Before the various other rivers empty into the Mississippi basin, the river is not so naturally deep and at low water rocks on the river bed and sand bars can rip up barges as if they were canoes. In the old days the cry "mark twain" signaled that the river was deep enough for the flat-bottomed river boats to continue. The same danger from sand bars would still exist today if not for the Corps.

The Coast Guard posts mile markers and navigation aids—blinking beacons and triangular or rectangular red and green markers—along the river's edge. Channel markers and lighted buoys float in the river and keep the ships in the deepest part of the river.

As part of this maintenance the Corps of Engineers publishes very detailed navigation maps in two huge books. One for the upper river above Cairo, Illinois, the other for the lower river between Cairo and the gulf. The maps cover about five miles to a page and denote sand bars, day markers and lighted buoys, underwater cables and pipelines, overhead power lines, underwater obstructions, islands, dams, dikes, roads near the river, railroads, towns, and almost every rock. Everything.

And now finally I am on the map. I can see ahead of time which routes to take, whether to stay in the main channel, take a quieter chute between an island and the shore, whether to go for speed and vie for space with the barges or to chop down the miles by taking short cuts along the slower-moving chutes.

It all begins at mile marker 868, twelve miles north of Minneapolis. Eight hundred sixty-eight miles north of Cairo, Illinois. I can see just how far I have to go.

The river seems to have narrowed somewhat since the area around St. Cloud. It may be my imagination, but easing toward Minneapolis I feel that the river is not so formidable. Am I just becoming more expert and more confident, or is there a point in growth where regression occurs? Don't little children sometimes stop acting their age and regress to about two years old? I don't know, but the river is definitely easier to take.

Rounding a bend I see my first glimpse of the city. Buildings tall but ghost-like rise in the distant haze. Bridges hang over the river and drop their shadows into the water. And on the water, the first appearance of barges. I was wrong about the fish early on in the journey, but I know for sure that these barges will be with me from here on down to New Orleans.

Minneapolis is the end of the line for barge traffic on the Mississippi. Or the beginning, depending on your point of view and on the barge's cargo. Oil from the gulf comes north from the gulf states and foreign oilfields to fuel and heat the north. Coal, grain, iron and steel go south.

Just north of Minneapolis barges are docked and are being loaded. Grain elevators are working. The harvest from these northern grain states is in and the elevators are full and what's in the elevators is loaded into the barges here for the trip south, on it's way to feed the country and the world. Clouds of grain dust rise up as I pass. I choke and cough and hold my breath. The workers wave. I'm asked the inevitable.

"Where are you headed?"

"New Orleans."

"All right! Wish I could go."

"I got room. And I could use some help paddling."

"Not this time. But good luck to you."

An old black man sits fishing on the rocks above the city. I can barely make out that he's black. I aim for him and when he sees me, he stands with his hands on his hips. He must be straining to see me and wondering what the heck I'm doing. He shouts something at me which I can't hear. Then he waves exuberantly and I wave back.

In the same way, a white man leaning on the rail at the quay of some promenade by the water's edge calls down his greetings to me as I pass.

It isn't much, perhaps. It makes me feel superb just the same.

I'm canoeing now as if I actually know what I'm doing. I pass under a bridge and I'm cocky enough now to let the canoe drift lazily under. I look up. Some men are looking down. They are working on the bridge above me and as I pass through they stop lest their sparks from blow torches and scraps of metal fall down on me. They are very careful for my sake. We have a five second conversation. Then I wave and get back to canoeing and they get back to work. Although I'm only in their lives for seconds, I hope they will hardly forget the day they saw the crazy black man on his way to New Orleans in a canoe.

I have this mighty urge to stop my canoe and get out and explore Minneapolis. I've only been here once before and don't remember it much. It looks to be a pretty city, with the sweet charm of a small town. Everybody who sees me waves.

But I've tarried enough: if I hang around too long winter will sweep in and settle solidly around me. Then the river will be sending big chunks of ice downstream along with the uprooted trees. I don't want to argue with ice floes for room. I think of the *Titanic*.

Already the air has grown colder. Clouds overhead are boiling together, fomenting winter and rain. I stop to put on my yellow rain suit. When I get going again the wind decides to play games with me, no doubt to let me know just how kind it has been so far.

The hills and trees north of the city have vanished from the west bank of the river, the wind, hiding behind a low warehouse-like building the same as it had hidden behind trees and hills, sneaks out and comes rushing down the slope and onto the river. It bangs into my canoe broadside and shoves it all the way to the opposite shore, right up on an embankment built of boulders. Scrape. *I hope nobody sees me.*

I finally make it off the rocks and canoe a while along the east bank but I know, by the map on the floor in front of me, that just ahead, on this side of the river, lurks the Falls of St. Anthony—whatever that is. I know enough, however, to keep away and that the locks are on the west side. I have to get back over. I have to.

But the wind doesn't want me to. Too bad! I have to.

Too bad for me. The wind says no and I'm not as strong as it is. It shoves me and says stay put, like a bully proving who's stronger. I stay put.

All at once the wind lets up, just enough and long enough for me to get away from the rocks and back out to the middle of the river. Then, still toying with me, it comes back.

So. You want to play, eh?

The answer is yes, and I have a way to outsmart the wind. At least this time.

Instead of aiming the canoe straight downstream with the flow of the river, I aim slightly into the wind, diagonally across the river, aiming for a point down and across on the opposite shore. I'll use my paddling as the keel of a sailboat and the wind won't be able to push me sideways. The river will be the wind in my sails and I'll go forward and across instead of into the rocks. And the harder I paddle, as long as I keep my canoe's nose into the wind, the more distance I'll make toward the west bank.

It works. I'm smarter than the wind. What do you know; I'm actually getting the hang of this. A few muscles and a decent head on my shoulders and I think I might just make it.

14

TWENTY-NINE LOCKS AND DAMS span and block the Mississippi at varying intervals between Minneapolis and St. Louis. They are there to hold back the water and turn the rage of the river into the lull of lakes, called pools by the Corps of Engineers, which built and operates the locks and dams. Twenty-six pools. One canal. Two locks at the water falls. Twenty-nine locks in all, and all of them put in place to make the river navigable all the time. To control the amount of water that flows, the depth of the water in the pools, the amount of flooding. (After St. Louis the river—at least lock-and-dam-wise—is on its own. Enough water falls in from the tributaries of the Mississippi basin to keep the river deep enough for navigation. Flooding, however, is a different story.)

My first time with the locks, the virgin experience that shaped my future times in the locks, came at St. Anthony's Falls Upper Lock and Dam. It is the first lock on the river and I didn't know what I was supposed to do.

I saw the lock from a long distance away. It loomed in the haze like a giant roadblock, a mass of steel and concrete lying quietly beneath a tangle of bridges and railroad overpasses. The activity on the lock was slight, but like a criminal approaching the roadblock and wondering whether to crash the gates, detour around the thing or just go on and feign surprise and nonchalance, I approached with caution. I didn't know if there was a fee or if canoes were even allowed or if a volley of rifle fire would come just after the whistles went off and the sirens and the searchlights scanned the water looking for me.

Just to the left, to the east of the dam, the river rushed roaring into the crevasse of the waterfall. The river which has been so quiet, so serene up until now, rages suddenly with the fury of a mountain river carving canyons. White water plunges into the crevasse, spills and splashes down below and sends up sprays of cold mist. The roar sounds like jet engines with nowhere to go, screaming for release.

I made sure to stay far away from the falls, from the roaring, from whatever current might grab hold of me and my canoe and not let go until we had been sucked toward the falls and hurled into the abyss and smashed to smithereens.

Over very close to the bank and up near the lock, the water is much calmer. I stayed there and drifted up to the edge of the structure, just creeping along the concrete wall of the lock and hoping someone or something would tell me what to do, whether I had to pay or get out or what. I didn't know if they'd let me through in this canoe or if I'd have to wait hours until enough boats or barges were ready to pass through to make it worthwhile for the engineers to open the gates.

A sign told pleasure craft to wait by the ladder in the wall and yank the chain to signal the lockmaster. I was a pleasure craft, wasn't I? I yanked the chain and waited like a good little boy along the wall.

A voice came scratchily through the loud-speaker stuck up high on the wall. A woman's voice. Like Emily, I thought, another woman to save me.

The sound of the voice was reassuring. Had it been a man's voice it would have sounded barky, gravelly. But this voice was actually pleasant beneath the grating of the loudspeaker, and soothing.

"Good morning."

I didn't see a microphone so I just shouted back as loud as I could at the loudspeaker.

"Good morning."

"Welcome to St. Anthony's Falls Upper Lock."

"Thank you."

"Are you locking through today?"

"Yes, please."

"Give us a few minutes to fill the chamber. When you get the signal, paddle forward and hang onto the floating cylinder in the wall; you'll see it. We'll lower you down and when the gates open, you're on your way."

And that's basically how locking through works. And this woman, whom I never got a glimpse of and only thanked through whatever she heard me through, took me by the hand and guided me through the lock. Whoever you are, thanks.

When the signal was given, a green light and a horn, the mammoth steel and wooden gates opened their jaws and I let myself be swallowed up. The gates closed eerily behind me.

This is how locks work: because of the dam, the water level of the river is higher upstream than it is downstream. In order for a vessel to get through, it must pass smoothly from the higher level to the lower—or vice versa if going upstream. The locks effect this by flooding, taking the vessel into the locking chamber between the two sets of fairly watertight gates (much like a whale takes in a mouthful of fish as food and then expels the water before swallowing), and then the vessel is lowered to the level—or raised—to the same height as the water the boat will pass into next. The gates open and the vessel is on its way.

I sat in the canoe and held onto the cold metal cylinder in the wall. As the water was expelled from the locking chamber and the level dropped, the floating metal cylinder began to drop with it. I dropped as well. The gates behind me held back the river. Almost watertight, they still allowed some water to fall in and I could see how high the river rose behind me because of the way the water continued to spill slowly into the chamber.

What if the gates break and all that water comes crashing in here on me?

One of the men working the lock came out to chat with me

while I waited. We talked about this adventure. He wished me luck, of course, and told me to be careful but he expressed no desire to come along. Not in a canoe, at least.

I said, "This is a lot of trouble for a guy in a canoe, isn't it?"

And he said, "Not at all. That's what we're here for."

I felt good and warm then. I felt like I owned the place. I finally could see tax dollars doing something I appreciated, something for me directly. This man let me know that, yes, he worked for me.

We talked until I began to drop away from him. Finally, when I had dropped too far below to hear his words, he just looked down and watched me. I wondered what he might be thinking about and how crazy he might have thought me to be. I looked up and he was smiling. I had dropped nearly fifty feet.

The gates opened and I canoed out confident, like I knew what I was doing. We waved. I didn't have much time to think.

The Falls of St. Anthony hold a double set of locks and dams. The upper lock that I just passed through, and the lower lock that I entered almost immediately.

It had begun to drizzle and I put on my yellow rain hood. I got to the chain in the wall and yanked on it. A man's voice this time.

"What the hell are you doing out in a canoe on a day like this?"

Just think. If that had been the greeting at the upper lock, my future with locking-through would have been a disaster from then on, ruined. But because of the woman I was not intimidated by this guy. I told him I was going to New Orleans.

Again someone came out to keep me company. I don't know if that's standard procedure or if a canoe in the locks is so unusual that someone has to come out and gawk. I was glad for the company, however, and said the same thing to him about how much trouble it must be for just a canoe. He wasn't as cheery as the first fellow, but he did say it wasn't too bad, as though I had meant effort for the folks who work the locks gates.

"You just throw a few switches and push some buttons. It's all automatic."

I locked through and I was again on my way.

Five miles down the river I came to Lock and Dam Number One. No problem. I was an old hand at this by now. Locking through was suddenly the easiest thing in the world. Nothing to be scared of, no matter how imposing the structures seem. All you have to watch for is the current going in and make absolutely certain that you stay close to the locks and the walls and away from the current that will suck you, if you're not careful, into the dams where you will be ground like burger meat.

But get into the locks and you're safe. The lockmasters are there to help. They keep you company. They come out to talk to you. They wave and wish you luck. In essence, they take care of you while you are in their charge. *En masse* they are possibly the nicest group that earns tax dollars. I've never heard anything but praise for them (which can hardly be said for soldiers and the IRS and most politicians).

And yet, they are part of the Corps of Engineers and because of that, as much as I respect them, I harbor a fundamental grudge against them. They have enslaved the river.

The river is now, at least between Minneapolis and St. Louis, as tame as a silent partner, a minority shareholder. But in the old days, the Mississippi called all the shots. It was wild and rebellious, capricious and unreliable and stubborn. The canoe, the paddlewheeler, keelboats, the river carried them all, but the river decided when their traffic was okay and when enough was enough.

The river above St. Louis had a mind and soul of its own and in times of flood the water rose high and the riverbed lay deeply below. The water often raged and those lesser beasts of olden days ran great risk of being dashed to pieces. In times of dry weather and low water, the river calmed but ran so low as to be impassable. Submerged boulders would chew up the hulls of the wooden steamers, and each storm sent new obstacles and created new hazards: sand bars appearing out of nowhere, trees ripped up and knocked over to form dangerous snags that those old boats couldn't handle, islands suddenly larger than before, altering all the maps. The river teased.

In the 1830's Uncle Sam stepped in to help create order out of the whimsical chaos of the river's will. The river was far too valuable in settling the western frontier to let it run unbridled. Like an expensive thoroughbred colt, it couldn't be allowed such reckless freedom. So the first primitive improvements began, the blasting of rapids with dynamite, removal of sand bars and shoals and the closing off of the side chutes that the river had used for resting. These old chutes and sloughs meandered lazily and diverted water away from the main branch. Closing them off confined the river's flow to the main channel and maintained the deeper depths required for navigation at times of low water.

In 1878 Congress authorized the 4½-foot channel on the upper river. Riverboaters could be sure of a depth of at least 4½ feet and the first navigation locks appeared on the river at canals built to circumvent dangerous rapids.

In 1907, Congress ordered a six-foot channel, maintained primarily by the construction of rock wing dams that jutted out from shore toward the center of the river to further constrict the water flow and force it into the navigation channel. It was not, however, enough to save commercial river traffic. By now man's own ingenuity had come up with cheaper transportation, and the steamboat on the river began to fade away. Unless something could be devised to make commercial river boating easier, less risky and much cheaper, the river would have its way. It would have won the struggle to be free.

But innovations in lock and dam construction and operation won the day. Dams were developed with roller-gates that fell into place like window shades, and the mechanical workings of locks and dams yielded to push-button control. Diesel-powered river vessels came to work. More powerful, more efficient than the steamboats, these new rigs were all business. It soon became obvious that the upper Mississippi could once again be suitable for productive commercial traffic.

Those powerful towboats and big barges would need, of course, a dependable waterway. So in 1930, the Army Corps of Engineers went to work to construct on the river between Minneapolis and the mouth of the Missouri River a series of locks and dams that would yield a navigation channel nine feet deep and at least four hundred feet wide. Between 1930 and 1940 the engineers constructed—miraculously it seems even to me—and put into operation most of the twenty-nine locks and dams. If it didn't make me so sad for the river's sake, this magnificent feat would merit praise.

What the engineers did was to destroy the river and in its majestic place was left a series of slackwater pools. This means very little flow, no current, and hard work for a man in a canoe because the river pouts and will not help much. You paddle every mile of the way.

And the locks—wouldn't you know it!—are almost uniformly the same dimensions: 110 feet wide by 600 feet long, with only a few exceptions. They turn the river into a giant's stairway, dams for the risers and pools for the treads that lift or lower the barges 420 feet in 669 miles, if the barges go all the way. And thus the river is harnessed and rendered useful.

I'll admit it: the construction *is* a marvel and the navigation is easy. Furthermore, the Corps itself did something for which I'll be forever grateful and which certainly made my journey easier: they constructed a great number of small boat harbors along the way which allow easy access to and from the water, access to towns along the route which come in handy when supplies and restocking are needed. In addition to that, the Corps bought land and combined their purchases with lands already owned by the US Fish and Wildlife Service to create a giant campground all the way to St. Louis. I can camp anywhere I please for as long as I please and know that, except for the areas around towns and cities and developed commercial sites, which are few, the river and the land are mine and wild.

But I'm a generous man. I will share what I have with others. And if these others are bigger and tougher than I am, so much the more readily will my generosity show itself.

So I have no trouble sharing the river. I willingly yield my place, actually get out of the river and politely wave when the river is needed by those towboats and barges as they go by proudly, like great river beasts.

15

THE HORROR STORIES are nothing at all like the real thing. They are inexact, distorted on the down side.

I've seen these things sluggishly plying the river for years at St. Louis. They roar in their labor and crawl past, and though the water slaps the shore loudly after the barges have passed, the feeling is absolutely nothing like being out on the river with them.

My first barge/towboat combination was a small one. I traveled downstream. The barge was moving upstream and so came at me rather quickly. Since it was my first, my virgin experience, I went at it carefully. The barge passed without a hitch. Or so it seemed.

But then came the wake. I saw it mounting into swells and rolling wave after bigger wave toward me. Quickly—and wisely—I paddled to shore, climbed out onto the rocks and watched. The waves lapped at the rocks and at the canoe and as they grew in size they slapped up at me and over my shoes. I held onto the canoe by the line in the stern and let it take the waves alone. I climbed higher up on the rocks.

The whitecapped waves on Lake Bemidji had nothing on these man-made waves. I thought the canoe would splinter on the rocks. I pushed it farther out and away from me. I thought maybe the gods wanted a sacrifice and would settle for the canoe in my place. But the canoe came back; it always came back, as if the rocks were a magnet or the canoe a masochist or simply out to get me. When it came back, the canoe leapt at me and creaked as if in pain. I wanted no part of it and moved a few inches farther up the rocks. Then the waves diminished and went away and the river was calm again.

I continued on down and eased into Lock Number One, which was ready for me since the barge had just passed through.

Lock Number One was a breeze. *How can something that holds back so much water be handled so easily? By me?* The man hanging over the rail talking to me treated me as though I actually knew what I was doing. I had that feeling myself.

I felt significantly lower when I canoed away from the lock, lower in the sense that the level of the river felt about thirty feet below what it was when I entered the lock. The river was very low and the dam gates were raised to let more water through. The water rushed through swiftly. I was under control, though, and feeling more and more expert, and the water didn't look too rough, only swift. I paddled right out into it and hopped on the dinosaur's tail for a ride. An exhilaration, but quickly over, which was all right. I felt great but was getting tired.

The river calmed around the bend and narrowed. Fishers along the high bank and steep slope of the west shore called out to me. They were fishing for walleyes and nothing too big had been caught. I rode past too fast for a chat and I crossed the river to the other side. I wanted to land at the nearby boat ramp marked on the map. It was raining and I was cold, especially my hands, and I told myself to get a pair of gloves first chance.

But I felt really fine inside, the way a child does when he finally gets something right and his dad pats him on the head. I was learning something, gaining a new skill and confidence and coming to love the effort and the challenges. So far it seemed as though around every bend a new unknown lurked to be discovered and dealt with, challenged and conquered.

I found the boat ramp and pulled out. It wasn't dark yet but soon it would be and I could stop here and try to get a fire going. But everything was too wet.

I dragged the canoe up out of the water and when the rain finally stopped, I took off the yellow suit. Vinyl gets awfully hot and steamy, even in the cold.

Looking around I saw that this place was some sort of city park, green grass, trees, downed limbs, little barbeque pits for picnickers, and a parking lot. There were few cars, however, and no people out promenading on the paths. I was the only one out.

Later on I met Troy and Rick while I foraged for something that would burn. Absolutely everything was wet and the wind kept blowing out my matches and nothing would catch fire and if I didn't get some flames going soon, I would never get warm.

These two guys had pulled up and sat in their car like teenagers hiding out to drink their beer. They were certainly old enough but maybe hadn't gotten over those teenaged attitudes and needed to get away to do their drinking. They never said how long they had been out and watching me, but they had definitely come prepared, armed with a cooler jammed full of ice and beer. Committed beer drinkers want their brew cold, no matter what the weather.

They offered me a beer. I downed it quickly. The beer was cold all right and I stood shivering beside their little blue wreck until Rick invited me inside to warm up. I folded myself up and fell into the cramped back seat next to the cooler of beer. Leaning against that thing I was even colder and Rick started the engine and threw on the heater full blast.

Two guys—now three—with nothing to do and nowhere to go. Rick had just been in Alaska visiting his brother and canning fish. Troy had recently gotten booted out of the Army. He wasn't too upset about it; now he could grow his hair long again. Both of them on the edge of the cracks and if they fell in, they would end up in a life of drifting and odd jobs like supermarketing or gas pumping or selling refrigerators. They wore without knowing it the vague expression of world weariness, the look of misfits wondering what to do next. They sat in that car with one foot in the bucket of freedom and fun and adolescence, the other foot in cement, and I doubt if either realized the horrible side effects of their non-conformity. Part of me wanted to warn them. Part of me wanted to know what made it my business anyway. Part of me wanted to cheer their misfitting just as they were applauding mine. The American dream isn't for everyone, is it, and who says it's so dreamy anyhow?

Still, when they asked me why, I couldn't help but offer a disguised sermon.

"Well," I said. "It's just something to do, and you've got to do something to stay out of trouble."

The ex-GI agreed. He grew sullen and looked sorry. He had caused enough trouble in the army and now didn't know what he was going to do.

I drank my next two beers without saying a word. I felt sad for these men. They were good guys, sharing their beers and warmth with a stranger, a fellow non-conformer, and yet life and happiness require more than merely being good guys. These two fellows were trapped. Couldn't they see it? And I wondered: *Just how non-conforming am I? Isn't education a safety net? Is talent? Just how brave, then, and reckless am I? After all, can't I find a good-paying job when I need one—yes—and can't I jettison this canoe and this gear, walk to the nearest road, hitch a ride to the nearest town, find a phone and call home for a ride out of here? Yes.* On the edge of the same cracks that the unfortunates fall through, I'm able to step back to safety.

I got out of the car like a man finding something he didn't expect in his reflection in the mirror, wrinkles and grey hair, and he doesn't know what to make of it.

I wished them well and good luck. It's what they would have said to me if I hadn't beat them to it. They told me to be very careful, and without saying so I wished the same for them. Then they were gone.

It was good to be alone again. In a way, it's the safest place to be. Certainly the easiest.

I went back down to the landing and stood there in the mist and fog and semi-darkness. My concern for the boys vanished as a beastie slithered silently on the water like an apparition rising suddenly and coming right at me.

Not long before I had seen a movie in which a run-away barge screams out of control in the night and shoots up on shore and destroys everything in its path. This thing was coming at me in exactly the same way and I couldn't move. I stood frozen to the spot.

Suddenly, the beastie changed its mind; the towboat grunted and veered to the right, heading upstream and away from me. I released the breath I held. The barge had been close enough to hit with spit.

The beasts: towboats and barges. They cannot turn on a dime and when they come to a sharp bend in the river they must slow down almost to a halt, nose into the bend and push the back end around until the whole beast aims straight in the desired direction. Then they can go. The maneuver is called flanking by barge men and it's best to learn all about it and be on the correct side of the bend—or out of the river altogether—when this is going on. The flanking motors kick up a heck of a lot of water and if you get caught between the towboats and the bank, it's like being caught in a box canyon when the dam bursts and there is no place else for the water to go.

Flanking wake is much more deadly than running wake, which is pretty frightening enough. The normal wake of a powerful towboat pushing a stack of barges stretches out for almost half a mile after the beast has passed. Waves rise as high as twelve feet from crest to nadir and if you get anywhere too close, the wash from those big engines can flip you and your canoe like a light and fluffy buttermilk pancake.

All I knew about the beasts at that time would fit in a thimble. Dangerously powerful and sneaky, but that was about it. Usually they roar their approach and you can hear them from miles away, but sometimes you'll mistake their bellowing for the wind in the trees or the roaring of the river itself. And sometimes, if the wind is blowing in the wrong direction carrying sound away, or if your mind is dreaming of warmth and sun in the Caribbean, you won't hear a thing. They can come down on you and be breathing down your neck instantly. This means you have to stay constantly on the alert, looking over your shoulder pretty often to get early warning about the beasts' downstream approach.

Open barges loaded with coal, covered barges of grain, tanker barges filled with petroleum. Ten, fifteen, twenty tons of freight—no problem! A far cry from the capacity of the old steamboats which used to ply this river. They were not nearly so efficient but I bet they were very picturesque and lovely to look at.

The area around St. Louis, or so tell the paintings, once resembled a parking lot of white steamboats. In the late 1800's the river was the scene of vast excitement. Paddlewheels slapping at the water, whistles announcing the arrivals of the river boats, the docks crowded with cargo just unloaded or about to be loaded, passengers, swarms of people down on the riverfront just to watch. The excitement of ordinary activity in those days before television and organized thrills.

Nowadays the barges cruise by and they offer no thrill for the observer; they arouse only slight interest and curiosity. How many crewmen are on board? How comfortable is the living? What do they do and how long does it take? But mostly they are hardly noticed unless you happen to be on the levee and tossing rocks into the river, or dipping your toes and ankles in on hot summer days, or trying to catch a fish. Because then you can feel the barges pass. The river disturbed from its serenity awakens with a start, blames you and your rocks and toes and fishing line, and sends noisy waves out to grab at you, scare you and at the very least to get your attention. You can't help but notice the passing barges.

If you're out there on the water when the barges pass, that's a different story altogether and you're lucky that you do notice them. You cannot allow yourself to get used to them; the beasts don't like to be ignored and consider it an indignity. They will have you for lunch. They'll hardly know they've been disturbed at all except for the thumping sounds you and your canoe will make as you pass under and bang against the steel hull of the barge. Then the towboat engines will grind you up like a garbage disposal, and you'll only be the memory of a good meal.

On the upper river the powerful towboats push loads that measure six barges long and three across. The pilots can't even see you if you're up too close to them and directly in front. They are too busy watching the river and their radar screens. When you appear on the green screens as a little blurry slash of light, you're no more to the pilots than a big log. They don't swerve for logs.

For obvious reasons, you'd better not be out on the river after dark. But in the daytime, if you give these bad boys a wide berth, they are gentle. The pilots wave down from the wheelhouse at you and the crew, if they're not busy with their work, will wave and holler. You can never hear what they're trying to say.

Whenever the big barges pass, I always found some excuse—time for lunch or a need to pee in the trees—to stop and get out and let them go by unmolested and unchallenged. And if it wasn't time to eat or pee, and if I was lucky, there'd be a side chute or slough to duck into and I'd let some little river island hide me from the roar and wake of the beasts.

Until later, of course. Later everything changes. The river widens and deepens, and there's no place to pull out, no hideaways. Or maybe confidence swells and the head puffs and the fears vanish. There's no need any longer to get so far out of the way. You're not afraid of much of anything and you begin to feel like an expert at last.

16

The river. Big hearted like your grandmother. Stern like those stories of your best friend's father. Double edged like a broadsword and sharp as a razor carving its way through the terrain even as it snakes its way into my being, creating a deep rift and immediately filling in the void as it goes. A strange kind of cleft, one that strangely unites instead of dividing. A river that unifies north and south the same as it connects east and west—rather than creating an impasse—even though this linking bridge is two thousand miles long and a great distance across.

The river has changed many times since Itasca, and will change a lot more before the end. Passing between Minnesota and Wisconsin the river is a monster. Because of the dams, the river backs up in places and spreads out more than two miles across. What probably once was a narrow channel in the old days is now a massive lake that has swallowed up acres and acres of land. The Mississippi River proper has been confined to the navigable channel while the waters surrounding it go by various other names: Sturgeon Lake, Lake Pepin—twenty miles long and so wide you can't see to the other side—Robinson Lake, Big Lake, Spring Lake. And in the middle float those scattered islands that were once rises of high ground. Now that the lowlands have been flooded, ridge tops become islands. None of this would have been created without the dams blocking the flow of the river. The dams have fragmented the Mississippi, altering its character in places, slowing it down, widening it, turning the upper river into a long string of lakes, but no matter what they do to it, no matter how many faces the river puts on, the Mississippi remains only one river. Different phases in an old man's life which, because it touches the lives of so many others along the way, actually connects those lives. A great-grandfather, a church elder, an old man sitting day after day on the same bench in a small town. You might never have paid much attention to him. But he has his effect.

The river can't help but connect, like the old man touching lives however subtly. Or like a national purpose. Like a favorite baseball team. Like poverty. Something shared. A common understanding. Different in intensity and meaning perhaps to each who share it, but a common language that holds together like a delicate infrastructure. No nails, no glue, just some sort of mysteriously strong bond. Like baptism.

The river flows through towns as different from one another as Minneapolis and Portage des Sioux. In some places it runs wild, in some places it is wide and standing still. For some the river means industry, for others beauty, or leisure boating, or duck hunting. But it's all the same river, all things to all men.

I've watched this river forever. It is as familiar to me as a relative. But now all of a sudden I see beyond the surface and river becomes friend. The river shows me more of what it truly is. It allows me an understanding that I could never have gotten without the risk of intimacy. As I strip the varnish off my own exterior and expose hidden layers, the river reciprocates and reveals to me what I otherwise would not have known.

That, then, is what I must be after, seeking an understanding of the river and through the mirror of friendship, an understanding of myself, and through the special unity offered by the river, a better way to see.

17

THE RIVER LAPS LAZILY at the sides of my canoe, gently slapping a greeting and rocking me as I drift with the flow of the water and coast for a few moments. The waves are meek and comforting today.

I promised myself early on that I would not make race an issue out here. I would try to live my life on the river as I so far have lived my real life; I would not make my being black a part of my success or failure or too great a factor in how I perceive things. After all, I have never considered being black my most significant feature; when I think of myself, black is not the first descriptive term that comes to mind. And yet, how could race not mean a little something extra out here? As my old friend Robert had told me, and he was true so far, here I was traveling from the high north where blacks are pretty scarce and slicing into the deep south where feelings toward blacks are often none too sweet—historically at least. And people will see that I'm black only moments after they see that my canoe is green. Maybe even before.

It's not, I hope, what they'll remember later, and long after I'm gone, maybe they'll talk about a black man in a canoe, but perhaps they won't. Perhaps they will pick up on some other aspect of me and will choose to remember what I'm doing out here, what a sweet smile and happy soul I have, and how I let them treat me kindly. People in this country only need a chance and an excuse to be kind, and they respond.

Not too long ago a girlfriend tried to enlighten me. She told me I was the dumbest, most naive simpleton she had ever run across, a danger to myself and a step in the wrong direction. I had told her that I had not experienced much bigotry, and she blew a gasket. She violently told me that yes I had and that unless I recognized it I would never be able to do anything about it. And in a way she was right. And I may indeed have been blind to it or too stupid to see, but "if a tree falls in the forest. . . ." If you don't perceive a thing, no matter how real or concrete the occurrence, if it doesn't enter your consciousness or affect your awareness, how real could it be? (The converse is true as well.) Or better, what difference does it make?

I told her I didn't allow people to deal with me on the basis of my race. I am more than black and my attitude says so. My *attitude*! I think that plays a big and greatly unappreciated role in how we are treated, and in how we face our world and our selves.

When as a writer I am rejected, my first reaction questions the stupidity of the editor, my second question concerns the writing itself and the realization that maybe it wasn't what the editor was looking for, or maybe—perish the thought—simply not good enough. Never had the rejection been racially motivated. When I was accepted to the university, it was because I was qualified, not because I was black.

When a man downright doesn't like me, I'm sure he has his reasons; I'm not always so likable. But when he doesn't give me a chance, I find a way to force him to. Certain things, no matter how small, you cannot allow. Idiots screaming bravely from passing cars excepted, people should not get away with stupidity without challenge.

Racism—sure it exists, I know that. But its effect and effectiveness depend as much on the reaction as on the action.

I stopped for breakfast one morning early in La Crescent, a dinky little town parked at one end of the bridge that reaches over to La Crosse, Wisconsin. The town isn't much for size but it offered a choice of spots to eat, including a place for pizza. I opted for the one that had the most character, a plain looking diner removed from the center of town. A little place, frequented mostly by locals. The lady tripling as waitress and busboy and cashier seemed to know everyone who walked in, and she greeted each one with a different remark, some personal little tidbit that marked the customer like a brand. Early morning laughter to get the body stirring until the coffee comes.

The breakfast nook was two rooms worth of booths and a counter up front, and three shallow rows of tables in the rear. Everybody in there looked like a farmer or at least somebody who worked hard for a living, laboring with hands and arms and back, and maybe I didn't look too out of place among them walking in with dirty jeans and smelling like a herring. The looks they tossed my way were the recognitions of a stranger. No one stared for very long and if the waitress took a bit longer to get to me and take my order and return with my breakfast, I understood. She was too busy chatting with the regulars to be bothered with a stranger. And when she came to me she somehow had mislaid her friendly face and became a woman with a job to do.

While I waited for my breakfast of chicken livers and scrambled eggs and fried potatoes, a group of three insurance salesmen came in. I don't know if they really sold insurance. They wore ties and jackets and possibly sold farm equipment or maybe held office jobs over in La Crosse, but they reminded me of insurance salesmen. I've yet to see one dressed in a suit that fits well and is not wrinkled, a suit that looks good and is in style and shoes that are more than comfortable. A woman was with them and she wore the female equivalent. They sat in the rear.

At the counter an old man was treating his wife to breakfast out but they sat and ate without saying a word to each other, although both spoke happily to the waitress when she came their way. I guess they had lived together so long they had nothing new to say to one another, or else they just knew. The wife passed the salt and ketchup when the husband needed it. He didn't have to ask for it.

My food arrived and I asked for a clean fork and for mayonnaise for my potatoes. I said please and the waitress smiled. I noticed after that that no one else used the word. She hurried with the fork, but the mayonnaise took forever. The waitress had stopped to talk to three sturdily built women in the booth nearest the register. They were loud and laughing and wore jackets that said River Rat across the back. I was a river rat by then and I wished for a jacket like that.

No one in the place paid any undue attention to my existence or my eating or my being different.

I ate quickly and comfortably and paid. A middle aged man with a puffy face came up to pay as well. I hadn't noticed him with them, but he looked like a part of the group of men wearing those badly fitting suits. It turned out that I was right. This man, at least, *was* an insurance broker, and while we waited for the waitress to finish talking to whomever, he brought up the weather and asked me where I was from. I told him and said what I was doing and he laughed, pointing out the women in their jackets, and he said:

"You should have a jacket like that. Instead of River Rat it should say River Nigger."

He thought it was just the funniest thing and he laughed so loud that everyone looked in our direction. I didn't know if they had heard what he had said and wanted to see my reaction, but they were definitely watching and I felt I could not ignore this man and let him slide by unchallenged, even if he had meant no harm by it. It might, after all, have been a real attempt at friendly though misshapen humor. So why scream and shout?

I put on my toothiest grin and my best African accent and I said rapidly, "I'm from Nigeria. You mean River Niger. Aha-aha-aha!"

I let him struggle to grasp that one and I paid. His face went blank for a second and then knotted into a frown. By the time I got outside he must have figured out what I was really saying: your little joke upsets me and is not funny. And saying it in a way that does not threaten him, that does not attack him and so he cannot defend with anger and arrogance against it.

He hurried out to get me, grabbing me by the arm and saying, "Hey! I didn't mean nothing by it. It was just a joke."

I put my lips together and squeezed them tight and nodded once, but he wouldn't let it drop that easily.

"You're not from Nigeria, are you?"

He wore the most quizzical expression and he was so sincere that I had to laugh.

"I told you where I'm from."

I could almost hear the gears grinding in his head.

"Why'd you say you were from Nigeria? Did what I said bother you that much that you'd rather be from there than here?"

I hadn't meant that, but if it works. . . .

"I know I shouldn't have said it but you know how it is. You hear things and you repeat them and you get used to it. You don't even stop to think." Then he stopped to think. "Unless," he said and his head hung a little lower, "you're the one who's offended. Then it's a different story, isn't it?"

He went on to tell me about the final two games of the World Series which I had missed because of the journey and which had eroded into a fiasco. Grown men throwing tantrums on the ball field and behaving like children, little cry-babies because things weren't going their way.

"And you could see them, right there on camera, saying F-you this and F-you that and I didn't appreciate it. It was uncalled for and I didn't like it one bit. And I'm not a prude, mind you. I was in the Navy, you know."

Twenty years as an insurance broker had done little for him but cause his hair to fall out and make him drink too much. Those little capillaries in his nose and cheeks inflamed his face and gave him the appearance of constant sunburn. Business wasn't too good. Premiums too high. A lot of businesses just can't afford insurance anymore. It's cheaper for them to go out of business, he said, but what can you do, he wanted to know, except close down the law schools for six years. Too many lawyers with nothing to do so they sue sue sue.

But twenty years ago, back when he was in the Navy pulling submarine duty and rearranging the Vietnamese coastline, life was leaner and not so cluttered up.

"Maybe it was Vietnam," he muses. "Maybe that's what did it to us. We could have won that war, you know, and Korea too."

"I guess you miss those Navy days." I'm beginning to feel compassion for this man when only moments before I was feeling contempt. It saddened me that I had made him feel so rotten over a harmless little joke.

"Those were the happiest times of my life."

And now he's back where he started. He's wound around full circle and he gets to the point of this conversation. He tells me about the stint he served in Puerto Rico. A simple story really about a beautiful heiress from Philadelphia who had come to San Juan to get over her grief. The two had met and spent all of their free time together. They slept together in the same room, in the same bed even, but never once did they make love.

"It wasn't that kind of relationship."

Instead, they would tell each other secrets, things they would dare tell no one else. And only once in a while if ever in your life does there appear a soul you truly trust with your own soul. And most likely she's a stranger you'll never see again. And since those days in Puerto Rico, he's not seen the woman ever again and had only received one letter from her, the one that said, "We shouldn't see each other again because we would only try to force something to happen that will only warp the memories." He sent her flowers after that, and that was the last they corresponded.

But in San Juan on hot days when the slightest breeze from the sea felt like a miracle, they would walk and sip rum drinks and talk forever and she told him of the man she was there to forget. The man she loved but whom she could never have because of her family. The only man with whom she had ever. . . .

The story stops while he clears his throat and swallows.

"The only man that she ever, you know," he whispers now, "climaxed with." His eyebrows lift. The whisper disappears. "His name was Raoul and he was a black man and she told me she loved him very very much and she cried and cried and I said to her, 'There's no reason why you shouldn't love him.' And I meant it."

I reckon he did at that. And, I suppose, every man out here who has waved at me so far and wished me luck would get to carving at the core of American racism that lies inside if given the chance. The chance to be helpful. The chance to be friendly. The chance to know that we're not so very different, none of us from the others. I hoped so, anyway. I was traveling south, and because the South still doesn't get very good press, in the back of my mind gnawed a little apprehensive wondering.

Working on that core of American racism is certainly an easier task man-to-man, but on a grand scale chipping at it is as laborious as carving granite. Or so it seems, and I struggle with the confusion the same as I struggle with this river.

If only the racism could be tamed as easily. I should call in the Corps of Engineers for the task.

I waved goodbye to my friend the insurance broker and hoped he would find better days ahead.

Cruising steadily southward I moved into the stretch of river that divides Iowa and Wisconsin, and then Iowa and Illinois. The landscape changes and there are high bluffs all around blocking the wind. Trees overhanging still wear their autumn colors but the fire has gone out of them and subdued hues of amber and gold linger in afterglow. From high atop one of the bluffs I look down on the blue water winding and coiling like a giant anaconda. What a sight to behold! And what a heady thought knowing that I'm out there in a boat the size of a peanut.

It's peculiar. The littlest things make the biggest impressions. I zipped through Iowa in a hurry, like a man on a mission. Only a few memories surface:

Cheese and crackers and smoked carp purchased from a gasoline station that also functioned as the town's grocery. I had never had carp before and heard only horrible things about it. It's a scavenger fish and will eat anything, but so is a catfish and I love catfish. The man working the station promised I would like the fish, and I really did. I was ready for a beer.

The beer that quenched my thirst didn't come for another fifty miles or so, but I was glad I waited.

I pulled into Dubuque and half expected it to be a reprise of La Crosse, Wisconsin, another river town with old buildings fighting to stay alive in the shadow of new offices and hotels. La Crosse had felt old and sleepy and deserted to me, but I had cruised that place in the early morning. The town was just awakening and what few souls were out were the grumpies with another working day on their minds.

I arrived in Dubuque in the middle of the day. The streets weren't bustling but at least they were alive. It was almost lunchtime.

I gave the city a quick inspection. It sits on a bluff and many of the residential sections of town are steeply hilly. Main Street however is flat as a tabletop and just as straight. I stepped into a dim little saloon on Main Street between 9th and 10th Streets and I had my beer.

Seated there drinking a draft beer and munching barbeque-flavored potato chips was a wiry fellow who probably should have been out working somewhere. He was the only customer and he and the little woman who ran the place were watching soap operas on the TV. She was a dwarf who reminded me of the type of feisty woman you find running saloons in movies about the old West. She didn't talk much, just served up the beers and minded her own business and kept her eyes on the television while I'm sure her ears caught everything that was ever said in here. Finally, after enough questions and her very brief answers and after enough comments about the soap opera, she loosened up and started talking about this saloon. I think what opened her up at last was the request for another Budweiser. She was all out.

"The Budweiser man," she said, "was due here on Tuesday, but he never showed up. He doesn't like coming around here because the orders aren't big enough. Only a case or so at a time. It's not worth the effort for him."

Being from St. Louis I couldn't imagine a place being out of

Budweiser, unless of course the bar couldn't keep up with demand.

"No. Lite Beer from Miller," she told me, "is the best seller here, followed by Pabst. That's all they ask for."

So I asked for one too. A Pabst. I don't drink light beers. Too thin.

"Bottle or draft?"

I took mine in a bottle because, it had been pointed out to me, bottled beer comes colder than draft beers. To disprove that, she poured out a glass of draft Pabst and gave it to me free and it seemed just as cold as the beer in the bottle. Unless there had been a remarkable difference, I probably wouldn't have been able to tell anyway, just as I probably only *think* I can tell the difference between light beer and real beer. But I was happy she thought I could, happy for the free beer, and happier still that she cared enough what I thought about the beer in her kegs. And she knew I would not be a regular customer. I had already told her I was just passing through in my canoe.

The man next to me perked up suddenly. There was a commercial on the TV screen and he took a break from the soaps. He was excited about the trip and wanted to know everything.

"What's your ETA?" he wanted to know and then he explained it for me. "Estimated time to arrive."

"Whatever it takes," I said and that seemed to impress him all the more.

"How about them locks?" he asked. "Bet them damn things take a lot of time. You probably spend as much time stuck in them as you do paddling."

I laughed and invited him to tell me about himself.

"Me? Nothing much. I'm just making it."

The soaps came back on.

"How about you?" I asked the bartender. "You making it okay?"

"I do the best I can. Nothing fancy. I try to attract a little business, put in a little live entertainment, but if it's any good it's too expensive, and if it's bad it's just not worth it. The people around here don't notice much anyway."

She sounded like a woman biding her time, saving her money and just waiting for a chance to clear out of here. I had a feeling that she might be here a long time.

Back out on the street I spotted a Chinese restaurant. I crossed over and went down to it and when I got inside the decor struck me as odd. Red everywhere and Chinese lanterns hanging, the restaurant looked like practically every other Chinese restaurant in the western world. I don't know why I expected anything different but it still struck me as odd. And then I knew why. There wasn't an Oriental face in the place. Actually, there was one but he was a customer. He was all dressed in white and looked like a yachtsman, and when I, trying to make friendly conversation, asked him if he had been sailing today, he jumped back startled that a stranger would speak to him and snapped his no with an expression that told me to leave him alone.

A pretty woman dressed in black satiny fake oriental clothing came out to show me to my seat. She carried a menu under her arm but she wasn't smiling like most restaurant hostesses. I should have known better.

I said, "You don't look Chinese." I was trying to be funny, but she failed to see the humor. If she had been a lioness, I would now be headless.

Whew! Dubuque, Iowa.

I got a couple of egg rolls to go and left.

There is a part of town not far from city hall that is closed to automobile traffic. It's lined with shops and has a little clock tower in the center. People hang out here at lunchtime and I stopped to sit in the sun for a minute. A black man passed. He waved exuberantly at me, too much so to be just a friendly wave. He was actually happy to see me, the way Americans get after weeks in a foreign land when they finally hear English spoken. The man waved and kept going. I said to myself again, *Dubuque, Iowa*. It felt really strange.

I next came to Davenport and the sunset that awaited me there. Stripes of blue and swirls of pink and purple, all coming from out of the black of night that sat directly overhead, and fading into an orange glow sitting on the horizon. And I thought, *Some things make everything else worthwhile*. Like those beans and weenies of the first night. Like Robinovich and Emily. Like this sunset streaked with fire and magenta and awash with blue and violet. So simple, yet so spectacular.

In Muscatine, Riverside Park sits right on the river. If you slide into town late and pack up early, you could camp there and no one would ever know. Or you could cross the park, cross the road and sleep comfortably in the Hotel Muscatine. An old hotel, nothing fancy, this dark squat box made of bricks sits on the corner and watches the river run. It probably once was a grand hotel but now you can only tell it's a hotel by the sign out front. It houses a travel agency as well as a coffee shop, and I went inside to eat breakfast.

The specialty of the house at dinner time: French cuisine. On the walls hung reproductions of French fine art, Toulouse-Lautrec and the like. And still the place looked like a simple coffee shop. Grey carpeting, booths and wobbly tables. I sat at a wobbly table.

An old lady was running about with the energy of an Iowa tornado taking orders and serving food and working the register and having quick conversations. She even acted as bouncer: loitering in the lobby of the hotel was a scuzzy character who looked about as bad as I must have and maybe even smelled as bad. He had parked his bicycle outside and had come in to use the men's room and to sit. He sat in one of the telephone stalls outside the coffee shop and smoked a cigarette. When he had finished that he got up and just stood around. Maybe he was harmless, maybe he was a bit wacky, but the old lady kept an eye on him and when he became too much for her to bear, she left the coffee shop and threw the fellow out.

I said to her after I had eaten my omelette, potatoes and toast, "That guy looked almost as raggedy as I do."

She winked and smiled and said, "Yeah, but you're paying."

I sat and listened to a grey-haired man in a grey sport coat and brown pants. He was talking about purchasing farm equipment to a curly-haired fat man, probably his son, who wore glasses and a blue polo shirt and blue jeans. The son seemed like a successful rural car dealer. He fidgeted a lot, but it was the old man who said he had things to do.

"So much to do," he said. "I can't keep it all straight. Already in the last five minutes my head is clearing and I can't remember what I'm supposed to do."

I know I should have felt sad for this old man, growing old and losing his memory and talking to his son who didn't particularly want to hear what he was saying. But instead of compassion, a wave of jealousy rushed over me. I knew that when this old man, when all the people in this place recalled this day, they would remember the old lady and the hobo she had thrown out. They wouldn't remember me.

I wanted to be as much a part of their lives as they would forever be of mine. I didn't want to waltz in for a moment and then out again without leaving an impression, but that's what I was doing. I didn't know how to do otherwise, not without intruding and waving a banner and shouting: Hey, look at me. I'm canoeing down the river.

What I was out here was alone and would be until the end. Maybe this was the journey I had in mind. A selfish one, a journey that would have its effects totally on me. A journey of one-way rewards.

All of a sudden I wanted to share something with somebody and by the time I shoved off in Fort Madison I was feeling so alone as to feel frightened and fed up and wanting to go home. That old dread had returned.

Clouds grey and heavy hung on the sky. I put on my yellow suit when it started to rain. The wind began to blow and the canoe to pitch. But I wasn't thinking about that. I couldn't stop worrying about being so alone, and being alone had never disturbed me before. I actually like it and always have, but now suddenly being alone had turned into loneliness. I tried singing, but that only made the rain come down harder.

Not far ahead I see smoke coming from the trees of an island. My map tells me it's Devil's Island but it's supposed to be uninhabited. *What could the smoke be from?* People of course and I drift closer to the shore of the island and hope somebody will see me. A wave, a hello shouted from the bank, anything. I just want to wave and smile.

They did me one better. As I passed they were calling out all sorts of things, but I couldn't hear any of it. The wind was whistling too loud under my rain hood. Finally they gestured at me. There were two of them and they both came right to edge of the river and beckoned for me to come ashore. It was all the invitation I needed and I turned in and paddled hard to reach them.

The river doesn't seem to be moving so fast when you're on it. Paddling makes the canoe go faster than the river itself, and as slowly as the trees slide by beside you, you think you're not going very fast at all. But as soon as you turn and head to shore you find that you should have started your turn an hour ago. By the time you decide to aim for a point directly beside you, you've already passed it and have to work like mad to get back upstream to it. When you're facing upstream you can feel how swiftly the river is moving under you.

I put everything I had into swinging the canoe and digging in the water to get back to them. But I couldn't do it and when I reached the shore I had missed them by quite a ways and had to climb over fallen trees and through the brush to get back to the clearing where they stood by the fire. I ripped my rainsuit.

"We saw you coming from way off up there. We saw that yellow suit."

"But we didn't know you were in a canoe though."

They were standing by the fire getting warm. They were father and son and they were commercial fishers who stretched nets out into the river overnight and came back the next day to check their catch. They lived up in Fort Madison and I asked them right away what their names were.

"I'm Rod and this is my father Vernon."

They asked me mine and I told them.

"What are you doing out here?"

"Going down to New Orleans."

They hardly reacted.

"Wish we'd brought out some hot dogs like we usually do. But we aren't going to be out here long today. Just cleaning these nets and going to get them back out there and go home."

The fire sputtered and threatened to go out. Vernon searched for more wood. I watched how he got the fire started again even though everything was wet.

He laid leaves on the big smoking log to dry and when they had dried they caught on fire. The twigs and sticks he'd placed around the leaves caught fire too once they had dried and the draft from the breeze fed the flames with air. In no time the fire was a blaze again and I stood over it to keep warm.

They went back to clearing their nets of leaves and sticks and debris, stretching them and laying them down neatly so they wouldn't be so tangled up when they went to set them out in the river.

"What kind of work do you do?"

"I'm a writer."

"You going to write a book about this trip?"

"I hope so."

"You going to put us in it?"

"You bet."

They looked at each other and grinned.

I stepped over closer to them to watch what they were doing. The nets were about a hundred yards long each and to clean them in time to get them back out into the river they had to move fast. Their hands were tough and skilled and only Vernon's age slowed them down a little.

Eventually they went off in their flatboat to set the nets. They drop them in the water and secure them in place with long poles. They mark the nets with empty plastic milk jugs and from then on when I saw those milk containers floating in the water I knew they were more than rubbish trashing the river.

They had told me to keep the fire going.

When they came back and we were all standing by the fire again, Rod told me he had been to New Orleans. He hadn't always lived in Fort Madison, but for some reason he had always come back to it.

"You can't stay away from the river too long," he said.

They laughed at the rip in my rain suit.

"Looks like you could stand a new rain suit."

Vernon showed me his. It was ripped as badly as mine.

"They don't last too good, do they?" he said.

"I've seen some," Vernon said, "that are made of thick tough stuff. They last a little longer but they rip up too. But they're better than these cheap ones like he's got."

Next they criticized my shoes.

"What's that on your feet? Tennis shoes?"

"Something like that."

"You ought to get you some boots like these. Then your feet wouldn't get wet."

"I didn't know they were going to get wet, but you know every time I cross the paddle from one side of the canoe to the other, a few drops at a time fall into the canoe. Those few drops turn into quite a puddle after about ten thousand times."

"I can imagine."

"And when it's cold my feet turn to ice."

"What you been doing at night? Camping and building fires?"

"Yeah."

"Well you ought to stay here tonight. This fire's already going and all you have to do is keep her going. And this ain't such a bad spot for camping."

I looked all around and he was right. The clearing was sheltered on all sides by trees to keep the wind out and the branches arching overhead would shield me from the rain. And it was going to rain.

"Going to be a big storm tonight," Vernon said. "Rod is right. You might as well stay right here."

"I think I might."

And I did.

"Well we got to be going. But we're going leave you with this radio so you can have a little music tonight if you want to." He searched his other pockets. "Where'd that extra battery get to?" He found it and handed it to me. "And when you leave in the morning. . . ."

"If you do," Vernon said.

". . . . leave the radio right here." And he showed me a place in the fork of a tree branch where I could stand the radio up.

I watched them go off across the river, one man sitting in the johnboat, the other standing. They were really river rats, their boat hitting those high waves and the bow being lifted high out of the water and crashing down. They didn't slow up at all.

Too quickly they vanished from my sight and I was again all by myself. But this time I had a physical piece of someone else to comfort me in the night. I turned on the radio and dialed in the strongest country music station I could find. It came in from Keokuk, fifteen miles away. Their weather and mine would be the same.

I climbed back through the brush and over the trees and paddled my canoe up to the little cove. I dragged it up on shore, took out my necessities for the night, and left the remainder safe under the overturned canoe. I saw that the wind and the rain were coming out of the northeast and angled the canoe to keep my gear dry. Then I pitched the tent and collected a mountain of firewood for the night. I wanted to keep the fire going as long as I could and on until morning if possible so I would have a way to warm myself and boil the water for my breakfast cereal.

It hadn't been very late in the afternoon when I landed here, but after a while, talking to Vernon and Rod, and a while longer bringing the canoe around and fetching firewood and making camp, it was nigh unto darkness by the time I ate and settled in the tent ready for bed. I turned on the radio.

Country music and reports of rain on the way, which I already knew, and the story of Hurricane Juan beating up the Gulf of Mexico and sending wind and rain up the Mississippi Valley. I knew about the wind and the rain but both seemed to be coming out of the north and east. Very quickly, as if he heard my doubts, the weatherman explained that the wind and the rain were coming out of the south and west. And very quickly after that, the rains came.

Weathermen and birds are the first to know. And if you're an attentive listener, you can detect the rain's advance as well. Listen for the birds. They twitter and chirp so pleasantly that a storm is the last thing on your mind. But two by two the birds fly off and hide. A genetic memory from the days of Noah, perhaps, but they feel the storm in the air and take cover. I wonder where they go. They disappear so thoroughly, only a few lollygaggers stay to make music. Diehard musicians hate to go home.

And then the wind swooshes up and swishes in the trees. The rain is never far behind. But if you still doubt and need further warning, lightning flashes silently and as the storm draws nearer, thunder comes up to join the lightning flashes, closer and closer to each successive flash until at last they happen nearly at the same time. The storm is here.

This storm was more than a storm and I wondered if the tent could take it. Each wave of the storm brought with it more rain, more wind, and when the storm had finally gone by, water still fell from the branches swaying overhead.

Luckily I had parked in the trees. If not, the wind may have been too much and I would have gotten even more soaked than I did. And soaked I was. The vinyl groundsheet that was supposed to keep water out, didn't. And neither did the nylon fly hanging taut across the top of the tent. I was up all night, catching sleep in short spurts, moving about the tent trying to find a new dry spot. I didn't catch much sleep but I did manage to keep the fire going. Every so often I unzipped the tent and tossed on another log. By keeping the fire alive during the night, the wet wood I tossed on it would dry and eventually burn.

When the rain stopped at last and the batteries in the radio had gone completely dead, I fell asleep. In the morning the fire had gone out, but there was just enough smouldering of the last big log to put to use what I had learned from watching Vernon.

I crawled from the tent stiff and wet. I stretched. There was still water dripping from the trees above and enough of it that I thought it might still be raining and I considered getting back inside for a little longer. But the river was still and calm and I could see that it was not raining. When the wind stopped blowing, the branches stopped swaying and the water from above stopped falling. I knew it was time to get up and get going. In fact I could have gotten started hours ago.

I scooped up wet leaves and scattered them around the smouldering piece of wood. I blew on them hard until finally the coals glowed red and little flames leapt out. The leaves smoked and finally caught fire and I piled on the wood. Soon I had a very decent fire and I felt very proud of myself.

I made breakfast, checked the sky for more bad weather and

took camp apart. I would have felt better if there had been sun or even a little blue in the sky, but there was none and I still felt fine. I set the radio where I was supposed to and took off. I wanted to leave a note but it would have gotten too wet to be legible or would have blown away.

The morning was beautiful and so was the river. I passed a few floating milk jugs and knew what they were. I steered clear making sure not to disturb the nets below. As I got out of range of the island it occurred to me that once again I had been the receiver of kindness, but at least this time I had made an impression, if only by creating anticipation of a book. But how would it last? The anticipation, until there *was* a book. The impression on them, I didn't know, but not as long as the impression made on me. That would last a lifetime and I wondered, is it always the receiver who is impressed the most? Is it because he benefits most from the contact, because he is most affected?

I had no time to dwell on that then. The wind galed up ferociously and knocked me about. The rains returned and the river told me to get out.

I angled for the town of Montrose and for the briefest of moments actually considered going on all the way down to Keokuk, ten miles down river.

If I hadn't stopped for the night on Devil's Island the storm last night might have caught me in a less sheltered spot. There certainly would have been no fire already built and with every piece of wood wet, getting a fire of my own started would have been an awful task.

And this morning when I awoke, if I had gotten started even a half hour sooner, I would already have passed Montrose and would have had to wait out the coming rains huddled up in a little ball on the bank somewhere.

As it turned out, I got to wait out the rain in Hoenig's Riverview Tap, a bar facing the river and the only place available for longterm loitering except the laundromat. The town is only seven blocks deep and eight blocks wide—and that's stretching it.

I poked my head in. A lady with a mop turned.

"Are you open yet?"

She nodded and brought the beer I asked for. I started to

undress, first taking off the torn rain suit and then the wet hooded sweatshirt I wore underneath.

I sat on the stool at the end of the bar closest to the door and just hung around watching soap operas on TV when the game shows had disappeared. I had seen more soap operas since I started this trip than ever in my life. But today I didn't mind. Anything to take my mind off my plight. The rain was not letting up. The beer chilled me so I switched to coffee to warm me and drank coffee after coffee after coffee until I was sick of coffee. Then I had a bowl of chili. Local workers came in for lunch and still I sat there. I was there when they came in, I was there when they left. I caught a few queer glances, but no one said a harsh word about my hanging around.

When I felt I'd had enough, and when the rain had stopped and the river looked calmer, I dressed again in my somewhat drier clothes and headed back down to the river and the canoe. I even put the canoe back in the water and thought I could get underway again. But on closer inspection I realized I'd be a fool to try it—expert though I was.

A young couple came down to park and neck in front of the river; they watched me instead. It took a while but I finally realized I'd be going nowhere today. The river had said no. Don't go. And I didn't.

What I did was to search for a place to spend the night. Failing that, because there are no hotels in Montrose, I searched for somewhere to stash canoe and gear while I hitchhiked somewhere that *did* have a hotel.

A fellow in the lumberyard told me I could leave my junk with him and he'd lock it up for the night while I went back up to Fort Madison. That was the closest town with a hotel. Or Keokuk down river. It would have to be Keokuk. I couldn't go backwards.

And then, in my boldest move ever, I asked him, "You don't know anybody with a pick-up truck, do you?"

I could see he was thinking and wondering what I had in mind.

"I got a pick-up."

"You do?" What luck! "Are you going down to Keokuk by

any chance? We could put the canoe on the truck and drive it there."

I crossed fingers and toes, and he said, "Yeah, we could do that." He spoke so slowly. "If you don't mind waiting a little bit."

Of course I didn't. Especially when he said I could wait in the lumberyard office. It was warm inside.

He was a thin man with a drooping mustache and long hair. He told me his name was Elton or Elden (you can ask a man his name and you can ask him to repeat it, but you cannot ask him to spell it) and I think he was related to the man he worked for—son-in-law, or something. They were inside talking and then Elton went to do his work.

I stepped into the warmth and shivered from relief from the cold and wet. I said, "It's freezing out there."

He said, "Ain't too bad if the wind don't blow."

"It's nice and warm in here. Feels good."

"Yep." Then the phone rang.

Elton came back around and said politely, "You ready?" as if he had changed his schedule to accommodate mine and wouldn't go anywhere until I was warm and ready and said so. And maybe he had urgent business in Keokuk, but I rather think he pushed up his trip to the city to keep me from having to wait around long. He did tell me that he would have to get back to the lumberyard and then turn around later and go again to Keokuk where he lived.

We drove down into Keokuk with the windows rolled up and the heater on full blast and Elton told me how hard it is to find work around there. Rural economies were hurting because of the bad situation the farmers were in, but you do the best you can and keep hanging on.

He told me about Keokuk once being the cocaine capital of the U.S. I found it hard to believe, but he said that all the cocaine coming into the country used to come through here.

"Keokuk used to be a wild place," he said, and I'm sure he meant about a hundred years ago. We passed a low shopping mall. "Used to be a big time hotel right here, biggest whorehouse around."

Then as we searched for a cheap hotel for me, he told me about the bar scene in town.

"I used to go out all the time till it got so dangerous. Not worth it anymore. People start a fight over just nothing, getting stabbed and shot. I stay home."

He pointed out the lesbian bar and the gay bar and the cowboy bar and the redneck bar and then he told me the wildest story about his days on the road when he and a buddy of his were driving to California, somehow came across a pile of cash (gambling in Las Vegas, I think) and how the buddy swiped the money. I'm not sure if I got the story straight, but somehow the buddy ended up broke and hitchhiking and Elton ran across him in the desert. Elton just kept going and never looked back.

He told me straight-faced and without a ripple in his voice about the agony of hell he and his wife went through when their little child lingered through some horrible illness and finally died.

I didn't know what to say so I just shut up, but my heart hurt. Is it that only kind souls get stepped on or just the contrast between their goodness and their pain that makes it so ironic? This man going out of his way to find me a cheap enough hotel—and we stopped at a few—driving me around and showing me the town, taking me down to the Coast Guard station, this man surely deserved only good fortune. Why did his baby die? Why was it hard finding a really good job?

At the Coast Guard station I asked and received permission to leave my canoe and some of my gear on the Coast Guard dock. I took some things with me and Elton dropped me off at my hotel, a pretty fair walk from the center of town. Then he waved goodbye and he was gone, his head tilted back as he drove and his chin stuck out.

I wanted to go home with Elton, meet his wife, share a meal. Instead I was left wondering if I would ever cross his mind again.

In the bathtub I washed the leaves and sand off my tent and pitched it in the hotel room to dry. I hung up wet clothes all around and my sleeping bag too. I took a sit-down bath and then a shower and scrubbed and scrubbed until I was nearly clean. I lay down on the bed and tried to sleep, but the emptiness inside would not let me sleep. It nagged at me until I cried, sobbing from the sudden yearning to have children. I don't know why: to teach them, to tell them tales. To share with them the parts of me that are important so that whenever I'm away and even long after I'm dead they will think of me and carry me with them and I will forever be a part of their lives.

I must have fallen asleep for a few minutes. When I awoke the longings had yielded to hunger. I dressed in clean clothes and cowboy boots and set out to find—naturally—catfish for dinner.

I would have thought that since this was a river town and a Mississippi River town at that, catfish would be the easiest thing in the world to find. It wasn't. I walked all the way into town searching for a restaurant that served catfish. I asked everyone I passed, but I was just out of luck.

The man in the shoe store told me to try the Holiday Inn. They used to have catfish there, he said.

The bookseller at Copperfield & Co. recommended the Blizzard or the Buzzard or something like that. "The new place that just opened across the street," she said as if she thought I lived here in town. "I haven't eaten there yet, but they say the food is good."

While I was in the bookstore I bought a present for Robinovich, a book which later on got soaked. I sheepishly hesitated to give it to her and lied that I'd had it a long time.

When I crossed the street, there was no catfish. But just to make sure, the waitress said, "Wait and I'll go ask and find out." And she came back with the bad news. She hunched her shoulders and threw open her hands. "Sorry."

"Me too," I replied.

I stopped one more fellow and asked by mistake for good fried chicken and he recommended the Colonel. I suppose he would have sent me to Mc's if I'd wanted a good burger.

So I walked on down to Main and 7th, to a place called the Chuck Wagon. I had given up and was hungry enough now to eat anything.

The motif was cowboy: paintings on the wall of cowboy scenes, deer antlers and Texas longhorns, a big harness hanging with a mirror where the head of the animal goes, and another harness with fake flowers instead of the mirror. All the tables were red and all the booths were wooden, and each booth with its own hatrack on the end. In the other room was a large picture of the power plant dam crossing the river here.

The restaurant was packed, just like a good restaurant ought to be.

"May I help you?"

"Can I get something to eat?"

"Certainly."

"May I check the menu first?"

She gave me one and then she left because if I was looking at the prices and couldn't afford them, she didn't want to embarrass me. That was very kind, but I wasn't checking the prices; I was looking for catfish and when I found it, I released a big sigh.

"Would you like a table?"

I wondered if she was always this sweet and polite.

She led me to my booth and I sat down, giving her back the menu. "I know what I want." And the waitress came and I ordered. "A huge piece of catfish."

"The catfish steak or the whole fish?"

"The whole thing. Deep fried." And I added, "Please."

It came with french fries and slaw, pickles and tomato and lettuce, a roll and butter, and cottage cheese with pineapple mixed in. I don't even like cottage cheese, but I ate it and it was delightful. The entire meal. Even the butter. And a Pepsi full of stinging bubbles to top it all off. I couldn't have asked for anything better.

Maybe they would have ruined a steak or botched linguini with clam sauce, but they did catfish to perfection and I walked out of there a happy man.

I slept well and set out in the morning feeling fine. I even got a ride from the hotel down to the river from two teenagers who had been up all night cleaning and stocking shelves in a grocery store. They were driving around having their morning beer before going home to sleep. They were looking for some excitement before going home because once they went to sleep it would too quickly be another night of work for them as soon as they got up in the evening.

They dropped me off and I set the canoe in the water. I collected my gear from the Coast Guard office and chatted for a minute or two. I asked about the weather and the river level after all the rain. It wouldn't have mattered, of course, even if they told me of floods and high water everywhere. I loaded up and took off.

The few uniformed men standing outside waved after me and before long I was out of sight.

What an abrupt change from yesterday! Today it was breezy but not violent. The water was calm. And I was feeling superb. The sun was shining and the air around me was very warm. I paddled long graceful strokes and moved swiftly out to the center of the river, catching the current and gliding smoothly downstream. Men working at the river's edge stopped to watch me and to wave. The whole world seemed to be waving and smiling and I was once more a very happy man.

18

Something as simple as a wave can be a gift from the gods if it comes at the right moment. You're tired and can't go on, your spirit sags because nobody knows you and nobody cares. Then all of a sudden some stranger waves, a smile follows and you are bathed in warmth and glowing of sunshine. Your soul soars.

I waved to every person I saw and I always tried to wave before the other person did. I rarely succeeded. Even the barge pilots waved down on me and this made me feel especially joyous. I was one of them. A river rat. A river ***man***. And we shared a river in common.

I paddled away from Keokuk and as if to say, Hold on; get back down to earth, the winds refused to let me go my own way. A big green and rusty channel marker floated in the middle of the river and I seemed to be heading straight for it. If I didn't maneuver around the thing, I would hit it and who knows what would happen.

I aim to go around to the right of it but the wind pushes me left. I adjust too late; I'm going to hit it. My first thought is the embarrassment. The Coast Guard men might be watching me with high-powered binoculars and after talking about my bravery and skill, they will laugh and think I'm a goon if I hit this thing. If I tip over and fall in they would think even worse things.

Tip over and fall in? It hit me then just what the real danger of hitting this buoy would be. I might fall in, lose my gear, sink this canoe, drown.

I paddled as hard as I could but it was no use. I was going to hit it. The best I could do was brace myself and hold the canoe steady.

The water around the buoy rushes past it like rapids and roars like waterfalls. I got caught in the swift flow and the water pulled me right at the buoy. I dropped the paddle to the deck of the canoe and held onto the sides. The canoe, luckily, swung around and banged into the buoy broadside. I hit and bounced and spun away undamaged.

Whew! I took the paddle and hurried to the east bank of the river and stayed there a minute catching my breath. I laughed right out loud.

When I got going again I realized that the wind still would not leave me alone. I tried to get back out to the center of the river, but the wind said no. I was stuck and before I knew it I was off the main channel of the river altogether and gliding to the left of an island. The river here didn't seem much slower so I took it easy and enjoyed the forested banks. The river was so gentle I could hear fish plopping in the water and see them leaping for flies and for joy. Herons squawking before me like heralds to the king's court. They stayed some distance in front of me, stopping to let me catch up, squawking again, and then lifting out of the water, their wings beating heavy and slow, their necks extended like arrows pointing the way. When they got going the necks pulled in and their feet hung long underneath, and then retracted like a jet's landing gear. They sailed high into the trees guiding me to the king and I finally saw him sitting high in a tree. Majestic, imperial, heavy and yet perched delicately on his flimsy branch he peered about the countryside like an arrogant snob. It was his right.

A bald eagle looking for fish and watching me slide under his gaze. I want desperately for him to leave his roost and soar high, beating those immense wings and then diving like a missile for his lunch. But he won't accommodate me. He's too regal to perform. I don't mind. Seeing him is enough for me and I watch him over my shoulder until I can't any longer. And I think (with apologies to Shelley) *If he's here, can winter be far behind?*

This is certainly no winter day or even late autumn. It's spring and I feel like singing.

I sing in a loud voice until I see in the distance a man standing on shore. He's fishing and I approach him.

"Good morning."

"Good day to you." He reels in. "Why'd you stop your singing." He was smiling brightly and he knew why, but I made up a good excuse for him anyway.

"I didn't want to spook the fish."

"Well, I thank you," he said.

I was drifting slowly and pulled into shore just above him. He didn't move to assist me. He cast out again and jerked his rod tip a few times and reeled in slowly.

A gentleman fisher he wore a tweed cap instead of the usual baseball cap you see around here emblazoned with the logos of transmission companies and diesel truck outfits. And he puffed a pipe. He took his fishing seriously, I could see, for he didn't sit and doze or relax. He actually fished.

"How's your trip going?"

"I'm going to New Orleans."

"I guessed as much." He cast out again. "I asked how was the trip going?"

"Fine," I said. "Just fine."

"My name's Calhoun," he said. "What's yours?"

I told him.

"You're not from around here, are you?" I said.

"How could you tell?"

"Well, I guess you don't sound like anyone from around here," I said after a chuckle. "Where *are* you from?"

"Just like you. Here and there." A regular mystery man. "I travel around a bit, seeing the world, meeting the people, listening to their stories, looking for something different, something new."

He pulled in his bait and took a good long look at it and he shook his head as though there were something wrong.

"You know, I just can't get the feel of these things. I do most of my fishing with a fly rig but I've been hearing tales about folks pulling catfish out of this river as long as my leg and weighing fifty pounds or more."

"I've heard that too," I said, "and I've seen some pretty big ones but I don't know if they really get that big."

"Those whopper granddaddy catfish. I believe the stories, but maybe I'm fishing the wrong part of the river."

"Yeah, down south would be better for catfish, I bet." But I couldn't say why. "What do you usually fish for?"

"Oh, just about anything I can take with a dry fly. Salmon up in Scotland. Steelhead out in the northwest. Rainbow trout just about anywhere I can find them."

"It's good?"

He stopped his fishing more to feel the memory than to remember it. It must have been a satisfying one.

"Let me tell you," he said. "When you're wading out in the stream and the water is swift and cold and the bottom is rocky and slick and you're fighting hard to keep your footing and stepping slow and you're squinting with the sun in your face and you're cool from the hips down and hot from the waist up and feeling just right, oh! there's nothing like it in the world. It's not just fishing; it's making love. You're making all the right moves, whipping your rod just right, your body is relaxed and your wrist flexible and you're moving into the right position, slipping a little bit, finding your balance, tension, release, tension again. Aw! it's beautiful. You know, or you think you know, the right fly to use, what time of year it is and what stages the insects in the water are in, how the fish are feeding, what types of nymphs or flies the fish are hungry for, whether you want to fish the ripples around the rocks or the still pools in the shade, cast upstream and let the fly drift back down to you, yeah that's really fishing; fishing for the thinking man and if it works just right and that fish strikes, it's absolutely beautiful. You're riding a horse, not fishing. The feeling is all in your hands. And in your heart. Exhilaration. No. It *is* making love, the way you're playing that fish, milking it of its energy, making it come to you, and your reel just squeals and sings with delight and excitement."

Deep sea fishing in the Bahamas. I was there again, feeling the fishing as Calhoun described it. Out in a boat, fighting sea sickness and boredom rocking on an endless expanse of blue, nothing but blue all around, maybe a cloud or two to add a dash of difference, when all of a sudden the monster takes the bait trailing behind the boat. The line flies off the reel and the reel zings in a panic. You play the fish for all you're worth until the fish exhausts itself and in a last gasp for escape the fish breaks the surface of the water and leaps high.

"The fish," Calhoun was saying, "leaps in agony but at the same time in ecstasy, proud in his defeat to the very last. And your heart is beating a mile a minute."

"Yeah." I was as dreamy as Calhoun.

He caught his breath. He was smiling. It took a moment before he returned to this river and this day, and then as if it had only been two seconds since his last cast, he flicked his wrist and let fly his line and sent his lure back into the water with a little plop.

"So," he said. "What stories have *you* got?"

After that emotional outpouring, there was nothing. What could I say to equal his fishing? I hesitated and he watched me from the corner of his eye.

"One more cast and then. . . ." He cast out, reeled in and came up empty. "How about a cup of coffee?"

I almost said no. I said, "Coffee?"

And he pointed to a fire off in the trees with a little grill resting over the logs, and on the grill a coffee pot. It hadn't been there a minute ago. If it was, I don't know how in the world I could have missed it. This man was pretty spooky.

"Sure," I said. "I'll have a cup."

We sat and he poured out coffee for me. I held the mug in both hands and close to my face. I inhaled the smooth smell of the coffee. I don't much like the taste of it, but coffee smells wonderful. The steam bathed my face.

We talked about the weather, about the beautiful day. I said what a surprise after the last couple of nights and Calhoun didn't know what I was talking about.

"The storm that's been beating me up for the last two days."

He still didn't know. He apparently had missed it, although he said he'd been in the area a couple or three days. He was really beginning to spook me.

"I guess you meet a lot of people on the river," he offered to change the subject.

"Not really. It's the wrong time of year for that. Too cold. Not many people out in boats or on the banks fishing. But in the summer I bet it's just packed."

"I guess so," he said. He sipped his coffee and peered out over the top of the mug at me. "Then I suppose you must get pretty lonely."

He saw that he'd touched a nerve.

"I do sometimes," he said. "All alone, traveling about. It's a great life, but sometimes I just want somebody there that I can share it all with. Know what I mean?"

A few days ago I would have said no. Now I guess I did. I told him so. I told him all about it.

"Yeah, that's funny," he said. "You would think the man on the receiving end would sort of get complacent and come to expect gifts coming at him from all sides. But that's for a selfish man, which I can see you're not."

"But I am."

"Not really. But I'll tell you this: it's not always the selfish man who receives. At least not *only* the selfish man who does. Sometimes it takes a pretty big heart to receive, to let someone share with you. You have to put your pride and your ego aside. And you'd be surprised just how much giving you're doing while you're getting, because some people are just dying to give and have no one to give to. And when you let them, you give something in return. Like listening to me ramble on and on. It delighted me just having you listen to me explain about fishing. I'm not sure how much I was giving to you, but you were giving me plenty. That's why I'm saying you should never refuse a gift. It lets the giver give."

I thought immediately of Emily and some of the things she had told me. I nearly said her name out loud and hoped she could hear me think it. *Emily*. Too bad she and Calhoun hadn't met. They'd be great together.

"What about your loneliness, Calhoun?"

"It comes," he said, "but it always goes. Maybe I'm just getting too old for this kind of life and need to settle down and get a wife and some children before it's too late."

"You don't want to stop this great life you've got, do you?"

He thought about it a bit. "No, but. . . ." There was lightness in his throat and he said it rapidly. "But I could take them along with me. How about that?"

"Sounds good to me."

He flung his coffee to the ground but held onto the cup. He slapped his thighs with both hands and jumped to his feet.

"Well," he said. "You've got to be on your way, and I've got to get back to my fishing."

We shook hands and I gave him my address and told him if he ever got my way to give a call.

"Will do," he said. "And if I catch one of those big ones I was telling you about, I'll send you a picture."

I handed back my mug and thanked him for the coffee. He said, "You're most welcome."

And as I got into my canoe he said:

"There is something you can do for me."

"What's that?"

"I want you to go to California. There's a river there. The Fox River. In redwood country. Up by Eureka. I want you to get yourself a good fly fishing outfit and go to that river and fish for steelhead trout. Fish it really hard and get yourself a really good fish. Nine, eleven pounds. Fight him hard and bring him to net. And then I want you to release him. It'll be the hardest thing you ever did, releasing him. But do it for me."

"You got it." I must have said it too lightly.

"I want you to promise."

Too many promises I've made and not kept. I didn't know when I'd get back to California, and certainly not to fish. But he seemed to want it so badly that I said okay.

"I promise."

And he was satisfied.

He shoved me off and out into the water.

"I know you'll do it. And if he's not quite so big, well that's all right."

He was laughing when I saw him last and then very quickly I didn't see him anymore. Either I was paddling and moving very quickly, or Calhoun vanished in the trees.

I thought about him all day. He brought back my waves of doubt and the pangs of loneliness which I had gotten rid of, but when they came back he was with me to alleviate them. Finally I had found a stranger that I knew for sure would take me with him and make me a part of his life. And I thought about Emily again and apologized to her for forgetting that I must now be a part of her life too. And probably, I was thinking, even the smallest contact with a new face means something, however slight and I shouldn't belittle it. As long as I am a positive addition.

These people are my friends. The littlest touching of hearts is all it takes. They are friends for life and I, at least, will think of them often.

I move on down the river and soon I am called to shore by a couple of other fellows offering me a beer. I really don't want one. After the coffee a beer won't taste very good, and out here in the hot sun it might make me lazy. I stop to take it anyway.

The conversation is ordinary. I hear once again about those Cardinals and the World Series and I'm told to have a couple of drinks on Bourbon Street for them when I get to New Orleans. And they wish me luck. I feel I already have it.

They go back to chopping wood and I get back to canoeing, sliding on down the river past Hackley Island and Taylor Island and Buzzard Island and Hunt Island, Huff Island and Blue Goose Island. And there *are* geese all around, migrating to somewhere and on the look-out for hunters.

The sun has reached the tips of the trees when I pass through the locks and reach Canton. I am finally in Missouri and I have to stop. Just to touch home soil. So I wander through the streets of this little-bitty town and hope that these people will see that I am one of them. Maybe they will offer me refuge. I don't know. Your mind goes funny when you get to the homeland.

I am greeted by graffiti on the corner of Lewis and 3rd, a dingy corner not worth mentioning except for the writing on the wall. Niggers Den, it says in bold letters.

A man stands near-by working on his car and he watches as I pass by. He doesn't speak. I pull my tired back up straight and tall and walk up the center of these deserted streets like a cowboy looking for a gunfight. Nobody waves.

Strangely enough I find refuge in Phnan's Inn, an oriental restaurant. I was looking for a phone but I find Phnan instead. And he seems more out of place than I do. An oriental man and his mother who had come to Canton, Missouri to open an oriental restaurant. Actually the sign and the menu offer both oriental *and* American food.

His mother, when she comes out to meet the man canoeing down the river, speaks with a heavy accent. She is definitely old world and very polite, extremely sweet. Her son speaks with an accent too, but not an oriental one. He sounds just like every other farmer in the area.

I ask where they are from.

"Illinois. My family used to run the ferry that goes from Canton to across the river, but we thought the restaurant business would be better."

"And is it?"

"Not quite," he answers stoically.

I hadn't imagined it would be. America is wonderful, but it's not so open-minded as it may seem, and if I were looking for a business to go into, it would not be an oriental restaurant in the boonies. Even if I *did* offer hamburgers and lo mein.

His mother brings out the spring rolls I ordered and she stays on to watch me eat. The rolls are very good, which probably is all she wants to know. She smiles happily.

Her son tells me about the couple last year who floated down the Mississippi in some sort of raft made of all kinds of junk they collected along the way. People are doing this sort of thing all the time. It wasn't exactly what I wanted to hear.

I ask him if he knows where I can camp for the night near

here and when he tells me it seems as if he has memorized the shoreline for the next ten miles. I have already forgotten that his family ran the ferry for so many years.

He tells me where there is grass and where there are railroad tracks. He knows precisely where the Bunge grain elevator stands—to the mile—and where I can camp without harrassment from the cops. I'm amazed by it all and take it all in but I don't camp where he advised. I go on down past that spot. I don't want to get out of the river just yet. It's just too peaceful. Evening is advancing and the sun is going down but I want to stay on the river as long as I possibly can. I want to cross the river to be in the sunlight as long as I can before the sun sets behind the trees, but if I stay on this side, I'll get the sunrise in the morning.

Too quickly the sun goes down and I have to find a place to pull out. I don't want to. The river is glassy and I skate as if on ice. Birds are singing the forests awake and the evening air is filled with sound and song. The whip-poor-wills call and are answered by the bobwhite's whistling in the distance. I want to sing too, but if I join in these others will quit. I'd rather have theirs.

I want to continue on but I have to stop for the night. It's dangerous out here on the river after dark. But I do want to find the perfect spot before I get out for the night.

And what a night it is! Have you ever seen it so still and beautiful and clear that the stars reflect on the river? Way off to the left the lights of Canton where I came from. Down river to the right, around the bend, the glow from La Grange where I'm headed. Just near by, the night flashing of the government's daymark to guide the barges after dark. They don't stop for night. And up and all across, stars and stars and stars. I hate to sleep, dead tired as I am, because I don't want to miss this dazzling display. The night offers giddiness and joy. It's like sneaking away when you're a kid and eating chocolates in the safety and solitude of your room. My room tonight is this dark and quiet night. The only sounds: leaves falling and the gentle sloshing of the river against the channel marker fifty yards away. And the hiss of the wet wood drying and sizzling and trying to burn in my fire. *Does it get any better than this?*

I'm so tired and aching and sore that sleep will be a relief and I'll sleep and sleep and sleep without a worry or a care or the ghost of insomnia. I'll curl on my side and not toss or turn once tonight. After, of course, I watch the fire glow out. Just a few minutes more.

19

I WOKE UP answering my own question. *No. It absolutely does not get any better than this.*

Breakfast and then a moment's peace beside the fire.

I can hear the early morning screams of red tail hawks, the chirps of golden eagles searching for the early thermals and floating on them. The sun rises higher in the sky, the air warms, and the day glows bright blue. The hawks are thrilled to be alive and know they can soar and I can't. Their screeches are not as shrill as their working shrieks. These are softer, less piercing, happier. This time of day the birds take off from the night spent alone and flap those few hard beats that propel them up, the only effort they may perform for hours. For a short spell they play. In groups of two or three or more they glide in circles wider and wider around, joyously. Then they fan out and take off one by one to hunt and soar alone.

This day I, like the eagles, am truly thrilled to be alive. The day speaks to my soul, and I hear and answer with silent song. *It must be Sunday.* And God answers back. I hear his voice but not clearly. Too many things are in the way and distract. I long for just a few minutes more to sit and relax but I am compelled to pack up and enter the river. God is waiting for me there.

The morning thundered with explosions of birdsong. The music overpowered me and was too beautiful, almost too much to bear. I entered the river and made for the center, but there I could hear no sounds at all. I came a little closer to the shore and skimmed along an eerie zone of half silence from the river, half nature's serenade from the shore. And the birds I could hear I could now see.

In the woods a bird that I had never seen before appeared and chirped to me. Black on the top with white streaks, white on the bottom with a rose throat. (A rose breasted grosbeak, I found out later.) A beautiful little bird with a sweet whistle.

A cottontail hopped close to shore and then back again.

Streaks of red flashed across my vision, undulating and disappearing. I heard a familiar call, the song of the cardinal. I was let down. *Only a pair of cardinals.*

Only a pair of cardinals! What a moronic thought. The cardinal is a beautiful bird. Bright red crested males with black throats. The female is dusty red in color and they always travel in pairs, male and female. They sing to one another tossing a song back and forth and I had seen them a million times before and watched their play, they were all too familiar and I was not impressed. But I should have been and I knew it. I pitied myself for being so stupid.

But this was no day for pity, no day for calling myself names. This was a day the Lord had made, a day for rejoicing, a day to find the joy and beauty in the ordinary and familiar as much as in the exotic and the new.

Two squirrels were chasing each other up and down the trees in the woods. I drew closer as I passed but they paid no notice. What fun!

I passed La Grange and thought about stopping in, finding a church and going to Mass, but no. No Mass could ever be as fulfilling as a day in this cathedral.

The sun rose high quickly and the day grew very warm. There was the gentlest of breezes to keep me cool. And on the breeze floated the voice of God. And I talked to him.

It was not a prayer, no more than the whole morning was a prayer. I did not pray. I was talking to God and He was talking to me and I heard Him and I felt Him in my heart and we communicated.

A red fox scurried down to the edge of the water and ran along the shore. He keep pace with me and seemed to be watching me, keeping up with me. I had never seen a fox in the wild before. I didn't want him to ever go away. I didn't want this day to go away. This feeling. Just a few years longer. Just a few more hours, minutes, moments. I hope that when I die I have those words on my lips: just a minute more. Not out of fear of death or out of wanting to live on and on, but because I will have been so thrilled with this life with all its ugliness and pain which does not in the least overshadow the warmth and glowing of peace and joy and moments like this morning on the river, and I will ask for just a few more minutes of it.

The fox knew I was there and kept looking my way. Agile and funny little creature. And then he was gone.

My heart sang out its rapture; my soul soared on the wings of eagles. The glory of heaven was revealed to me on the water and I felt invincible.

It must be Sunday.

20

I HURRIED to get to Quincy. Duck blinds had been built out in the river, not quite out in the middle but pretty far from shore and I didn't know how in the world they had been set up there. I didn't have time to investigate. I wanted to get to Quincy and find a telephone and share this day with the folks back home.

In such a hurry was I that I stopped off in a little log cabin village called Quinsippi. It was some kind of recreation of life in the pioneer days that people could come out and visit, but no one lived there. I had thought I might be able to find a phone there but I was wrong.

So on to Quincy, around the tip of Bay Island and down to the concrete boat ramp. I pulled my canoe up and took my canteen with me and I searched the streets of Quincy for a pay phone.

This being Sunday, everything down by the river was closed. I had to walk up into the main part of town and I chose Vermont Street's steep hill to climb. On the corner of 4th and Vermont, I found my phone and I called everybody I could think of.

Unfortunately not everyone was home, but I did talk to my mother and father, my sister, Robinovich and Walter. I didn't call them out of loneliness. I was feeling too wonderful for that, excited and giddy. I called out of a sense of sharing.

I must have made it sound pretty fine. Walter canceled his afternoon plans and drove up with Tim to meet me in Hannibal.

When I could think of no one else to call, I walked farther

into town to find some place to fill up my canteen. The Park View Restaurant on Hampshire Street took care of me. A long restaurant, not too wide, a bar on the right hand side, those familiar booths on the left (they must all get the booths from the same place), and tables down the middle. The place was dim and quiet. I sat on a stool at the bar and asked politely if I could fill my canteen. The woman I asked had to ask permission of someone else and I could just see my mood of the day going down the drain as she came back with: "No. We don't serve dirty stinking low life in here."

But to my surprise she came back and said yes and even offered to fill it for me. I thanked her for her trouble and bought a bag of potato chips. It was the least I could do.

I caught a little bit of history as I made my way back to the river. The park I passed through, the one with the red white and blue memorial to locals who fell in the World War, is the same park where Abraham Lincoln debated Stephen Douglas in 1858, the same year, incidentally, that Minnesota, the cradle of the river, was admitted into the union. In those days, while the river might have been the spine of the continent, it was practically the rump of the nation. We were thirty-two states strong when Lincoln was losing his debates, and of those only six lay west of the Mississippi, and only one, California, did not border on the river.

Same river, same country, and yet bring Lincoln back to this same spot where he stood and he would recognize nothing. Not even the river—wider, deeper, quieter, less traffic.

"I know this country—or I should. I grew up in this part of the world, became a man here, lived many years here and yet, I don't recognize the place. Nothing is the same."

Bricks instead of planks, asphalt and concrete instead of dirt packed hard and rutted by wagon wheels.

"But I guess the most important changes have been in the people themselves."

The thumb of his right hand hooked in his waistband, his left hand grabbing onto the lapel of his long black coat, he would express in a tired smile his satisfaction.

"That's a good thing, such a wonder as I would have hoped for and expected. We are a people as good as any other, good at heart, a great people, quick in a joke and quick in a fight, but we are often so slow to learn."

Should I tell him just how slow? Should I break his heart and tell him yes, we have changed, yes, nothing is the way he remembers it, which in a way is great, but his plea for emancipation turned first to confused jubilation and then became muffled cries beaten silent and hung out to dry and evolved into quiet anguish and self-destructive frustration, wailing in the darkness, acceptance and the futility that follows and then finally a fatigue so simple that it could not be ignored any longer? Deprived of sleep for so long, the hope twitched into restlessness, the moaning and spirituals rose from the gut as demands, acceptance roared in a blaze, a passionate and riotous outcry.

And still the work started is not finished completely, not done to perfection or even to satisfaction. Are there no blacks in the frozen north because they still need to huddle together? There is relative safety and strength in numbers, fear in scarcity and isolation. The need to huddle and circle the wagons exists still. Boston. Philadelphia.

I've not been a part of much of it. When I was a kid I thought only of school and play, school and play. I hardly knew I was black. Through innocence I missed the turmoil. Through good fortune I missed the discrepancies and the deficiencies. An attitude was forged that the outcome of my life would be my doing alone. How wonderful for me, but so shallow to think even for a moment that such is the case for all. I wish it were. The shadow beside me would wish it too.

I could feel myself growing itchy and anxious for the journey into the South and I hurried to it.

Lock number 21 stood in my way. I paddled my canoe slowly up to it. A large rock dike jutted out from shore and I swung wide to avoid the crazy water swirling around it. The current flowing hard toward the dam sucked at me but I pulled hard away from it. At the head of the lock's retaining wall, a tow boat and barges waited.

This was my first experience with lock and tow boat at the same time. It wouldn't be my last. I wasn't sure if the boat was parked and if I should go to the right of the sleeping beast and risk his waking up and then not having enough room to avoid the heavy gravity of the current that wanted to suck me into the gates of the dam, or should I squeeze by on the left.

I got my answer in a hurry. The *Ulysses* (owned by the *Spartan* Transportation Corp. naturally) throttled up and churned up a ton of water and I chickened out immediately. The beast had awakened and I would not attempt to pass him at all. I aimed straight for the rock levee and climbed out. I tied off a tree and walked up toward the lock.

Good thing. I found out what was going on and got to see it firsthand.

The locking chamber is only 600 feet long. Each barge is nearly 200 feet long. The *Ulysses* was pushing a stack of barges three across and six deep and in order to go through, the load had to be broken in half, the front three by three shoved into the chamber, locked through and yanked out the other end with cables and winch. Then the second half locks through.

The *Ulysses* had just pushed the first half in and was waiting for the process to continue while I watched.

As I looked on I talked to the lockmaster who at first thought I was merely another visitor who had come down to the locks to watch the action. I told him I was part of the action. But when he heard that I was waiting my turn in a canoe parked just out of sight, he turned so casually as if not to be impressed at all and said, "Oh yeah?" I had expected more surprise.

"There was a guy through here yesterday—or maybe the day before—and I think he was in a canoe too, doing the same thing you're doing."

Excitement mixed with deflation. It could be a good race and it would be great to talk to another nut, and at the same time I was disappointed that I was not the only fool left in the world. After I thought about it of course I knew just how much of a fool I was. This other fellow was precisely what I wanted everyone to be, a little wacky, a little different, a little daring. I should have been happy for him and in a way I was. Too bad though that he had chosen to be crazy in the same way I had chosen to be crazy.

Once the *Ulysses*, roaring like a freight train and spewing forth billows of black smoke and soot into the air, got clear and out of the way, I rode my canoe into the lock and waited. And waited. And waited.

The lockmaster leaned over the rail to inform me that we were waiting for the *Viking Explorer,* a huge white cruiser that had passed me yesterday evening at sunset and that I had passed shortly before now at the docks in Quincy. It looked like a tycoon's yacht sitting in the harbor at Monte Carlo, or a small ocean liner. It was taking on passengers at Quincy and I'd have to wait for her.

So. These guys aren't here solely for me afterall. The real world creeps in any way it can.

Once the *Viking Explorer* has joined me, we have one more vessel to wait for: a raggedy, beaten up old sailboat, loaded down with all sorts of trash and junk. The mast is down and lashed to the deck. The boat is powered by a puttering old motor that sounds like somebody's grandfather, and the sailor himself is just as seedy as his boat. When I wave at the *Viking Explorer* all shiny and white and clean, everyone on deck sends down hellos and smiles. When I wave at the sailor, he turns away. I shout something friendly at him; he ignores me.

Long stringy hair, greasy and dirty even from this distance. If he's shampooed in a year or bathed, it was done in the water from his bilge. I'm happy now that he doesn't wave, this grungy goon.

The *Viking Explorer* steamed on ahead. Passengers lined the rail to wave down at me. They might have waved at the goon as well, but he was too deep inside himself to notice them or care, and they felt his indifference and didn't bother with him. They went on in luxury and comfort and hit the horizon in a hurry and vanished. I had sort of hoped they would pull up and invite me on board. Anything not to have to share my river with the goon in the sailboat.

He chugged ahead of me when I pulled over to let the *Viking Explorer* pass. And when I saw that his top speed was six maybe seven miles an hour, I was determined to keep him in sight and not let him beat me to Hannibal.

I dug deep into myself and poured on the energy. The race was on.

Sixteen river miles. The goon had a good lead on me, but I

had plenty of time to catch him. This would be a race of strategy and stamina, not mere speed.

I sprinted and caught up and ran alongside for maybe a mile. Very quickly the river bends left and I slip to the inside and inch ahead. The goon steadily ignores me and the competition and chugs along like the tortoise, slow and steady. I, on the other hand, am burning out. The anger begins to subside and the initial burst of energy that gave me speed and shot me into the lead fades and I wonder:

Didn't I eat breakfast this morning?

My lead, which wasn't a very great lead, shrinks and eventually vanishes. But it was enough anyway. Sometimes you don't need to win. Sometimes it is enough to compete. Sometimes it is wonderful simply to give your all, to gain the upper hand for a time, and then if the enemy outnumbers you to yield to superior firepower.

I can coast and take it easy now. I gave it a good effort.

To hell with that. Valiant effort. Noble try. It's leaving the backdoor ajar so that dirty thief defeat can sneak up on you in the night. If defeat comes looking for me, he'll not take me without a kicking, biting, screaming fight.

The hare awakens from his nap. The tortoise has sneaked past and out of sight. Time to get moving.

Determination replaces energy and I fire up the engines and get that canoe going. Choice: The map shows Goose Island right in the way and if I keep to the right I can stay in the current. If I go left, however, the distance is shorter and I will avoid whatever barges might be out there to slow me down.

I take the short cut and lo and behold! the goon has taken it too and his little putt-putt engine has quit on him.

Can I give you a hand? Want a tow? Ha-ha-ha!

I slide right past. One backwards glance and I'm gone. And right away the goon's motor putters awake again.

I'm far out in front when Goose Island offers another choice. There appears to be a straight shot through again to the river's main channel. If the river is high enough there would be no problem, but the map shows that this little diversion gets cut off by a narrow strip of island. If I go that way I *might* get cut off. But it is shorter.

I don't risk it; the goon does. Instead I follow around the bend of Goose Island and swing out and around the tip. And there, to make the choice the right one, two couples landing on the island in a john boat. If I had gone the other way I would have missed them and they were all smiles and laughter and spending a Sunday outing hunting for ducks or geese and having a good time. I promised I would have a drink on Bourbon Street for them too. It must be a popular thing to do for people when you're going to New Orleans and they're not.

I come back to the channel and there he is. The goon has passed me once again. I slide behind him and cross the river. The current is here but I don't stay in it long. A barge beast is coming and I duck behind a group of islands called Whitney to hide. The water is slow here but I manage to cruise fairly quickly. Once the barge has passed, I can hear the goon puttering in the distance.

The day is still and the sounds carry. The sun has been up all day but now it arcs toward the tree tops and the horizon. The day ends in peace and stillness, but it remains warm, warm as springtime. Those summer spiderwebs that hang on nothing in the air stretch across the river and suspend on barely a breeze. They stick to me when I pass through and tangle around me. No spiders though. I'm too large for them to get excited about. I only have to worry about the annoying stickiness of the webs, and today I don't care.

What a day! I take time out from the race to once more admire the day and beauty and the splendor of the river. I know now, if I didn't know it before, that there is a God. I've seen Him all morning and heard Him. I know where He lives and have visited.

And just what if my imagination is toying with me again? What if God truly does *not* exist? What then?

Then so what! Isn't it enough to live as though He exists? Isn't it plenty to marvel at the creation, at the beauty and to love the Creator? We can love so dearly a character in a novel or film even when we know for absolute certain that the character is a figment of some imagination. And yet he has the power to change us, to make us feel and think and desire. Why not God, then, who if He does or doesn't exist is still responsible for so much?

Better to experience love and beauty out of the hands of the Imaginary than to take it all for granted, say "uh-huh" and let it pass, call it nature and therefore ordinary and ours and no big deal.

But what a day! What glory! What passion in my bones because of pleasures as simple as a fox, a couple of squirrels, the trees, the birds, the breeze, and the smiles of strangers. I want to thank *some*body.

My voice followed my heart, only not so mellifluously. I sang until my music was overridden by the steady puttering of the goon's engine. The race was still on and I found myself out in front. The towboat or the goon's own boat and engine must have given him trouble. He was well in back of me but gaining. I didn't turn around again. I put my back and my shoulders hard into my paddling. I knelt in the bottom of the canoe instead of sitting cross-legged on the seat. Sweat poured off my head and dripped down my arms. I was cooking.

I slowed to catch my breath and to shout hello to a few kids playing down by the river. Their parents were barbequing up by their summer homes that sat near the water. They were lounging. The smell of the meat cooking drifted out to me and I was hungry. They ignored me when I asked them to toss me a steak and instead offered me their children.

"Want some company? These kids we'd love to get rid of." They were joking of course. "Hey! You're really moving."

"It's hard work," I said, "but somebody's got to do it."

I didn't have time for much else. The goon was closing on me.

I had been hugging the shore but now I moved out into the deep water where the current would carry me and I would move faster. There was one final bend in the river before Hannibal and I was making fast for it. Trying to keep the zigzagging to a minimum, trying to keep on a straight line, aiming for a distant point and adjusting my direction periodically, I was motoring, crossing sides with the paddle deftly and swiftly and not missing a beat. But still the goon gained.

Suddenly there arose a tumultuous outcry of shouting and cheering from the trees. I was in the middle of the arena and this was my moment of victory. The spectators were going wild with excitement. I pushed on at the urging.

And yet I was alone. I looked and saw no one. The voices died away. But I was sure I heard them.

I slowed at the letdown but kept going.

There. The voices again. Shouting at me. Not a crowd, but definitely someone calling to me. I still could see no one, but I would have sworn I heard my name even.

I picked up my pace once more but so did the goon. I tried to ignore the voices from the hills or the trees, but I couldn't. If someone was calling to me, I at least wanted to wave. But where?

Dead in front of me a high bluff rose spectacularly. The sun had passed over it and now the trees atop stood in silhouette. It was from that the shouting seemed to come and I raised my arms high over my head, the paddle held in both hands and I must have seemed victorious.

But the victory wasn't won yet. My back was aching now and I was tired. But I made the bend and saw the two bridges that meant Hannibal. The goon and I were dead even when we went under the first bridge, a railroad bridge. He was out in the very center of the river, I had edged closer to land. I thought he was going on past Hannibal and definitely wanted to beat him to the second bridge, the finish line.

He came closer to shore. He was going to stop in the city also. But he wasn't going to win. One more mile. That's all I had left, all I had to fight for, all I had in me.

And I did it. I fought off the sedentary years and my failure as a long distance jogger and I gave it the last full measure of umph and desire and I crossed under the Mark Twain Highway Bridge first. The winner. I beat the goon.

But as always, no matter what the achievement, there was a price to pay.

21

HANNIBAL, MISSOURI. Mark Twain's town. Home of Huck and Jim. Like a pilgrim arrived at Mecca, I fell to my knees.

There is in Hannibal a small harbor and a marina. Not a grand marina like the one in San Francisco, stocked with gleaming yachts expensive and ghostlike in the advancing fog, a marina well kept and private. In Hannibal the marina is tiny and empty this time of year, and when it is crowded, it is a parking lot for power boats stopping off in town for an afternoon or a few days, but mostly there are the small johnboats of local fishermen. Only a couple were parked there in the grid of grey floating walkways when I arrived. The rest had probably been loaded onto trailers hitched to the backs of pickups and dragged home for the winter.

The loading onto trailers gets done at the concrete boat ramp that leads from the road down into the water, and there is where I landed. I pulled myself from the canoe at the foot of the ramp and I sloshed in the low water pulling the canoe up the ramp behind me. I stumbled a few steps and I fell. My knees had locked on me from kneeling so long and my back was so tight and tired from the strain of racing that I couldn't straighten up. I couldn't walk, I couldn't stand. I knelt there like a pilgrim before the shrine and then rolled over and sat on the damp concrete at the edge of the water. Good thing for the retaining wall or the waves from the river kicked up by the barge passing would have soaked me. I couldn't move. Good thing too that Walter was there. He handed me a Budweiser in a tall bottle ice cold and beaded with water from the ice chest in his truck. I emptied the beer in about four seconds. Walter took care of the canoe and tied it in a berth while I tried to uncoil.

Funny thing: Walter had been so adamant *against* my attempting such a voyage. Now he was as ecstatic as I was exhausted. From high atop the bluffs overlooking the river, he and Tim had watched my approach to Hannibal. As I made that last bend and sprinted toward the bridges, it was their screaming that I had heard.

Now they were screaming again.

"I wish you could have seen it. You looked marvelous. It was beautiful. We saw you coming from a long way off. At first I thought you were one of the things floating in the river. Then you came closer and closer and you looked really good."

They were still laughing and howling in the aura of my triumph which had suddenly become theirs, my thrill was theirs now, my trip even. I however was not so elated. I was in tremendous pain, and the pain did not transfer.

Furthermore, I felt rising up from my toes this creepy sensation warning me that something horrible was about to happen.

I thought the ill feelings would go away if I had another beer. I drank one. It did nothing for the misgivings which I was trying to ignore, but while I drank I managed to unfurl my body and walk. Stiff, but at last mobile.

The frolicking began despite my queasiness. We three climbed into the cabin of Walter's pickup and set out on a tour of Hannibal. Ostensibly searching for a good place to eat we took every back street and zoomed up and down every hill in sight. Hannibal is a very hilly town. A few streets are broad, but most are not. The buildings are old and brick and could have been there when Tom Sawyer himself was out looking for something to do.

We settled on looking for someplace to eat. By way of celebration, eating and drinking are about as good as anything, although Walter had another thing in mind as well.

I wanted catfish. If I could find catfish again as tasty as the fish in Keokuk, I could eat only catfish for the rest of my life. And there's something about being on this river that makes catfish a delicacy. It tastes better. It was all I could think about eating. Walter wanted steaks. We ended up at a pizza joint, Cassano's Pizza, on the western edge of town.

The farther from the river we drove, the worse I felt. I worried about the canoe and the gear in it. Normally when I parked at the foot of a town and went exploring, I kept a fatalistic attitude. In Hannibal, because I had gotten so far from the river, I worried.

We eased into pitchers of cold beer and pretty good pizza. Pepperoni and onions. Not many people stared or held their noses at my grubbiness. Mark Twain looked down nobly from the wall.

The quotation beneath his head read: *Yes, even I am dishonest. Not in many ways, but some. Forty-one, I think it is.*

I put my feet up on the chair opposite me. We laughed and joked and I answered my friends' questions about the journey so far. It should have been quite a relaxing respite from the river, but it wasn't. I didn't need a break from this river. The river had become my best friend and if he wasn't sick of me yet, I certainly wasn't tired of him. I preferred the river to the company of men and understand how those mountainmen of old could hunt and trap for six months at a time and more before coming down again to be with men, and then ache like the devil to be away from them again. Men talk too much and they say the wrong things. They intrude on your feelings. The wind and the trees and the river, the mountains and birds, they talk, but they whisper. They talk through you. They speak to your feelings and let you feel what they have to say.

"Come on," I said. "Let's get out of here."

I was ready to get back to the water, but it was night when we got outside. Too late and too dark to get back to the river and slide downstream and search for a place to camp. I saw what was coming.

Instead of searching for a campsite, we sought out a place to sit and drink. A hotel bar on the highway back to St. Louis, dimly lit and uncrowded. We sat at the bar and I drank something tropical. A major mistake. By the time I switched to bourbon, a cleaner and more honest drink, it was too late. Disaster was already in the making and I helped create it by not being honest. I should have stayed on the river.

I did not want to be in that bar. I did not want to be out drinking. Without saying why—without even knowing why—I became belligerent and when Walter wanted to talk about some things we did years ago, I became testy and arrogant.

"I don't want to hear about something that happened years ago. I don't want to live in the past. Life is now. I want to do my living now and in the future. What happened before is gone; it's another life almost."

Walter brought up sports. Just as arrogantly, I hit him again.

"Except for tennis, I don't like watching sports on TV. I don't want to be a spectator. I'm not like most people, content to look on while others are doing."

To counter, he reminded me of a day we played basketball one on one and I only beat him by two points. He claimed this made me only two points better as a basketball player than he was.

"On the best day of your life," I told him, "you couldn't keep up with me on a basketball court. In fact there's nothing that I've ever done before that I can't beat you doing."

"How about soccer?"

He used to be a very good soccer player.

"I never played it," I said.

"And tennis?"

"Give me a break! You can't beat me in tennis. And you know it."

"Who always wins when we play?"

"Because you play such boring tennis. You hit those dinky shots and all I can do to keep interested is blast like crazy. But if you want to put some money on it. . . ."

"Any time," he said. "Any time."

Tim sat quietly drinking his beer. He wisely ignored us. Walter was growing angry. And I was beginning to feel like a rat. Not only was I saying such stupid junk, but Walter had been so sweet—coming up here to meet me, buying dinner and drinks and wanting to share my thrills like the good friend he is—and this was how I repaid him.

I should have stayed on the river.

We calmed down and we drank until midnight. We drove into the darkness of Illinois across the river and then back again. Whatever it was we went looking for, we had not found, and then it was time for me to sleep and for Walter and Tim to head back to St. Louis. Tomorrow was another working day.

Walter paid for my hotel. A smelly room with a king sized bed. I took a hot bath and watched TV before trying to sleep. I nodded off, but I never found sleep. The sleep I wanted and the rest I needed played a hiding game and only came out to tease me off and on. And in the morning I felt simply horrible. Clean, but horrible.

The hotel and the shower this time had been cheating. In Keokuk it had been absolutely necessary and the river okayed it by giving me a ride and a Coast Guard station and a wonderful dinner. I had awakened feeling like a champion. In Hannibal I woke up feeling like a cheat and a loser.

I dragged myself down to the river, but even seeing my old friend didn't give my spirits a boost. Normally it does.

I passed by Mark Twain's boyhood home, walked along the fence that Tom Sawyer made famous. There was Becky Thatcher's house and other old buildings, but I didn't care. I hardly noticed any of it and I just didn't care. I wanted to get on the river and hurry down to St. Louis, be home and be done with the whole damned thing.

Just another hundred twenty miles. I could make it in a few more days.

I arranged the gear the way I wanted it in the canoe and situated myself. I took a deep breath, hoping that would help to get the juices flowing. But no. The thrill was simply gone. It had quietly sneaked away like an imposter before discovery and left not a trace. The goon in the sailboat had likewise left and even the thought of him would not inspire me. I shoved off but moved out slowly. Physically I was not hung over, but mentally yes and with the residual lethargy that hangovers produce in the body.

I had gotten a late start. By this time of morning, if I had camped the night before, I would already be in the rhythm of the day. The stiffness of the night would be working its way out of the body and the mind would be relaxed and refreshed and eager.

Not so today. The stiffness held tightly knotted in my lower back and the pain in my shoulder felt like real pain, not soreness that would work itself loose as the day wore on. And my mind was dead.

A yellow truck came honking up behind me. I was holding close to shore and there alongside me was this truck rigged with special wheels so it could run along the railroad tracks. The driver honked his horn and waved down at me. He was smiling, and I waved back. I may have even smiled in return, but it was without emotion.

There are rules to ruggedness and I had broken them. In my heart I apologized to the river, but my lips were dumb. I felt humiliated and could not speak and only asked that I make it home safely. I was close enough now to walk almost and in more or less familiar territory. The feeling of being near home gave me a little strength and I canoed on into the shadow of St. Louis.

22

THE REGULATIONS ARE CLEAR and precise concerning precedence at the locks.

> The vessel arriving first at a lock shall normally be the first to lock through, but precedence shall be given to vessels belonging to the United States. Licensed commercial passenger vessels operating on a published schedule or regularly operating in the "for hire" trade shall have precedence over cargo tows and like craft. Commercial cargo tows shall have precedence over recreational craft. . . .[1]

Roughly translated this means that men in canoes go dead last after all vessels that will not or cannot share the lock.

Lock 22 was no easy creature. Something told me to pull up when I got there. It could have been those huge black plumes of towboat exhaust. The towboat was on the downriver side of the lock and waiting to enter. I tied off, climbed up the rocks and walked across to watch. The lockmaster asked if I was planning to lock through. When I said yes, he told me I'd have about a three-hour wait. I thought I was going to die.

[1] US Army Corps of Engineers Regulations. Section 207.300 Ohio River, Mississippi River above Cairo, Ill. and their tributaries; use, administration, and navigation. Article (d) paragraph (1)

"Got to get the *Clyde Butcher* through first," he told me. That was the towboat and barge just about to enter the chamber. Running six by three plus the tow, it would have to be broken in two before completing lockage. "And by the time she's through," he went on, pointing downriver farther, "the *Hoosier State*'ll be up here."

About two miles downriver sat the *Hoosier State*, another big towboat and barge that was drifting slowly up and would be here as soon as the *Clyde Butcher* was on its way.

My facial expression must have been a pitiable one. Or else the river had accepted my apology. The man I was talking to saw how desperate I was about to become and told me to wait.

"I'll see what I can do," he said. "I'll radio down to the *Hoosier State* and if they're willing to wait off that far wall we might be able to squeeze you through."

It was worth a try. Anything was worth a try. But I had one tiny question.

"Will I be able to squeeze through on *this* side?" I indicated the side closer to shore, because I didn't want to be forced out into those torrents of wild water coming through the dam gates. Otherwise, three hours wasn't so long to wait.

He told me not to worry. When he came back he told me the *Hoosier State* would give me time to get through.

When the time came I hurried back to my canoe. I held on for dear life when the *Clyde Butcher* roared and churned from the chamber. The water around me swirled and pitched me about, but I kept steady and paddled into the chamber. Once I was lowered down, the bad news came to me. The gates swung open and I saw that the *Hoosier State* was already here.

"Here's what you're going to have to do. Paddle over to the other side and hold onto that far ladder. See it in the wall over there? When the gates open, hurry on out."

I had thought I'd be able to dive to the right and be totally out of the way until the *Hoosier State* cleared the wall. Now it looked like the *Hoosier State* and I would be sharing space for a few seconds. I'd be fighting the rushing water from the dam, and the water churned up by the towboat as it pushed the barges into the chamber.

"Okay, but tell them not to turn on their engines until I'm long gone. Okay?"

It wasn't meant to be and here I felt death squeezing in beside me.

When those gates opened, I shot out of that chamber like a rock from a sling. I was paddling for all I was worth. The *Hoosier State* was coming on in and looking to eat me for lunch. Those big engines kicked on and the water swirled up. And the engines were not on full power. Just a little nudge. But it was too much for me and I screamed out to the crew on the barge decks:

"Don't kill me."

They all looked on as I fought wild water from both sides and used all the skills I had so far learned. I slid off my seat and knelt in the bottom of the canoe. This gave me more stability and control, and I needed it. I rocked from side to side violently and rose and fell on the big waves like a roller-coaster. I was panicky, but under control. The excitement rushed to my head and heart and did things to my stomach. The thrill was back and I heard singing.

I felt like a champion. The fear turned to exhilaration. The singing was my own.

Water splashed into the canoe and I got wet. But I hardly noticed. The ride, which lasted maybe twelve seconds, had got my blood flowing again. The river had bent the rules for me and allowed me to lock through despite the regulations concerning precedence, and the river had taken care to give me a thrill without tossing me over. The river was not as angry with me as I had thought. I was forgiven.

I was still planning to quit the river at St. Louis. If this was indeed an adventure, the outcome didn't matter so much, and the distance didn't matter so much either. What mattered was how I behaved, and I had done all right. No worse than anyone else would have done, but no better either. I had set out with little to prove, and that I had managed. I had taken a city fellow and turned him into a fairly skilful outdoorsman. I had shown a little determination and fortitude and I was comfortable in the woods. A bit more skill with the canoe would have been nice, but all in all I didn't think I'd feel too bad about giving up. I did have this pain in my shoulder to point at, and the stiffness in the back and in the knees. I had excuses plenty.

But the river kept throwing favors at me.

And questions.

When I landed at Louisiana, Missouri, an old black man and his wife were there at the riverfront to greet me. He must have thought he was my father, or something.

"Son, what the hell do you call yourself doing?" he wanted to know.

I didn't say I was going to St. Louis.

"Canoeing to New Orleans."

"What the hell for? Don't you have anything better to do?"

"There's nothing better than this."

He shook his head. He didn't understand.

"And you think that little life jacket is going to hold you up when you fall in?"

"I'm a pretty good swimmer. It'll hold me up enough."

This old man had a son who used to be in the Corps of Engineers, he told me and I cringed, and he would wear huge life jackets that came up high on his chest and shoulders.

"That's what you need, something like that."

While he chastized me, his wife took photographs. Just like a mother and father.

"I hope you know what you're doing," he said.

And she defended me. "I'm sure he does."

And he saw he was getting nowhere with me, and no support from his wife so he invited me to lunch instead. Just like parents.

"You hungry? Let's get something to eat."

We walked up through Louisiana, which is another of those old towns made of brick buildings, low and all seemingly attached to one another. Off to the sides the streets were shaded. There are a lot of trees. The downtown sidewalks are those old high ones left over from seventy years ago, the ones that are high like steps. That old bank on the corner looked like John Dillinger might have visited here once.

We walked up a few blocks and found a sandwich place, and I

must have been hungrier than I thought. I ate a hamburger, a bowl of chili, and french fries.

The old man ate nothing; his wife, watching her weight and her blood pressure, took a turkey sandwich on toast with mustard. She chewed on only one side of her mouth.

A pair of young black women came in. The old man sitting with me got up and began to tease them and the little girl with them. He didn't know them. I could tell that. He was just a friendly old man who enjoyed making other people laugh. He asked the women if he could buy the little girl an ice cream cone. The girl's mother said thanks.

"Young lady, you sure are a pretty young thing." He wasn't talking to the little kid.

The woman said thanks again, and then they left.

He came and sat with us again. His wife steadily ate her sandwich. Either she hadn't heard his flirting, or she was used to it after all these years and wasn't threatened by it.

They were a sweet couple. You could see that by the way they ignored each other at times. But when she asked for a little cup of milk, he got right up to get it.

He was very interested in my trip and wanted to know about camping and those barges and mostly about snakes. That would do it to him, he said. He didn't like snakes. They were worse than the river, and the river was not to be messed with. It frightened him just looking at it. And thinking of me out there in a canoe, he said:

"Boy, you got to be crazy."

Then he wanted to hurry back to the river. He worried that someone might steal my gear. I told him I wasn't worried about it, but he wanted to make sure anyway. He didn't want my trip to end that way.

Apparently he didn't want my trip to end at all. Again like a father, while he was telling me how crazy he thought I was, he wanted to know if I needed any money. I told him I was all right.

"What you need," he said looking at my wet feet, "are some big rubber boots. You're going to catch pneumonia."

The thought had occurred to me as well, and I told him I'd

get rubber boots when I got to St. Louis. I had forgotten that at St. Louis I was quitting.

It was late in the afternoon when I left them. They were waving and taking pictures and he was telling me to be careful. His wife seemed pretty cool about the whole thing. Mothers, I think, have more confidence in their sons than fathers.

I wanted to look extremely expert under their gaze so I moved out swiftly and confidently. I didn't want them to worry.

The swing bridge was open for barges to pass, but I slid through and pretended it had swung open for me. I took the bend and Louisiana was out of sight. And then I was tired.

I didn't go very far, maybe another hour. I slipped into a little cove where Little Calumet Creek empties into the big river and I made camp. When darkness fell, groups of fishermen or hunters in their johnboats came up into the inlet and drifted up the creek on home. I built a nice fire and sat in the darkness and watched the orange and yellow dancers. Each time they tired, I urged them to leap higher and dance livelier and I gave them more wood to feed on.

The stars overhead lighted the sky with swirls of sparkles. So many stars, so bright and so bunched together. *What man could see shapes enough to give names to the constellations?* With the night so black and stars so bright and so numerous, I couldn't even pick out the constellations I knew.

I was dead tired. All the days on the river, all the canoeing, all the hunger piled onto me that night. I was hungry but too tired to cook. I opened a can of stew and shoved the whole can into the fire. Every once in awhile I'd stir the stew. I took off my shoes and propped them up on sticks stuck in the ground and hung them over the fire to dry. I ate and the stew tasted great. I watched the fire dance down in a diminishing pirouette. It was time to sleep.

A barge passes in the night. It sounds like a freight train in the distance. A bright light startles me, a light brighter than the sun but white like a prison spotlight. It comes off the river and sweeps past. It's gone. In a moment it sweeps this way again, stops on my camp and then disappears. *UFO?* I'm up on my knees and looking out. The light now is on the opposite shore, still sweeping, still searching. The chugging roar from the towboat gets nearer and nearer and then the barge is directly opposite me. The light comes on again. I can relax. It's the searchlight from the top of the towboat searching the river for debris and islands and sandbars and checking the shore for distance and for markers. But that roar is horrible. Will I be able to sleep?

I've camped too near civilization. Another roar from inland this time. A real freight train. And the whizzing by of cars from the road not very far away. All through the night the noises keep up. The road, the towboats, the river sloshing against the bank. I hear it all and yet I sleep the good sleep. When I awake, I'm feeling pretty good. There is nothing like a hard day to make you sleep. Nothing like sleeping out on the ground to make you know you've been asleep. Nothing like hunger to make food taste good.

I got going quickly. There is another lock a few miles downriver and I wanted to get there before the morning traffic built up.

Lock 24 (there is no Lock 23) was busy, just as I feared. And there was no place to safely wait for the barge in the lock to pass by. I was told to go to the other side of the lock and wait behind the retaining wall.

At most locks there are a couple of smaller towboats that sit and wait in case they are needed to assist barges through the locks, or maybe to retrieve run-aways. At Lock 24 there were two of these towboats and I held onto the *Polly Jo* while I awaited my turn through the locks.

On deck a fellow named Billy was watching me. I asked if he minded if I held on.

"Hand me your line," he told me. "We'll tie her off and you can climb up and stretch your legs."

I did and it was great actually being on one of those beasts. And this was a small one. Two engines only about seven hundred fifty horses each. I walked on the deck and climbed up on top to look out at the river.

"Must be something to work on one of these things."

"It's not too bad," Billy said. "I used to work the tows going up and down the river. Now that's hard. Ninety days on without a break. At least here I can go home."

He lived up in Clarksville. I had never been there but I'd heard of it. There is a big skylift that will take you way up to the top of the bluffs and when you get there you'll be at the highest point above the river. It must be a wonderful view looking down across the river and valley. Trees and water from a hawk's-eye view.

Billy said it was a friendly place and I believed him. Every place along the river was friendly. He liked living here.

"You want coffee?"

I didn't, but I took a cup anyway.

"You had breakfast yet?"

"As a matter of fact, I didn't."

He made me a ham sandwich. Then he packed my lunch. Two more ham sandwiches and half a dozen oranges.

Normally I like the ham on my sandwiches sliced razor thin. I like a dab or two of spicy mustard spread out evenly, crisp lettuce, and a slice or two of cheddar cheese. The bread should be light rye and a beer to wash it down afterwards goes along very nicely.

The sandwiches Billy made had no mustard and no cheese. The bread was plain old white bread and he cut the ham in thick slabs. But they tasted as good as any of the delicate sandwiches I've ever eaten, and not because I was dying from hunger.

A squawky voice barked through the radio. Billy understood what I did not and he told me they were ready for me. We shook hands and he told me to come by and see him one of these days. Then I climbed down into the canoe and set off. Once again that feeling of leaving a friend plagued me. I think the feeling is one of fear as much as one of loss. There exists the fear that when you leave someone or someplace you run the risk of not finding a friend or a wife or a lover or a town quite as good as the one you left behind. In a few short minutes I had grown comfortable with Billy. He was my friend and yet I figured I would never see him again. *This going in and out of people's lives is hard. And dangerous.* But it's necessary. Otherwise you stay the same. Sometimes you encounter new and better, sometimes new and worse, most often new and different.

I saved the sandwiches for later in the day, but I started on the oranges almost immediately.

I stayed out of the shipping lanes and took my time, drifting a lot and peeling oranges and enjoying the sun and the warmth. There wasn't much sun, but it was warm. Those spider webs hanging on nothing floated through the air and across the water and stuck to me. I marveled at how flimsy they were and how unattached. I didn't fight to get them off.

It's a leisurely day and I try not to think. If I think, I know my mind will run back over the people I've met. I'll remember how wonderful they've all been and if I do that, I won't want to stop in St. Louis. I'll want to continue on meeting new people, trying my luck and seeing how long I can be a victim of their generosity. I'll want to see if sooner or later they and the river will turn sour and instead of being friendly to me will want to harm me.

My mind will run back over the river and the beauty I've seen. The changes in the river. I won't want to stop.

But I can't avoid thinking about the river. It's become a part of me and I a part of it. A duck floats dead on the water and I feel the pain of its death stabbing through me. A deer takes a swim crossing from a river island to shore, its antlers and head all I can see bobbing slightly on the water and seeming to float. I'm thrilled. I didn't know deers could swim. I hadn't thought about it before. He reaches land and now he looks familiar. He's up and running.

I see trash floating at the river's edge. I feel dirty and disgusted and angry.

I slip behind an island's shelter from the wind, and the trees are mine. I am calmed by them.

I am the river.

When evening comes and I approach Lock 25, even though it lies pretty and calm in the fading light, I hate its being there.

The river has changed once again. From the first locks until now, the river has been a wide creature, slow and heavy. As soon as I pass through the lock, the river narrows. It moves a tiny bit faster and the barges are closer, but I can cross the river with ease—to escape the barges or to cut corners and chop off distance or for whatever reason. It has gone from over a mile wide in places to only half that. The water is still dark grey and blue but it feels like a different river.

I cross the river to stay in the sun. The trees reach high into the sky and the sun is dipping below on the opposite shore. On my side the trees still spread out autumnal colors of fire: red, orange, yellow. A month ago this tapestry would have been spectacular. Now it is merely beautiful. In a week the colors will fade to brown and the leaves will fall. The trees will face winter naked.

I camp on private land. There is a barbed wire fence. I ignore it and build camp anyway. Before nightfall I even fish for my dinner. I sleep well.

From here on down, most of the land that edges down to the river is private land. I hate the thought of it.

As I canoe down in the weak morning grey, voices yell down to me from the hills on the Illinois side. The trees are too thick and I can't see anyone. I wave anyway, even though I can't hear if the calling is friendly or not.

I see a house partially hidden in the trees. Two men are working on the roof. I don't know if they see me. Farther on there is what looks like an abandoned boat house with a ladder reaching down into the water. It must have been some sort of boating club at one time. It's pretty dilapidated now.

Another old barn-like structure sits at the edge of the water. Signs painted say Martin's Landing, and in summer when there is a lot of recreational traffic this place must be some sort of watering hole.

I meet a couple of young duck hunters playing hookie from school.

"Man, you must be fucking nuts!" they tell me, and I'm beginning to feel it myself. I'm just so tired.

Still, they seem to admire me for the effort and that fuels me—even if, as they say, I'm going about it all wrong. I should have a couple of cases of beer and a little motor and of course a couple of companions, preferably women.

Farther down the river there are more signs of civilization.

There is a whole village of summer cottages jammed close together and all facing the river. It's deserted now, but in warm weather this must be a madhouse of noise and barbeque and children screaming and splashing. *Some vacation!*

A tree trunk stretches out into the river. I duck behind it and pull up on shore to wait for a barge to pass. An elderly couple watches me and when I see them I ask permission.

"We don't care. This ain't our land."

The barge passes.

"I'd get out too when those things go by," the man says. "Where're you going?"

I only seem to have one answer: New Orleans.

"Boy, that's great."

"You must really love the river," his wife says.

A weary smile. "Yeah, I sure do."

"We love it too," she says.

"We just come down here to look at it. Our boy's over here picking beans and we came down to watch the river."

"It's a beautiful thing, isn't it?"

"It sure is," she says. "Just lovely."

"Well, don't let us hold you up none," he says. "You're almost to Grafton. Just a couple more miles. You can stop there for lunch if you're hungry."

Just the thought of it makes me hungry. And tired. I don't know how I can go on, but I must. I shove off again.

And now I'm going to leave the Mississippi River for a while. I slip between two islands and down a narrow chute and after a struggle with the wind, I'm riding on the Illinois River. It's narrower and greyer and even a bit calmer in this wind. It will dump into the Mississippi two miles down and I ride it across to Grafton, Illinois.

I land at a muddy flat and trek through tall weeds to get to the road. I'm in back of Bill's Market and I go in to grab a bag of potato chips. I've got my canteen with me. I'm out of water completely and I'm looking for some place to fill up.

I'm still wearing my life jacket and I must be a little conspicuous. A man and his girlfriend stop to pick me up in a big old

Cadillac and they drive to the main part of town. I go into the city hall where a group of senior citizens is having lunch. I ask if I can fill my canteen and someone takes it out to the kitchen and fills it for me. And with a smile.

What's wrong with these people? Did someone let them know I was coming? Do they think I'm famous? Why is everybody so damned nice to me?

As I'm walking back through town I see a big sign: HOT FISH. That's the ticket. BUFFALO PERCH CATFISH. I must be in heaven. A smaller sign announces OPEN: FRESH FISH—STEAKS. I hurry to the place at a trot. My mouth waters and my stomach growls in delightful anticipation. I'm all set for a delicious lunch of hot tasty fish and cole slaw. But when I get to the door, still another sign stuck in the window said CLOSED and told me to eat a pizza. The final sign said FOR SALE.

I hurried out of Grafton.

The river, when I get back to it, is wide again and grey as steel. The sky overhead is cloudy and threatens rain. I stay close to the shore once I'm back on the Mississippi. A barge has sneaked up silently behind me and by the time I feel him coming there is no way for me to get out of his way in time. I get as far away as I can and just ride the wake. If they're going to be that quiet in this wind, I'm going to stay close to shore.

The shore is fortified with rocks and boulders. The Great River Road runs along here and I've been on it many times. I'm close to home now and in familiar territory.

I stop in a little town for lunch. Elsah is the town and Elsah Landing is the restaurant. The town has been preserved in all its quaintness and charm from a hundred years ago. The streets are narrow and trees overhang everything. The houses are all wooden and beautiful and well kept. There is more grass than concrete and the place is quiet and peaceful as a church.

I have a hearty lunch of black bean soup and potato bread. It's hot and sticks to the ribs and what I need more than anything right now is energy and warmth. It's about to rain and I want to get as far as I can before too late in the day.

Half hoping my boat has been washed away, I hurry back to

the river and put on the rain suit. The barges now come at me one after another in quick succession. I feel like I'm riding a bicycle on a highway with truck after truck after truck screaming down past me at dangerous speeds. One false move or careless mistake and I'm somebody's lunch.

The rain is here now. I don't really care. It's not really cold and what I feel most is exhaustion. I don't even bother to hide from the beasts as they swoop down on me.

Cars honk at me from the road and people wave, but even that doesn't cheer me. I wave back.

Finally I can go absolutely no farther. I land and drag my canoe out of the water. I'll stay the night here.

A jet plane flies low overhead. It's on final approach to Lambert Field in St. Louis. I'm almost home.

The rain comes down hard. I don't want to pitch camp in this muck, so I wait. I'm in the trees and out of the wind, but it's going to get cold. I know it. I can tell by the angle of the falling rain that there will be wind tonight. The thought weakens me.

I know exactly where I am. I'm only a few yards from the road and then only a half mile from Piasa Harbor. I can walk up there and kill some time, maybe find something else to eat.

Outside the marina I find a pay phone and call home. I'll be in St. Louis tomorrow and I'll need a ride. I estimate when I'll be there and tack on an hour. And then I go inside the boat shop. The owner's name is Wally.

"Do you mind if I stand in here and get out of the wet for a little while?"

He doesn't; nor does he mind that I'm dripping all over his floor. I try to stand in one spot.

He offers me coffee and I take it. Hot and black. I want to sit down but I don't want to get everything wet, and if I sit, I may never get up again. My legs are like lead and I work hard to keep my chest up and my ribs expanded so I can get air in my lungs.

I'm not the only visitor Wally has. This place must be a hangout of sorts. There are two fellows who work here, one of whom is about to hop on a motorcycle and ride home in the rain over wet slick streets. The woman who works in the office hangs around a few minutes after closing time, but then she leaves. And after the shop is closed, Wally lets in a few more friends.

Okie is a commercial diver and he operates a salvage outfit that raises barges from the bottom of the river, barges that somehow break loose and smash into bridges or other barges or in other ways find themselves sunk to the river's floor. He stops by with his girlfriend on his way home, which is one of the cabin cruisers moored in the marina.

"This fellow's going down to New Orleans in a canoe," Wally says. "I was telling him about that religious nut who came through here. Remember him?"

Okie nods.

This fellow apparently had ridden a bicycle from the west somewhere and when he got to the river he bought himself a rowboat, piled all his junk inside and rowed down the river.

"He said he was rowing for Jesus."

When he came through Piasa Harbor, he took the crankset from the bike, bored holes in the rowboat and fashioned a paddlewheel which propelled him when he pedaled.

"He was a pretty fair carpenter, but he was a sight."

Stringy hair and a little squirrely. But he got the job done and went pedaling on his way.

"I wonder what happened to him."

"When he got to that rock dam at Chain of Rocks," Okie says, "He got stuck on those rocks and I had to tow him out. Those paddles tore all to pieces while I was towing him. But he went on and fixed them up again."

Some guys, I guess, won't let anything stop them.

There have been others to go down the river. Wally told me about a group of school kids in a huge boat, twelve to fifteen kids and all of them paddling at the same time. They made good time and it was part of some stunt that got different groups along the way each to row part way and then pass the boat on to the next group.

And there was a painter who had come down from the north. He was painting the scenery as he went and living with the bears up in Montana.

And there was one brave sort in a kayak going upstream.

"You should have seen his arms and shoulders. Like rocks."

Wally's a big man, beefy, with white hair and beard, and a big smile. He talked about old St. Louis, about boating, about the river.

"When you get down to Kimmswick, there's another marina and it's run by a man named Hoppie. Hoppie's Boat Dock. Stop in there and talk to him. He knows everything there is to know about this river. That is, if you make it that far. When you get home tomorrow and get something good to eat and a good comfortable night's rest, you might not want to leave."

"The thought crossed my mind," I said.

He laughed, and I didn't like it.

He talked about labor unions and politics and communism.

"Seems to me it can't be too good if so many of them want to escape—or that they have to escape. They're not free to come and go like we are. And you never hear of too many people wanting to move to Russia."

I had to agree.

"Did you hear about that Russian sailor who jumped ship in New Orleans? Swam to shore and we took him back and then he jumped off again. Finally he said it was mistake, but you know as well as I do, nobody falls off a ship twice like that by accident. Be careful when you get down there. Somebody might jump off a ship and land in your canoe."

He seemed no more in favor of labor unions.

"Take the UAW. When you and I get laid off or fired, we go down to the unemployment office and collect our unemployment check. A hundred fifty dollars a week. If you're in the auto union and get fired or laid off, you collect the same hundred fifty from the government, but then you also get enough from the auto company to make up a total of ninety percent of your working salary. Now how can that be? If you take a job that pays fifty dollars, your unemployment check is reduced by fifty. Something's wrong somewhere. And the president of the Teamsters union is making about five hundred thousand dollars."

We talked for a good long time and finally he gave me my lesson for the day.

Wally owns a very nice boat, big and plush. Some time back a prominent magazine wanted to rent it as background for posing models to be photographed. Wally, knowing the damage that can be done by camera crews hanging lights and dragging cables all over the place, wanted to say no politely. The politest way to say no is to name an out-of-this-world price. But this particular magazine really wanted the boat and they agreed to the price. Wally was tempted, but he hung in and just said no. He wasn't interested.

They tried money and they tried the lure of prestige that the magazine supposedly would bring to Wally and his marina, but to keep his boat and his integrity intact, he stuck to his guns and said no thanks.

On leaving I promised Wally that I'd come back to say hello.

"Everybody says that," he said. "Nobody ever comes back."

I promised that I would.

I found my way back in the dark. I'd been gone for hours and was powerfully hungry. *Should I build a fire? Should I eat something cold?*

I put up the tent. Totally expert now I put it up in complete darkness, just feeling my way. I crawled inside and went to sleep. I didn't eat at all.

Outside the sky glowed orange from the powerplant across the river. A barge went by. The river sloshed gently. I slept like a dead man.

The last day. I set out early. The river was the same cold early-November grey that I had left yesterday, only now the water was choppy.

I had no more strength than yesterday but I found new energy because I was almost home. Barges were lined up along the rock levee. One or two passed going upstream, and going downstream far in the distance I could see one moving. But where I passed now, the barges were still, tied off and parked. I thought it must be another commercial dock and the barges and towboats were lined up here waiting to load or unload. But there was nothing here, no elevators, no railroad yard, no factories. *Maybe they were parked here for the night.*

I found out later that this was no barge parking lot. This is where they tied off to wait their turns in the lock up ahead.

Lock 26 at Alton. I didn't know any better so I slipped right around the parked barges and headed straight for the lock. They were understandably busy and had me use the alternate lock chamber, but I didn't mind. They were all the same to me. Just so long as I got to pass through quickly.

When I came out, I felt much better. I was on the last leg home.

The *Don Labdon* was heading up river toward the lock and I rode close to him. He waved and I gave him a hitchhiking thumb. He called down that he'd see me on his way south.

All along the way until past the next bend in the river, the area is commercial. Barge companies and oil refineries. The river looks like a massive industrial park. I zigzagged to keep away from the barge traffic and then I shot across to the Illinois side once more. There is a huge opening along the Missouri side and the water there changes color and rushes like rapids and swirls violent eddies. For a short time there are two rivers, the one colored grey and blue, the other muddy and dark brown. Then the two rivers blend and the brown one wins out. I was at the mouth of the Missouri River and I ran into the wedding like an uninvited guest, and was treated like one.

The Missouri is a much swifter river and it was like calm warm air running smack into cold violent air and the horrible storms they produce together. I was knocked around and out of control, part of the time going sideways down river, part of the time going backwards. A big sign warned me that I was about to enter the Chain of Rocks Canal, a deadwater canal built so the barges would not have to scrape over the rock dam four miles down the river. I didn't want to go through the canal. The dead water would mean hard and slow going, and as the canal is only a hundred yards wide, the barge traffic, which would be heavy, would give me fits.

I fought hard to stay out of the canal, and I made it. Now I had time to reflect. I had moments before passed a monument to the Lewis and Clark Expedition that traveled upriver—up the

Missouri River, a raging monster in those days—and if ever I thought I was manly or strong or brave or tough, I only had to think back to those Americans to know better. Upriver, poling those flatboats, not knowing where they were going or what they would find. Don't tell me about strong and tough.

And I was going to quit at St. Louis!

Okie's salvage operation was around here someplace and I had promised to stop in and say hello. He gave me coffee and I got a chance to meet his father, a wonderful old man named Kiel. He told me about St. Louis in the old days, about a mayor named Kiel and an opera house called Kiel and then he taught me about the building of the Eads Bridge. A monumental undertaking. Kiel had a book that showed how the builders worked under water and under the river bed in watertight caissons. The bottom of the caisson became an oversized diving bell with compressed air forced into the chamber keeping water out and supplying the workmen with oxygen. But the men worked too long hours under the high pressure and without suitable decompression on returning to the surface. The inevitable result, caisson disease—the bends—and its effects of excruciating cramps caused by dissolved nitrogen forming bubbles in the bloodstream during too quick decompression were dealt with by drinking heavily and taking patent medicines of the time. Of the six hundred men who labored under the river on the caissons, one hundred nineteen were afflicted, fourteen died.

But men were men.

Eads himself had spent half a life more concerned with clearing obstacles from the river, not creating them. He was not a bridge builder. He was a salvage operator much like Okie and he cleared wrecks from the river and cleared navigation channels. This bridge was his first, and he dared it. He succeeded, even after the world around him doubted him and told him his bridge would not support itself, let alone four lanes of road, a double railroad track and two sidewalks. But he was determined, even though many times he too wanted to quit and did, sending in his resignation and trying to recruit a replacement and finally taking an extended leave of absence and sailing to Europe and leaving the work in the hands of his assistants.

His bridge was a disaster. Less than a year after the celebration of the grand opening of the Eads Bridge, the bridge was bankrupt. It did not generate the tolls expected and the railroads it had been built to serve instead purchased interest in ferry firms and drayage companies and routed freight away from the bridge. Railroad tolls averaged only $163 a day, barely more than the income from pedestrian traffic. And so three years later, the bridge was sold at auction for two million dollars, a third of the bridge's cost.

James Eads pushed on with hardly a glance over his shoulder. At the mouth of the Mississippi River, using principles of his own devising, he constructed a system of jetties to aid the river's self-dredging capacity and thereby open the delta to navigation. The South Pass Jetties. Eads never stopped reaching.

I felt surrounded by men of courage this morning.

I could have stayed and talked to Kiel for hours and eaten his sweet rolls and potato chips and drunk his coffee and looked at his pictures of old cars on the walls. But I wanted to get home to St. Louis.

I promised I'd come back and talk some more.

And then I came to the rock dam. I was feeling pretty expert but those rocks were huge and the rapids they created were terrifying. I could hear the roar from almost a mile away. But what could I do? Certainly not turn around.

I aimed for the shallowest part, the easiest part and took it right through in a swift luge ride that left me only a little wet and very exhilarated. I would have screamed with delight, but I quickly lost control of the canoe in the swift water and the wind and all I could think about was aiming for shore and hoping the water was calmer there.

It was calmer, but the wind was still high and I fought hard and bravely to keep straight and make forward progress.

I rounded the bend of Mosenthien Island and expected to see the city and the arch, but there were only fishermen and trees and railroad tracks.

Farther on I took another curve and passed the mouth of the canal. I went under the Merchants Railroad Bridge and down toward the McKinley Bridge and then I saw him.

He had stopped on the bank nearly under the bridge and he was standing watching me. I put on the brakes and fought the current over to him, paddling hard upstream a little bit to reach him. He was wearing those rubber boots that I needed and he waded out to grab my canoe and pull me ashore.

"Thanks."

"No problem." A tall thin and good looking young man no older than I. "Where're you going?"

"St. Louis right now."

"Me too. And then New Orleans."

His canoe was silver and he had a seat with a back to it to recline on in comfort. The seat had broken and he was repairing it.

"I heard about you," I said. "Back at the lock at Quincy, Illinois. I was hoping I'd catch you."

His name was Kevin Miner. He lived in Texas and had started his journey in Minneapolis.

"Why are *you* doing this?" I wanted to know. I was curious to see if his reasons were at all like mine. Or nobler.

"Couldn't think of anything better," he said. He was taking time off from school and hoping to collect himself and find some answers, and he did this sort of thing all the time. He had once ridden his bike from Texas to Canada and I was impressed, although I wished his reasons for doing the river had been more active, less passive.

"I hear there's a McDonald's on a riverboat in St. Louis. Is that true?"

"Yeah, there is. I'll meet you there and we can talk. Do you drink brandy? I'll buy you a drink."

"I'll be there as soon as I fix this."

And I left him there.

I raced on ahead. Looking over my shoulder I saw him get into his canoe and start out. I dug in deep for speed. I was not going to let him beat me into St. Louis.

Kevin may not have canoed much before, but he is very good at it. I could tell. He paddled smoothly and his canoe knifed swiftly through the water. He was gaining ground on me. There was nothing to do but throw absolutely everything into it and race as if for glory. Only two miles more. I chanted like a coxswain. "Stroke. Stroke. Stroke." Under that rickety old Veteran's Bridge, then the Eads Bridge, past the riverboat restaurants and the big steel and shiny *Admiral* being refurbished and I was beneath the Gateway Arch, the memorial to Lewis and Clark and pioneers and the westward expansion. And *if* I was going to continue south on the river, I was psychologically if not physically halfway.

23

MY OLD FRIEND Robert told me once a long time ago that to be a winner you have to behave like one, to be a champion you need to look like one.

When I came into St. Louis I was greeted as the victor of a great race or battle. Robinovich was there at the riverfront, my mother and brother, sister and niece and a few friends. And somehow the press found out about me and the news people were there too. No time to enjoy my victory. For it had been a race—against winter, against Kevin in his canoe—and a battle against the river, against nature and against myself. No time to feel the fatigue and the pains and the bitter frustrations of wanting to quit, of knowing I'd done half a job, fought half a fight and couldn't finish. The attention was warm—and in a way warming—but I was yanked hard and too unexpectedly out of the river's privacy and solemnity and cast sacrilegiously into the fishbowl.

Isolation can be harsh but it can be beautiful at the same time. And you can't know how beautiful it is until you're back in the city and in the company of people again. Not part time people whose lives and yours intersect, but people who line the course. They define your life more precisely, and somehow you owe them more.

I showed no disappointment or pain. A little stiffness maybe when I climbed out of the canoe and dragged it up the levee, but none of the aching that burned in my shoulder and knees and back—and in my heart. I was smiling.

I let the television news team interview me. (They had waited patiently for hours. Two other teams had come but couldn't stick around for such trivia and left. A man in a canoe gets there when he gets there.) I tried to tell them how I felt when I was asked what it was like and why I had done it.

"I didn't expect anything," I said. "I didn't know what to expect. I just saw two thousand miles of water and I had a canoe—well, I didn't have one but I got a canoe—and I wanted to see what it would be like to try it."

Do I tell them about being two inches from quitting, or will they think I'm a fool? And if I'm talking about giving up, I can't very well talk about manhood and the American spirit, or about the modern life turning us into sissies, can I?

The ways out we dig for ourselves, the ways to save face.

"The effort is valuable whether or not I had actually completed this part or the rest even. It's worthwhile just doing it simply because it's—uh—you know, if you do it for one day it's worthwhile."

I truly believed that, but the words echoed as from an empty room.

"Anybody can do it."

No. Not anybody. It takes something special. Something I thought I had but I don't.

"It's there. The river's there. I've watched this river go by for twenty-nine years, and now I'm part of it."

That's what I wanted. To be like the river. Noble and brave and honest every inch of the way. And to actually be part of the river, well. . . .

But if I *was* part of it, which part? The dark side? The shadow that makes light bright, the weakness that gives strength character, the fatigue that makes perseverance gallant?

One good thing about the fishbowl, for all its invasions and intrusions: while it amplifies size and importance, it magnifies the flaws as well, the weaknesses and doubts and failings and exposes them.

But the very best thing about the fishbowl is that it offers no place to hide.

A radio station scattered me out live across the airwaves. Suddenly not only friends and family know what you're up to but strangers as well. The phone rings. People recognize you in the grocery store. They congratulate you. They wish you luck and well. Worse, they hope for you, they expect, they want your dreams to come true—for them. And you can't let them down. Not without letting yourself down too. That's the worst sin, the one you feel the most.

Of course peer pressure alone can't force a coward to behave like a hero. Or vice versa. The spark of heroics or weakness must glow somewhere inside first, and indeed it does—inside all of us are the makings of heroes and fools. Which we become depends on how we train ourselves.

With each hot and filling meal I ate, I remembered a few gesting words that Wally at Piasa harbor offered when he found out that I was from St. Louis.

"You'll probably get home, have a few good home-cooked meals, sleep warm and comfortable in your own bed, and you're liable to just stay home. Right?"

Yeah. And forget about the rain and the cold and the labor. And the river. Just forget about it.

I ate a lot and well and took nourishment but no satisfaction. I slept warm and comfortably all right, sleeping long and hard but waking up unrefreshed and so slept some more, dozing most of the day away and not because I felt so tired.

I knew what I had to do. In spite of what Emily had said and what I truly believed about the effort being all that really mattered no matter how far I actually came, I knew I would feel a failure and cheated if I did not try still harder. Robert had said that if I were to quit, "That sure as hell is going to mess with your mind," and he was right. And I was only *thinking* about not going on. I knew deep down that I'd get back to it. The river was calling me and I heard her voice howling out loneliness. The river missed me. I was her adopted son and I'd run away as though to be with my natural parents. I had no right to do that. She had taught me plenty. There was still more. And what about this dance of death, this ritual where a man sets out to test himself? What about the spirits of the men and women who had used this river before me and carved out this country, those that rode the river for fun and for profit and for salvation, the ones who worked the river, lived and died on it and on account of it? I couldn't forget them and fling spit at their graves. I knew what I had to do. Or else I could never look at the river again.

24

THE MISSISSIPPI RIVER: more than a river or a waterway, but a river system that extends from the Rockies to the Appalachians. The Mississippi gathers up the other rivers like foundlings, and this area of drainage covers nearly half of the United States, approximately 1,250,000 square miles. Great rivers like the Missouri and the Ohio, minor ones like the Illinois and Arkansas, and rivers you never heard of like the Rock and the Black and the Chippewa—they all flow into the Mississippi, the greatest river, either directly or indirectly, and the big river lovingly takes her charges down to the sea. Thirty-one states and two Canadian provinces she drains, discharging into the oceans more water than any other river but two—the Amazon and the Congo. From Wyoming to West Virginia, Montana to North Dakota to North Carolina, the rivers of the midsection of the country flow into the Mississippi and belong to her.

As highway the Mississippi is second to none. During the peak of river cargo transport, nearly ten thousand towboats plied upon the river, carrying billions of tons of freight annually.

Much more than any of this, though, more than a river system, more than drainage, more than highway, the Mississippi is legend. Too thick to drink and too thin to plow, the saying goes. More than river, less than god. The legend tickles imaginations worldwide and the word alone—Mississippi—conjures up images to everyone. When you call out her name, no one has to say what is it or where?

The river was born as a trickle out of a glacial lake in Minnesota. It flows north for a short distance, meanders through a series of lakes, turns and heads south. It grows wider naturally—not just because of the dams—and is over a mile wide naturally at Cairo, Illinois where the Ohio joins in. From there to the mouth, strangely the river narrows and deepens. At the Passes just above the mouth, the river is only half a mile wide.

And how she meanders. From Cairo to New Orleans the river channel is nearly three times as long as the river valley. That makes a crow-fly journey of about four hundred miles that takes the river nine hundred to complete. And as the river meanders, making huge loops around the land, it often cuts through the narrow necks of land and straightens itself, shorting its route to the sea. Always changing, always alive, always searching for the quickest route to the end.

The Mississippi carries fifty pounds of mud in each 1000 cubic feet of water. As it goes, it carries this mud and silt and deposits it in the delta at the Gulf of Mexico. In ages past this draying of soil created the river valley itself from Cape Girardeau, Missouri to the Gulf. The river deposited the land that it later carved through, adding to itself and determining its own end and then carving through it. In the past hundred years a third of a mile of new land has been added. The river has been creating itself and its path through time, but now that existential ability is diminishing. The Corps of Engineers has done its part, certainly to stifle the river's own expression, expansion and determination, but now studies show that the present mouth of the river lies close to the edge of the continental shelf. The mud silt and soil the river carries and drops now mostly falls to the edge of the shelf and tumbles down deep into the bottomless pit of the sea. What little continues to be built up is offset by erosion and that, too, the thinkers think, ought to be halted.

Men can learn a lot about the river and do a lot to it, but the legends of the river are not to be tampered with. Her facts and figures are written in stone. Her starting and ending points, depths and currents, wildlife and flora. But the legends are etched in stiffer stuff and are harder to erase.

There are those creatures beneath the surface of the river: alligator gar growing to ten feet long, blue catfish weighing a hundred pounds or more, funny-looking paddlefish with snouts broad and flat like shovels, and prehistoric-looking snapping turtles that are as gruesome as their relatives the dinosaurs. In the murkiness of the river, they can't be seen, only imagined. But they are real.

And then there are the ghosts of this river. The Indians who first came here from God knows where. The Spanish explorers. The French missionaries. The trappers and traders, pioneers and settlers, the merchants and rivermen, pilots on steamboats, keelboatmen and rafters, the farmers and slaves and plantation owners, the roustabouts and scallywags, drifters and gamblers. They were all gamblers.

The Indian tribes settled and left names that still stick along the Mississippi: Chippewa, Illinois, Miami, Biloxi, Alabama. Then the Spaniards who murdered those same Indians. The French who converted them to the Christian God. The settlers who tamed them and moved them out.

Dugout canoes, rafts, flatboats, stern- and side-wheelers. Of them all, perhaps the steamboat carries the most talked about ghosts—at least in legend. At St. Louis facing south I could hear those joyous whistles blowing, announcing the arrival of the next steamboat round the bend.

The flatboat took four months to travel from St. Louis to New Orleans. The steamboat could do seven trips in the same time. And on the steamboats which first appeared on the river in 1811, the travel progressed from expedient to downright luxurious, their main cabins done up with elegantly carved furniture and crystal chandeliers, carpeting and mirrors, fine china and silver in the dining rooms, and gambling in the parlors. Cargoes of cotton in the holds, and slaves.

These were the ghosts that were waiting for me. St. Louis and facing south. It's more than slightly possible that I was scared.

The river south of St. Louis is nothing like the river north. It's narrower. There are no dams. It flows swifter and with more water. No locks, so the barges can be bigger. No longer limited to lockable three by six, they run "six and seven across and half a mile long sometimes," as Wally at Piasa had warned me. His exaggeration was only slight.

The river south is wilder, more like it was ages ago in its primordial state. Big bluffs and swamps and farther from the roads that could take me out. Fewer towns, and all of the towns are southern towns. The South has gotten a lot of bad press and the images die hard. Nightmares of slavery and lynchings, separate but not really equal or even close, injustice, insensitivity, poverty, Lee and Pritt rotting on death row in a Florida jail for a crime they did not commit and how many others sharing the fate because of their color? And I in my canoe would be as exposed as a white schoolboy from Kansas in a convertible at a stop light in Harlem. Would my attitude mean anything now?

But wait a minute. This is still America I'm running through. These people are still *my* people. I'm one of their own and they will take care of me just as they did in the north. They won't harm me. They won't disappoint me. There is no friendlier lot in the world than these Americans, none more generous and I'm going South where hospitality, not cotton, is king. And as for the evil princes—racism and hate—the river and the ghosts will protect me. If I needed any more persuasion, I only had to look at the river.

The beast in the river still frightened me—the submerged creatures, the animals down below, the spooky noises on shore at night. But the old man river raging would give me strength and old mom river was protecting me from father's fury and teaching me to read his moods.

I couldn't let anything get in my way. I'd come too far—in distance and emotion—to be left stranded in no man's land. So what was all this talk and thinking about quitting? Because of a few bad days? Everybody gets tired. Everyone has bad days. Put a string of them together and you think the world is ending and you can't go on. *But I* can *go on and I will*. This was my moment and this was my river and if the truth be known, this was my life and my joy, the wildest and greatest and most exciting thing I've ever done.

One of the hazards of telling your deeds, recounting *this* adventure, is that the marvels cannot be hidden. They rise to the surface like bubbles and burst with tiny explosions of excitement.

Envy sidles up and shows itself without the masks this time and suddenly everyone wishes he could be doing what you've been doing. Tom Sawyer got a fence painted that way, but canoes can't carry so many. Unfortunately, my brother Tommy was one who wanted to come along now and have some of the thunder as well, although he tried to mask it as best he could. "If you need help, just ask me." I never did. "If you want some company, just say so." I never did. "I think I can be free if you want." I didn't. "I'll go with you. Okay?" And who can say no to his big brother?

At first dear Robinovich, when she heard, just shook her head. As the notion sank in like drugs, she lost control and laughed and laughed and laughed.

"I'm sorry, but I can't picture Tommy sleeping on the ground or roughing it," she said. She didn't know him as well as I, and I couldn't imagine it either.

Even as he bought a sleeping bag and a life jacket and a jug of bottled water so he wouldn't have to drink from my canteen and share my germs, Robinovich refused to believe that he'd actually go through with it.

"We'll get there and he'll find some excuse to chicken out," she said. "But at least I'll have company driving back."

We loaded up her car again with my gear, a new supply of food, the canoe once again on top and we drove south this time, away from the ugly industrialized portion of the river surrounding St. Louis, over halfway to Cape Girardeau. It was a chilly and grey damp day and while Tommy slept on the back seat and I drove, Robinovich threw questioning glances at me. She was convinced that I was making a grave mistake.

That night it rained cats and dogs. Robinovich was safely back at home and dry. Tommy and I were like two kids stuck at summer camp, strangers trapped in a cabin with nothing to talk about.

Luckily we had found a picnic pavillion to shelter us. No walls, but a roof supported by four beams and a cement floor. Unless the wind blew hard and the rain slanted, we would stay dry. I pitched the tent on the concrete floor and made ready for sleep. There were picnic tables and Tommy pulled one around. He was not going to sleep in the tent with me. He preferred the picnic table as bed. He wanted to be elevated and away from snakes and insects and crawling critters. I wanted to laugh.

How unalike we'd become! So different over the years and our lives taking such different directions with so little in common anymore that we had nothing to talk about. People ask me why we don't spend more time together, why we don't do things together and hang out together. I can only shrug. Brothers yet strangers. I wished for more. All I got was that uncomfortable feeling like a lack of air to breathe. You're trapped in a hot and cramped train compartment in Portugal with a crowd of foreigners. You don't speak their language. The train is slow, stops absolutely everywhere, takes forever. And it's night and you can't even look out the window. You feel caged. No relief and no one to talk to. Then to compound the discomfort, someone lights a cigarette. Hot and sweaty and no air to breathe. And those obligatory smiles of politeness to mask the discomfort. You're not the only one feeling the squeeze.

And then a compatriot comes aboard. He brings as much comfort as a man you owe money to from years back. A less experienced traveler than you, he feels more uncomfortable than you. And because you speak the same language he feels obliged to talk. It's the first English he's heard in, he swears, months. So he talks. And talks. And keeps on talking.

The night was like that. All that hot choking discomfort. I wanted to say something. I wanted to tell Tommy what he ought to know, what I could sense, but he's one of those older brothers who enjoys the role of the big brother. I couldn't tell him anything.

"It's going to get warm tonight and stuffy in this tent, but you ought to sleep in here anyway. Get used to it."

"Naw, I'll be all right."

"There'll be mosquitoes."

But he wouldn't listen.

I slept well through the night. The noise of the rain pelting against the roof of the shelter didn't disturb me any. Tommy couldn't sleep. The mosquitoes were relentless and chewed him up all night. And what, he wanted to know, was that thing that kept buzzing and strafing him all night like a dive bomber? I had seen it in the lantern light and it was a bat, but I didn't want to freak him out totally so I said nothing.

In the morning it was pretty warm. The early morning was still and grey. The rain had stopped. I had slept through my misgivings about camping with my brother and I felt great and ready to get back into the peace of the river.

Tommy was already awake.

"How'd you sleep?"

"I didn't." He snarled and was angry. At me, it turned out, for sleeping so well when he hadn't slept at all. "The mosquitoes tore the shit out of me. I didn't sleep a bit. All night long I felt something was crawling on me. I kept hearing animal noises and I got a cramp in my hand from holding your knife so tight. If something came, I wanted to be ready."

He had plenty to talk about now, but nothing I wanted to hear.

"Did you hear those trains rolling by all night?"

"What trains?"

"Jesus! Every two minutes a train went by. I called you a couple of times in the night and you were snoring like thunder. I thought you were faking. Then I got mad because you were sleeping and I couldn't. And that thing that kept flying by. What the hell was that?"

I shrugged, laughing.

"Fuck this camping shit."

"You want breakfast?"

"Hell no! Let's just get the hell out of here and get going."

He was making a major mistake. As big as refusing to sleep in the tent.

Those first impressions are certainly most important. His first night of camping would leave the taste of soot in his mouth. For him each night until the end would be a hated ordeal. And for me too, as I'd have to listen to him in the mornings. The prospect was enough to make me hate my father for not making campers out of us early in life. Of course, if Tommy lived through it all he'd be much better off, but I couldn't think that far ahead. I could only hear the agonizing and endless complaining.

Now he was about to get his first taste of the hard work of canoeing. How would he react to this?

The morning was as fine as any I've ever known, warm and foggy with swirls of smoky mist hanging inches above the water. Where was winter? Dark green flora was packed densely along the banks. Trees and shrubbery and vines overhanging, and weeds prettier than the ones in the yard. The insects that sang and swarmed in the night are silent. But the river is loud, and tan in the morning mist. It's wide and inviting. It was the kind of morning for sitting back and relaxing, toes in the water, the boat just drifting.

But Tommy couldn't shut up.

"Where do we put this thing in the water?"

We had camped well up on shore and had to carry the canoe down a distance to the water. Directly in front of us was foliage too thick to pass through without a machete, and the easiest entry was too far away. We went over the rocks that formed part of the dike stabbing out into the water.

We got the canoe down the hill and into the dead water that was mostly mud. Tommy wanted to drag the canoe over the rocks and I had to do most of the work to keep it from scraping. Then we had to get the gear down, which I did alone because Tommy had stepped into a soft place at the edge of the water and sank in the mud up past his ankle.

Now I was in a hurry. On the way to the water we had disturbed a nation of mosquitoes and they were up in arms after us and out for revenge and blood.

Finally we got into the water and onto the river. Tommy was at the bow. Right away he wanted to paddle for glory.

"Just sit a minute," I said. "Feel the river under you. Feel its magnetic power, how it pulls down on the canoe even while the water rushes past. Get used to the way the canoe rocks from side to side and don't fight it with any sudden moves. Don't lean too far to one side and leave the steering to me."

"Okay, okay. Let's just go."

He had canoed but once before and now that I was expert I wanted to instruct him. If we fell in, I didn't want it to be because of him. But he was impatient so I let him suffer through his ignorance and offered no more advice.

"I'll call out junk in the water, okay?"

"Right," I said.

A log drifted by bigger than the canoe. Half a tree that had been ripped up by the river and sent packing. It moved faster than we did until it hit an eddy in the water and spun around like debris in a toilet.

"Holy shit!" Tommy cried out. "What if that thing had hit us?"

"We'd be swimming now."

Now he wanted instructions.

"What do we do when we hit something? How about those barges? Which way do we go? How big are the waves they make? Those whirlpools in the river. Are they going to spin us around? Can they tip us over?"

Questions about the river and comments about the shore.

"Look at that. You can hardly see the trees, the fog is so thick."

At least he was beginning to recognize how magic and wonderful it was.

"This is great. When are we going to get out in the middle of the river?"

"As soon as you get the feel of this and you know what you're doing. As soon as we can see better."

The mist was getting as dense as the foliage on shore and I was taking it easy, going slowly and staying close to shore. I didn't want to get caught by a barge unseen until too late.

"What's that noise?"

I had heard it a few seconds before and was straining to hear. My first thought was of a barge coming at us. I couldn't tell at first if the sound was in front or in back. But then we started to get closer to the sound. The sound was not coming to us. I stopped all engines and drifted, my eyes straining to see in the mist and dim light of early morn. Nothing came in view but the sound rushed louder and echoed off the fog.

"There," I called out. "Let's move left."

It was a rock dike and the roar was the water kicking crazily around it. Even far out in the middle of the river the water was disturbed and angry and it roared like little rapids and swirled and caught the canoe and yanked down on it, spinning us. It would happen like this a thousand times more before New Orleans, but I never got used to it and always approached with nervous caution.

We stabilized and Tommy let out his relief.

"Damn! Does that happen a lot?"

"That was an easy one. Just wait."

When the first barge of the day came along, I moved into shore but we didn't stop the canoe or get out. We turned into the barge's wake and rode the waves. The river here was so much deeper that the wake was less troublesome and we could ride on them and I wanted Tommy to know what it was like.

"Shit!"

"Just hold on and don't rock around."

I kept the boat aimed in the right direction and the only major motion was up and down. Then we paddled on.

"And that was a small one," I said, meaning the barge. I could almost hear Tommy's thoughts.

As the morning wore on, his lack of breakfast bore in and he complained of hunger. He had a pain in the side of his stomach and his arms were getting tired. I told him to sit and relax. I'd do the paddling.

The extra weight of two men in a canoe stabilizes the canoe but makes it drag heavily in the water. Okie, I was told by his father, used to race canoes, he and another fellow and they were extremely fast. Two guys in a canoe should be able to speed along. But two men in a canoe with only one man paddling is double the effort and strain just to maintain any pace at all. Tommy was tired and paddled sporadically. I kept us going and was tearing my shoulder to pieces in the bargain. And all the while Tommy wanted to talk.

When I conceived of this journey and started out, I longed for someone to go with me, keep me company, someone to talk with and help with the work, someone to share this with. I went alone because no one would come along and I couldn't *not* go. I thought it might be a major mistake to try it solo but had to do it anyway. Now I saw how valuable solitude in certain situations can be. Some things absolutely must be done alone. This was one of them, and I ran over and over in my mind ways to suggest to Tommy that I go on by myself.

How much luck can one man have?

By the time we reached Cape Girardeau, Tommy was a dead man. I was too, but that hadn't mattered before; why should it now?

We were on the side of the river away from the city when the high retaining wall of Cape Girardeau came into view. The city sits up on a hill anyway. Why there'd be a wall so high up to keep the river out I didn't know then. But when we landed I found out.

"Help me get across," I said, but he was in no shape to give more than an appearance of aid. We made it across anyway. He climbed out and fell to the ground. I dragged the canoe up. I had gotten a pair of knee-high wading boots and for the first time could stand in the water without worrying about cold wet feet.

Tommy climbed the steep embankment and collapsed. I secured the canoe and followed.

"What are you doing?" I asked. By way of reply he could only moan. He was hurting and I wanted to ask, ***well what did you expect?*** But I pitied his plight and kept quiet. I let him lie there in his one-day's agony and left him so he wouldn't see me laughing at him. He's very sensitive and was feeling humiliation enough. I went behind the retaining wall that guarded the city from the river's sporadic fury and I saw why the wall was there. It was fifteen feet high of solid concrete and a set of steel double doors that close when necessary. And at times, evidently, it has been necessary: high up on the wall the flood levels of the river had been marked and dated. A sort of testament, a scar to be proud of.

I had heard tales of the river's rising fifty feet and more in places. Now I believed it. The river itself was twenty feet down the hill. And the wall rose another fifteen. The river had reached near the very top of the wall.

Cape Girardeau lies in the bootheel of Missouri, that little part that juts down and out into Arkansas. This is the fringe of the South. From here on I'd be deeper and deeper in it.

Cape Girardeau is a real river town, not simply a town on the river. The townspeople seem to have an appreciation for the beauty of the river—maybe because they know firsthand how it can overpower and destroy—and actually come down to the river to sit and watch it, to share lunchtime with it, to appreciate it. A couple of benches were placed there. Business types brown-bagging it had come down to eat. And one old river rat was sitting there along the edge of the wall with nothing to do but watch this old river roll south, and the barges too.

He wore a drooping mustache that made him look heavy and sad, and dark granny glasses that hid his eyes and made him seem like an aging former hippie. He didn't look at me when he talked and his voice was vague with longing to be somewhere else.

"I used to ride them barges. Up and down the river. I used to hitchhike across the country too. I used to be like you."

How to intrude without being intrusive. This was definitely the South. People south talk more than people north. In New England two sentences is an extended conversation and takes a crowbar to get started. In the South where the weather makes for a leisurely culture, the words flow with hardly any prodding at all.

"What brought you here?"

"Bad luck. And my sister lives here. I had an accident. . . ." he said and went on as easily as you please and told me all about it without my asking, ". . . and I get this disability money coming in and I'm getting my strength back. It was fine for a spell but now I'm restless again and I got to be moving on. Somewhere. But my sister and her husband has been so good to me and all. I can't just pick up and dump them like that."

A big barge steamed upriver, seven deep and seven across. Forty-nine barges attached to one super powerful towboat tearing up the water.

"Those things really scare me," I said. "I've heard about those big barge loads, but that's the first one I've seen."

"They come bigger. They come so big they take half an hour to push through a sharp bend in the river. And if you're not careful out there in that canoe you'll die for sure."

Everybody seemed to know about the river and canoes.

"So make sure you stay on the inside away from the curve 'cause that's how they get through, pushing into the bend and shoving out again and if you're on the wrong side you'll get caught in all that water they kick up and it'll get mighty rough." He smiled slightly. His teeth were crooked. "I've seen barges flip canoes and little boats like flapjacks on a grill and never even look back. Don't be stupid out there."

I suppose he thought it was stupid enough just being there but he wished me luck just the same.

"That fellow with you?"

"My brother. But he can't take it."

Tommy lay sprawled on the ground. He lay on the gravel in the shade of the wall. The sun had come out and he was basking like a lizard.

"Don't need dead weight with you," I was told. Then he got up and limped off, taking a closer look at the lizard.

It was not a late autumn day at all. It felt like spring, warm and sunny with thick lustrous clouds rolling overhead and creating shadows out on the river. A farmer came down to the river to spit at it and complain.

"Damn this rain," he said.

"Has it been raining a lot?"

"Too much. Just about everyday. The river's too high."

"That's good for me. My canoe will go faster."

"Bad for me. I can't get my soybeans out of the ground. The ground is too wet. And I got acreage right down to the river. If she keeps on rising, my fields will flood."

One man's meat. . . .

Tommy revived a little and I sent him to fill up my plastic water bottle. When he came back we went to grab a bite to eat at an old time grill. Everything in downtown Cape Girardeau seemed old time—if this was indeed downtown. A brick building on Water Street announced Port Cape Girardeau. Inside was Cafe Girardeau looking new and very out of place in this old building. And high up on the outside wall an advertisement was painted in red and white for Coca Cola. Drink Coca Cola, it says. Delicious! Refreshing! 3¢ Plain. Relieves Fatigue 5¢ Sold Everywhere. (North south east west, some bits of America are identical no matter where you go and have been ever since Coke sold for a nickel.)

I had french fries with mayonnaise on top, which revolted

Tommy, and a cheeseburger. Tommy tried spaghetti with meat sauce which was even more revolting, he said.

"This isn't a good day," he offered quietly. "At least I can say I tried it, but this is your thing. You're going to have to do it alone because I can't take it."

This was the quietest I had seen him in years. Gone were the bravado and the loud teasings and in their place came honest fatigue and defeat.

Inside I was thrilled. He had saved me the horrible task of telling him his adventure was over.

"Are you sure?" I asked.

"I'm sure," he said. "You're more of a man than I am."

I wanted to tell him that this was no measure of manhood, that some people are better suited for some jobs and the ones who can do this can't do that. But I didn't say anything because some people do see it that way and make those comparisons.

Then I put in a phone call to St. Louis and said,

"Momma, come and get your son."

I didn't have to say which one. She knew.

"It'll take a couple of hours."

"Don't worry. He'll be right here." And I told her where she could find him sprawled out against the wall and how to get there.

I was happy and sad at the same time, glad to be going on alone and unencumbered, but sad at his defeat. I didn't enjoy that aspect of it, and was happy for that too. I was no gloating sadist taking pleasure from another man's downfall.

I met a young man who was on a bicycle. He had come down to watch the river and was admiring me and the canoe.

"You're going to New Orleans, aren't you?" he told me. "I've hitchhiked there and I always wanted to go by river, but I never got the nerve. You must be quite a man."

I didn't respond to that. I let it fall dead like leaves.

He had that look of a child excited for adventure to just go—anywhere—and I could see that he really wanted to break loose. But he looked over at Tommy still dying and not quite dead yet.

"My brother. He couldn't take it."

"You can't just get in and drift with the current?"

"Not really. It's pretty much hard work every inch of the way unless you want to take months and months."

"Yeah, well," he said, not so enthused now. "I don't think my girlfriend would like it."

It took him a minute, then his wanderlust returned. He was dying to get out of this small town and do something great. "Man oh man! That's really something great."

He wouldn't leave me after that. I needed a few paper supplies and he walked with his bike at his side and showed me where the cheap store was. He waited there for me and then walked with me back to the river. He just wanted to be part of it.

Off in the distance as we stood there, I saw another canoe coming.

"Hey! I think I know that guy." I waved my arms overhead to flag him down. This time, with my boots on, it was I who waded into the water to grab his canoe.

"Kevin. I was hoping I'd find you again."

We hadn't really had much of a chance to talk before. We'd had a drink together back in St. Louis, but there were so many people around and so much commotion that we couldn't really talk.

"You just get here?"

"No. I've been here a while, walking around, writing postcards and looking for a post office. It felt really good to stretch my legs."

He had left St. Louis ahead of me but had gotten caught by the rains and had to hole up, spending a lot of time in his tent reading. Now maybe—I was hoping—we could talk a little, canoe a bit together, camp together, keep each other company and share the experience. I was wrong.

"I'm really getting tired of this," he said. "I just want to hurry up and get finished."

A small crowd had gathered around up on the hill and they were watching us. One woman came down to talk. Her name was Bonnie and she was a poet—the poet laureate of Cape Girardeau?—and she was very interested in what we were doing. She came down and talked about the river and about canoeing and about the same expedition of school kids that Wally had told me about and she being a poet loved it all. Then she said something that absolutely floored me.

"Did you ever think about not going to New Orleans, but taking the inland waterways across and into Texas?"

I thought she'd lost her mind. I thought that *she* thought that *I* had lost *my* mind. I gaped at her, looked at Kevin, and then broke into outrageous laughter.

"I'm lucky," I said, "if I make it as far as New Orleans. I wouldn't dream of canoeing another inch past there. I'm so tired and sore and stiff right now that I can barely think about canoeing any more even today. What I need is a massage and a few cold beers."

She couldn't help with the beers, but sure enough as I sat there on the embankment, Bonnie started to massage my neck and shoulders. Her hands were surprisingly strong and she kneaded my shoulders until the muscles almost hurt worse. But when she finished, I felt great.

Kevin said, "Well, I'm in a hurry. You two stay out of trouble."

And in a flash he was in his canoe and aiming for the passing barge. Canoe and barge pass under the bridge in the distance and become one and slip out of sight.

He's really good at this.

Then it was my turn to leave. I said good-bye to Bonnie and told Tommy I couldn't wait with him any longer. The boy with the bike had gone. He came back, Tommy told me afterwards, with his girlfriend. He wanted her to meet me. He'd been deeply impressed and it made me happy to hear it. I was leaving my mark.

But for now, I was back on the river and all alone again and enjoying the solitude and the river and the evening.

I camped that night on a sandy beach at the foot of Commerce, Missouri, right in sight of the sleepy town. It was nearly night and no one would see me until morning. I pitched the tent so the opening faced the river. The wind came from the north in little gusts. I built the fire and the smoke blew south and away from me. The fire blazed joyfully like dancing children at a Christmas party, but it was hidden from the town by the tent. I was so exhausted that I ate quickly and went to sleep. I didn't even add more wood to the fire or sit up to watch it die out and to reflect. I just wanted sleep to fall on me like rain and douse out my fatigue. Even the dogs' barking did not disturb me. When I had first heard them, I thought one might come down to visit and nose around, but one never did. Not that night.

During the night strange dreams visited instead and poked at me. The barges gliding by didn't keep me awake, but the river sloshing at the beach gave me the feeling even in my sleep that all night long I was being washed away. At first I thought the canoe would float away. Then as the river rose, I felt the tent being lifted and carried out to sea. Somehow the tent was watertight and floated intact and I slept afloat like some cartoon character deep in slumber. It was just a dream.

Suddenly the dogs barked and snarled. They came down on the tent and rushed inside. I lay coiled up and threw my hands up to shield my face but there was nothing I could do. Fangs and dog slobber dripping, mouths wide open and lunging at my face, again and again, closer and closer. At the final instant, just before the gaping jaws snapped shut and ripped my flesh, I woke up. Out of breath and sweating, I crawled out into the grey pre-dawn. I wanted to get right out of there—it was such an evil feeling, a bad omen—but the air was so still and pure and quiet. Not a soul stirred.

I composed myself and stuck my pistol in the top of my boot, just in case. There came a young dog down from the town but it was too friendly to be dangerous or even scary. It sniffed around and then quietly went away.

I built my morning fire and sat near it. There is something so comforting about a fire, something more than merely light or warmth, but something in the fire itself that is a quality of strength and power and at the same time soothing. Like confidence.

I made breakfast and felt like a new man. When I got on the water I was totally at ease. I was becoming a river man, more comfortable on water than on land. There was fog on the water but it didn't slow me down. Its grey wetness clung to me like clothing and it was warm and part of me just as I was part of the river. My senses were river senses. What I could not see, I felt inside. The river talked to me. I heard and felt and I listened. My ears were as keen as my eyes now and I could hear changes in the river, in the wind, in the trees.

Sound in the fog is as muffled and soft as the light. I felt the barges coming before I heard them, long before I ever saw them. There were two, one close behind the other. They were on me before I could get away from them and they loomed in the fog like ghost ships. I never saw the barges and not much of the towboats. The white of the pilot houses blended into the fog. Phantom shapes afloat.

Strangely enough, the wake from these beasts did not upset me. The river was getting deeper still. The water churning down to the bottom took much longer to rebound and had less effect. I could ride with the barges all the way now as long as I didn't get too close.

When the fog started to lift and I could see clearer, I expected to relax. It was very strange, but I couldn't relax any further. I was so totally at ease already. I stretched out my legs and put my hands behind my head and leaned back. The air was warm and overhead ducks or geese flew southwest in vee formation. Often the vees were not complete, a long line on one side and only a few birds on the other. One flock especially caught my eye as they honked across the sky. They plowed through the sky and the mist and each bird followed the bird in front like an army. But there was one silly goose that stayed apart. He would not be part of the others. He flew in the same direction but he would not follow. He stayed aloof and singular, but in a short while the part of the formation nearest him began to break apart and the birds began to follow this lone goose and the sounds of his fife. I took pleasure watching this rebel bird, and then they were gone.

Apart from that, the day was uneventful, peaceful and speedy until I came to the confluence of the Ohio River. The river which had been fairly narrow widened enormously here and suddenly I saw barges steaming upriver but not coming at me. The Ohio has its barge traffic too and vessels veered off here to carry cargo on to Cincinatti and Pittsburgh. I was jealous. The Mississippi should get all the attention and her towns should get all the cargo.

I stopped the canoe to watch this strangeness and climbed out to look. She was wide here all right. One bridge connected Missouri to Illinois, another joined Illinois to Kentucky. Up the Ohio a short distance lay Cairo. Farther on lay Paducah, another great river port. Part of me wanted to venture up to see just because the names sounded so familiar, but I didn't want the Ohio. Even the Mississippi rejects the Ohio. Looking at the two rivers I could see that they remain two rivers even after they've come together. The clear water of the Ohio hangs close to the east bank, shunned by the muddy yellow-brown waters of the Mississippi, and the two stripes flow side by side.

But the Mississippi is not a spiteful river, and eventually the two rivers blend into one. I'm in a different world now. The speed of the river picks up. There is much more water now, water that has come down from Pennsylvania and West Virginia and Ohio. The river widens from the initial rush, then settles down and narrows again, and now I've reached the end of the big map, down to mile zero. The map that has brought me down from Minnesota has finally run out.

I have another one, a new map for a new river. Mile zero on the old map is mile nine hundred fifty-three on the new. I'm on the lower Mississippi now and I can watch the miles click off backwards to zero. I've still got Missouri to the west, but on the other side is Kentucky. I'm on a new river, in a new world. I'm in the South.

25

My Old Kentucky Home. Plantations. Acre after acre of ripening cotton. The hot sun drying the fine golden silk of the corn tops and turning them rough and brown. Lemonade in the shade of porches and elm trees. Bourbon over shaved ice. Perhaps a sprig of mint. Riders cantering down the lanes. Lazy days in the heat and cool nights.

Up on this Kentucky ridge I look out over the river. The fire at my feet, the stars dancing brightly overhead, and the river a glistening silver band quivering down below. I can feel the laziness and the peaceful simplicity and the glamour of the images of the Old South without the ugliness. The gallantry, the courtesy, the hospitality, the surface of gentility. If only they'd been smart enough to pay those poor slaves and give them the freedom of choice. Would it then have been much different than the assembly line, or being a maid or a janitor? Probably not, and a way of life might have been preserved. Then again, the slaves would surely have organized, stricken and become unionized, wages would have risen and living conditions improved, prices would have necessarily shot up and plantations would have found no way to remain profitable. The aim to hang on to a genteel way of life would have missed the mark just the same. And the honesty of the bucolic world would still have been compromised and squandered and sold to industry.

Funny, isn't it, how images stick in your sight and blind out the harsh realities, confuse your perceptions and expectations. I wondered, up on that hill, what the South would hold for me and I asked myself one more time, *How much luck can one man have?*

I shook myself to rid myself of the paranoia. I was in the South all right, but I was more glad than scared. Robert had been right. He told me there'd be times when I'd want to quit the river. Those times had been plenty. I was grateful that night that I had been given the strength to carry on.

When things come so effortlessly, as they did to me as a youngster, the tendency is to accept the ease as standard; you never have to try very hard and you can quit in the middle without failure, knowing full well that if you had gone on it would have been a cinch. But as ease becomes a way of life, muscles atrophy, the edge dulls, and softness sets in. I was glad that this was not coming easily, that this was the hardest thing I'd ever done, that even with maximum effort I still might not succeed. I was glad too that I still had enough left in the gut to hang onto the challenge—even if I had to grab this beast by the ears to hold on.

The sun rose up high behind the clouds and the screen kept the light diffused and soft all day and the heat never got too harsh. What happened to winter? Autumn even? This felt more and more like early summer. Hot and humid with mosquitoes at night. The good thing about being on the river was that while the insects assaulted me on land, they stayed away from the center of the river. I was safe there. The weather was calm, I was feeling great, and I thought I'd have smooth sailing all the rest of the way. But I was wrong.

My map indicated that the river was supposed to grow narrow. I looked around and the river was as wide as it had ever been. The rain from the north and especially from the Ohio Valley and brought down by the rivers had swelled the big river. At times this abundance of water made for swift currents, but when the water was spread out too wide and far from the main channel, the river slowed up. And as it slowed, Kevin's disenchantment with the task rose up like a serpent out of the water and bit me.

"I'm really getting tired of this," he had said and now so was I. Not to the point of wanting to quit; I was far past that now. But I did want to hurry and finish. I wanted to do as many miles in a day as I could.

So far, thirty, forty, fifty miles in a day had been pretty easy. I wanted to step that up. Just how much, I wasn't sure, but I could start earlier and stay out later and squeeze in as many miles as I possibly could.

As if someone somewhere knew what I'd be thinking before I thought it, a miracle on the map appeared on the page in front of me.

The river zigzagged and meandered and turned back on itself. It looped around the land and bent back and would send me back in the same direction I'd come from, only shifted over a few miles by the loop. If I could travel straight I could cut off many miles of canoeing. At one point, a portage of two miles across the narrow neck of land would save me twenty miles by river. I decided to give it a try.

The river had taken on the grey color of the clouds above. The wind was moving in and there would be rain later. I hurried, but when I got to shore I found parked there an old van painted red with the Confederate stars and bars crisscrossing the side and back. *Uh-oh!* A giant rebel flag. Out here in the middle of nowhere. Tennessee license plates on the van. And at any moment I expected to hear a whooping Yee-Haw! rebel yell piercing the silence and electrifying my spine and hair and jolting me out of my boots.

I beached the canoe and searched quickly for a route overland for me and my canoe. If I didn't have the gear I could drag the canoe. Or I could take the canoe by itself and come back for the gear. Even if I had to make three trips, it might still be faster than paddling.

The rebel van wasn't the only vehicle around. There were three or four light pickup trucks parked nearby and a gravel road led up the hill. I figured the trucks belonged to fishermen. I had seen several out in their boats setting out nets.

I took the gravel lane up and over the hill and stood there looking down across the broad valley toward the river on the other side. If only I had had a shorter canoe, I could easily have carried the thing. A paved road crossed this little peninsula and I could have taken it that way. And if the canoe had gotten too heavy for me, I could have dragged it. The road was lined on either side by soft green grass just perfect for cushioning a dragged canoe.

About half a mile down the road however stood a pig farm. I could see the pigs fenced in and could hear them grunting and squealing. Not fenced in was a pair of big dogs running across the farm yard. They were barking loudly. I couldn't tell what kind of dogs they were, but I didn't much care. They were big and they had teeth. And I did not want to contend with them while toting a canoe. So quickly the portage idea dried up. Unless. . . .

Unless I can get one of the fishers to take me across.

I went back to the river and waited.

With the sun hiding more and more behind the clouds and those clouds getting darker and threatening to pour, I didn't have long to wait. But the trucks didn't belong to fishers. They belonged to duck hunters and when they came in they wondered what the hell I was doing. I mentioned New Orleans, of course, but I stressed the portage. They all thought it was a good idea.

"But how the hell you going to get that boat across?"

Actually, I was hoping for some sweet kind gentleman with a pickup truck to load me on and drive me over.

"I suppose you could always drag it, but hell. . . ."

They had places to go and ducks to eat. They backed a couple of the trucks down to the water, pulled their boats onto trailers and took off.

Can't win them all.

One of the men in his camouflage clothes came back to me. There was hope.

"Would you like a couple of ducks for your dinner?"

It wasn't what I was looking for, but still. . . .

"Oh boy, would I!"

He missed my meaning.

"Yeah, would you?"

"I certainly would."

So I followed him up to his truck and he tossed out three of the big birds. Their bodies were heavy with death and still warm. They drooped sadly. The blood clotted purple in the holes made by the shot guns, and the head of one had been blasted away clean.

I took the ducks but suddenly didn't want them. I didn't have the heart. I remembered how I had felt farther up the river when I passed a dead duck floating on the river near shore, how my heart had pained and how I had felt as though a burglar had been in my house, going through my closets and drawers and tossing my underwear all about: violated.

I lay the ducks in the canoe and took a photograph. In the Old West photographers always marked the deaths of the infamous with photos of the posed bodies. I felt morbid and strange. I took the pictures anyway.

In a little while two other johnboats came up and were cranked onto trailers. Each man in the boats was a fisher and they were through setting nets for the day. One was going home. The other, Gene Butler, was already home—sort of. He lived part time in the rebel van. Both men wanted to know where I had gotten the ducks. I told them.

"Well, you better get rid of them. Hide them or something. Game warden comes by and you're in for trouble."

"But I didn't shoot them. I don't have a shot gun."

"Don't matter. You got them. That's all that counts. And it

ain't even duck season in Tennessee yet. You'd be in for serious trouble."

So I took their advice and stashed the birds in the tall grass until I left.

Gene invited me inside the van for a cup of coffee.

It was home all right. Messy and a tight squeeze, but he had a space for sleeping, a little gas stove that he cooked on and that he used for making the coffee, a television set and a small storehouse of food. He offered me cookies with my coffee and gave me the cleaner of the two mugs he had lying around. The coffee was instant coffee and tasted like it. The cookies were old and soft. The second and third cups of coffee tasted better and better and cookies became delightful. And *not* because I was so hungry. Gene turned on the television and we watched afternoon cartoons into dusk like old buddies, and nothing could have been finer. It was cooling outside and the rain was coming soon but I was warm inside sitting on the floor of the van and drinking hot coffee and listen to Gene tell his story.

"I don't like these new cartoons. They're too violent and full of real people and robots. I like the old ones. Tom and Jerry and the moose and squirrel."

"My favorite is Bugs Bunny," I said and we felt the easy comraderie of shared taste.

It must have been a very lonely existence all alone in the night, no one to talk to. He was happy to have me visit.

For reading he kept a Bible handy. After so much bad luck in his life—with the wife and kids and work—he had turned to the Bible and it helped him through.

"It's not so bad," he said. "It's a lot easier living like this than going to a job everyday and not making much money."

But the dampness of the river all day killed him. His joints couldn't take it all the time. So he did construction work as well, working heavy machinery. Because he was good at it, he went back whenever he wanted and whenever he was needed. The favors worked both ways.

"That was the best thing ever happened to me. Getting the chance to learn to work that big machinery. I can always fall back on that."

But for now it was the river. Setting out nets, bringing in the fish and selling them at market in town. He had a house that he went to once in a while. His ex-wife lived there with him. She was down on her luck too and he let her stay with their two daughters.

I felt I could have stayed all night there with Gene. He probably would have cooked up some fish on his little stove. He didn't have room for me to sleep in the van, though he showed me a soft spot nearby to pitch my tent. But I couldn't stay. The portage idea wasn't going to work out, and I had miles to make before it got too dark. As it started to rain, I headed out.

"There's been a pack of wild dogs running through here, so you might want to watch out. I had to shoot one of them the other day. I didn't like that at all."

I remembered my dream from a couple of nights ago and I took a queasy feeling down river with me and paddled fast. The faster I got around the bend and down the other side of the peninsula, the farther I'd be from any wild dogs.

Wild dogs are usually household pets that can no longer be kept and the owners take them out to the woods and let them loose. Their packing instincts come back to them and they range in groups behind their leader and attack pigs and chickens and deer and any other weak animal for fresh meat. Who was it who said that once a meat eater tastes the succulent flesh of man, man is all it'll eat?

Wild dogs were growling in my imagination and I found strength to propel my canoe and I scooted along the water with the speed of a motorboat. In the shelter of the trees blocking the wind, the river was calm and smooth like ice and I skated over it with no effort at all. The speed seemed tremendous and then finally there was the satisfying rush of exhilaration.

A barge's bright beam scanning the river came out of nowhere and I realized it had turned to night and it was time to get off the river. I raced with the beast until it passed me. Then I strained in the darkness to see, trying to find a place to pull out. There was none.

The river had eroded the banks and created little cliffs of sand that hung there two, three, four feet above the level of the water. I needed a place where I could easily slide the canoe out of the water and up the bank. I had seen a few good places farther back before the light went out on me, but I now refused to turn around. I would find something up ahead.

I didn't and had to settle for a forest on the sandy cliffs. Everything was sand. No more solid earth and mud, but sand carried down by the river. When I jumped up from the river to the beach, the cliff gave way beneath me and crumbled into the water. Luckily I was wearing boots and could wade around in the shallow waters at the river's edge. When I found the lowest and most solid spot, only two feet above the water, I lifted the front end of the canoe and shoved it up on land. I hopped up and dragged the canoe further up. I made camp and built a small fire.

I thought about the ducks. I couldn't just throw them away. I decided to go ahead and clean them and cook them.

I'd never cleaned a duck before. I went turkey hunting once and bagged a wild turkey and plucked its feathers, but a friend had gutted the bird for me. Chickens I got from the grocery store came cleaned and packaged and ready to cook. But I learned quickly. I plucked feathers like a madman.

I stood at the edge of the cliff and used it as a table. I stood in the shallow water with my back to the river and pulled the feathers out big clusters at a time and flung them into the river. When they stuck too much to my fingers I rinsed my hands in the water. Little bumps like goose bumps from the cold rose up where I'd plucked the feathers and the skin was loose on the duck flesh and shiny and slick, not at all dull as on the birds from the market. I carried the three bald birds up to the fire and singed off the fine down that remained.

Now for the hard part.

I took ax and knife and the three ducks back down to the edge of the water and like a burly savage lopped off their heads, necks and feet. I made an incision like a surgeon and after a long hesitation—*the first one's the hardest*—reached my hand into the hole and grabbed hold of everything inside and yanked it out. Memories of high school biology. My face was scrunched in a grimace and half turned away. I didn't want any part of this yukky work. Guts and gizzards, heart and intestines, no longer warm but still bloody and slimy.

The second was easier. *You've done one; you can do the others.* But while my hand was inside one of the birds, there came the chilling howls and barking of dogs on the run. My heart raced. *Wild dogs.* I hurried with the last duck and got back to the fire.

In the movies before the shooting starts, they always check the bullets in the gun. I never knew why until now. I knew my gun was loaded. I checked to make sure anyway. And I added bullets to the two empty chambers.

Dinner time, but I was not about to cook those ducks tonight and fill the air around with the smells of fresh meat roasting and bring those wild dogs down on me. I was starving, sure, but I'd have to make do with a can of beans and a can of tuna. I was risking enough by cooking the beans.

I ate at an indigestion-making pace. I put out the fire and crawled into the tent. I zipped it up and wouldn't you know it? I ruined the zipper on one side of the flap and it wouldn't slide shut all the way. The space was big enough for some animal to at least get a head inside and know what was in there. So I didn't get to sleep until the rains came. When they came, they really came. Winds howled louder than the dogs and the rain beat on the tent like a marching band. I thought my little tent would get ripped from the ground and sent flying into the river, but it held fast. I slept knowing the rain would keep the dogs holed up somewhere trying to stay dry.

Sometime in the night I was awakened by the silence of no rain. Instead, I heard a strange sound that I mistakenly took for water dripping from the trees and onto the carpet of leaves on the ground. But the sound stopped. Dripping doesn't end so abruptly. In my half-sleep I would have sworn I heard footsteps. It sounded like a man outside the tent and I perked. *Schlip Schlip Schlip.* That sound again. It definitely was not water dripping. It sounded like the man was sawing a log or lightly chopping wood. In the middle of the night? *Am I camped on somebody's land?* Stupid thought. The real question should have been: who would be out in the night, in the rain, chopping wood or even walking around? Nobody.

Then there really was dripping. The wind came up and it

rained again. No noise but the comforting sounds of wind and rain. I slept again.

When I awoke again, it was to those same strange sounds. Footsteps and *schlip schlip schlip*. I knew what it was. The dogs were here. Walking around. The weird noises were the sounds of a dog lapping in a hole that had collected a deep puddle of water.

When the growling started, I clutched the gun. I held it close and ready. And I sat up.

What if they attack? Maybe they smell the ducks in here.

The ducks were in the tent, wrapped in plastic.

They must know I'm in here.

I stayed quiet, straight and still. I didn't even take a breath.

The sounds went away and I lay back down. I knew the dogs were still out there—somewhere—and I couldn't sleep. I was dead tired and wanted to sleep. I was scared. If I'd close my eyes to sleep, one eye or the other would stay open on watch. My hand was cramped from holding the gun so tight. I knew what Tommy had felt.

How I could have slept, I don't know. But I must have snatched forty seconds of sleep. When I next awoke I heard the dogs. They must have felt the warmth of my body heating the tent. They huddled up right against the tent and all around it for warmth and for shelter against the wind. I was terrified. I could see in my mind the dogs plunging through the tent, tearing at my face and body and ripping my flesh to pieces. I could feel it. And I was helpless.

Please, God. Send these dogs away. Don't let them kill me and eat me.

I knew I would die if they came in.

What am I doing out here? I should have stayed home.

I had no nifty answers now, and nothing neatly philosophical gave me any comfort.

What am I going to do?

Wait and hope and beg for God to save me. The easy way out. Just have the dogs gone when I got out.

Or shoot my way out. I knew where they lay against the tent. I could see the bulges they made in the tent walls, and I could feel them. One lay right next to my head and I lay thinking and praying. I poked at him and he growled.

But if I shot, there might be more out there that were not against the tent. Surely the ones I'd miss would come in after me or wait until I came out. And I couldn't stay in here forever.

I don't know how long I lay there. If I slept at all, I caught naps seconds long. Eventually it got to be light outside. Still early morning grey light, but light enough to see. I peeped out and could see no dogs. But I knew by their indentations in the tent wall the dogs were still with me. They were getting more comfortable and settling in as the wind came up forceful as a gale again. Even if I broke away, I couldn't get far on the river in that wind.

God helps those who help themselves. I knew my only way out would be a way of action.

It's light enough out. I can't stay here all day. It's time to go.

I'd come out blasting.

The wind abated and I took that to be a sign. I sat up, readied my pistol and unsheathed my knife. I was going to make a break for it. I unzipped the tent flap as gently as I could. Knife in left hand, gun in my right, I leaped from the tent and ran right to the edge of the little cliff. I wheeled about and kept my back to the river. I kept all danger in front of me. And I got ready for the attack. The showdown.

I must have looked fierce and dangerous. I've tried to picture it but can't. It's too funny and I always laugh.

The animal to my right came quickly at me. Blood in his eye and dog slobber foaming from his bared and angry teeth. I had disturbed his sleep and he came at me. I cocked and fired, cocked and fired and his forward motion stopped dead. He leaped and froze all in the same motion, then fell straight to earth like a dropped sack.

Another dog, the one that had lain at my head, came sleepily around from the left side of the tent. The noise had disturbed him and he wanted to see what all the commotion was about. He came around like a sleepwalking old man. It was a very old dog, brown and thin and mangy. I could see his ribs through his coat. His coat had no sheen and he seemed sick and feeble. He hadn't eaten in ages.

He came at me and stopped. He looked right at me and considered, just as I was considering what to do looking at him.

I don't have to shoot this dog. I can leave him alone. Maybe he'll just go away. I relaxed to wait. *But what if he doesn't? What if he suddenly attacks? What if he goes to get his pals?*

Where were they anyway?

I put the dog right in my sights and kept him there. I aimed dead for the center of his chest, just under his head and right between the front of his shoulders. It was a patch of dusty white fur surrounded by the light brown. I squeezed the trigger and fired only once.

Yipe!

I can still hear it. The dog let out a horrible cry of pain and startled fright. He buckled once, fell to the ground and then got up and hobbled away into the woods to die in private.

I stood for about two seconds, then quickly took camp apart and loaded the canoe. I didn't want friends of the dead animals coming around looking for me. I put in and pushed on, checking the bank all morning for dogs, but staying close to shore for the shelter of trees blocking the wind.

New Madrid lay sleeping in the morning light across the river. I tried once to cross over, but the wind said no. I would have stopped there for composure and breakfast but the river ordered me on, and on I went, not feeling any better about the night and mornings of dead things, ducks and dogs, until I had rounded the bend and down the other side of the peninsula. I stopped on a sand bar to pee and drink water from my canteen and have a little breakfast of granola bars. I began to feel pretty potent.

The sun came out strong and hot and chased the wind away. The river calmed and widened and I headed out for deep water.

26

Sun on my face, working on my tan. A breeze coming up from the south, from the ocean, a sea breeze to keep me cool. My skin tingles through the sweat and old grime. It also itches from the creepies. I haven't bathed lately. I feel at once all man and yet animal. I came to the river almost a boy in a way. Inch by inch I'm becoming somebody else. A taller man. And at the same time softer. I was nervous when I started the river and the river scared me. The river still frightens me, at certain times more than at others, but nothing like before. I have achieved some sort of synergy with the river.

That night the stars glittered overhead like puddles in the moonlight. The fire I had built reflected brightly off the water. I was in the little cove of an island of sand. I was sheltered from the wind and the river lay at the end of the cove and around the edge of the island. The water here was still and the air carried no noise, only quiet. No slapping of the river and no barge roars. It was in the still of this night that I finally got around to cooking those ducks and it was perfect. The day had been filled with wonder. I counted blessings as numerous as the stars.

The wild dogs had been a panic. I was still shaken as I coasted down the river. But right away, to help me regain composure, the river sent out a man named Clifford to greet me. He was a river man himself, had been a towboat pilot thirty years and now retired, but he couldn't get away from the river. He spent the warm days cruising the waters in a white speedboat and he came alongside me, cut his engines and reached his hand out to take mine. He held it in friendship before he ever started to pull. Our two boats came together.

Right away he knew what I was doing. He understood. The river was in him too and he didn't think it foolish at all.

"How many miles a day you doing?"

"About fifty. I'm going to start trying for more."

"Let's see," he said and he took out a pencil and wrote with it on the side of his boat. "Canal Street is at mile 94. You got about seven hundred miles to go." Then he started figuring, but his arithmetic wasn't perfect and I helped him.

"Fourteen more days," I said.

"Two weeks. If this rain don't slow you down too much. How you doing for supplies?"

"Not too bad, but I'll stop in the next town and get a few things."

"Caruthersville is your next town. Down about four more bends in the river. It's a small town."

"I guess you've been to them all."

"Many times," he said. But not enough, I guessed.

Working those towboats must be hard and after a while very monotonous. The river gets to be a burden sooner or later and an ugly monster after being so familiar with it for so long.

"Like a wife. You know it too well and you get tired of it."

But you can't leave it. You can't live without it. You'd miss it if you tried and your heart would break.

"Enjoy while you can," he said and I promised I would.

We drifted apart and he motored to shore.

Later on as it got dark, I made it to Caruthersville. A big blast blared from the horn of a big barge across whose path I had daringly crossed. I had cut across to avoid going into the bend and around, saving distance and time and my shoulder by following the straight line, but it was getting dark and I miscalculated. I came a little close to the barge—but not *that* close. The barge honked.

I felt stronger then. I knew I was gaining confidence and becoming cocky and bold, vying with the big boys for space.

Caruthersville, when I got there, was dark and dingy and felt in the night poorer than dirt. The riverfront was partly parking lot where the locals came to park and make out and watch the river, and partly wide open space that had that look and feel of buildings demolished and the lot cleared and abandoned. I had the sensation that I had arrived in the bad neighborhoods of some big city, the slums, and waited until deep darkness before I ventured forth. I felt really and truly and finally in the South and this was the South I had always heard about. Dirty and poor like the Third World, dark like the boonies and decrepit like the urban ghetto.

I needed supplies but I could not leave the canoe. This time someone was sure to take it and everything in it. People watched me with suspicion. I felt like a visitor from another planet. From the way they all stared at me, they must have thought so too. I waited until a few of them had left. I pulled the canoe up on land, turned it over and hid it. I hacked down bushes and shrubs growing nearby and laid them on the canoe, Camouflaged like a tank in enemy territory. I stepped back up the hill and checked my handiwork. *Not perfect, but it'll do.*

I walked through the town carefully. My boots slapped against the pavement. My jeans had come apart in the crotch and seat and my striped longjohns were visible. My flannel shirt was rolled up at the sleeves and the sleeves of my longjohn shirt stuck out. A sweatshirt was wrapped around my waist hiding the pistol stuck in my pants, and the cap on my head was grey from being so dirty and losing its shape from all the sweat. I walked carefully, not wanting to draw attention to myself. I didn't want cops to stop me, question me, search me, find me toting a gun.

No one said anything to me, but everyone stared. I walked too tall and proud to be a local boy. Everyone in a small town it seems can spot strangers. Strangers walk with an accent.

I didn't buy much in the grocery store. A bag of apples, potato chips, hot dogs, candy bars and a few potatoes. Then I got out of there. Walking back I had the itchy feeling that someone was following me. I heard nothing and never turned around.

I was tired and wanted to sleep. The last thing I wanted to do was search for a place to make camp, but there was no comfortable looking spot around here. Everything on the river side of the retaining wall looked junky and exposed. Lights from the grain elevators and from the boat ramp area put me too much out in the open for comfort. And as it was night on the river—logs, big rocks, funny currents—I didn't care too much either for canoeing farther on. It would have been a good night to walk to the rectory of the Catholic church I'd passed and ask politely for a bed or floor space, but somehow the thought sounded foolish in my head.

I sat down to wait for the entire town to go to bed. Then I

could pitch my tent. But no fire tonight. The cops would surely be on me and take me away.

The later it got, the more people came down to park and make out and do secret things. This small town was starved for places to go and things to do, and just sitting around was one of the major attractions. And what more romantic spot than the riverfront? Even if it was lighted and trashy and in the shadow of a grain elevator and right near the railroad tracks. There was, afterall, a little grassy spot with benches, an oasis of forty feet square in a desert of ugly. It was at least an effort.

As I sat wondering what to do, looking down the hill at my canoe, the feeling came back that I was being followed. Since I wasn't moving, the feeling changed to one of being stared at. There were several cars around, but there were more important matters than me to tend to. It wasn't that, and it took a few more minutes to find out what it was.

The river streamed by silently like a secret. It smiled in the light of the night and with the same teasing grin of someone who knows what you don't. I thought I was being mocked for my predicament, but that wasn't it.

I turned around and there she was.

"Hi. How're you?"

"Hello."

"What you doing?"

"Just sitting here."

"All by yourself?"

"Afraid so. Just sitting and thinking and waiting."

She was all by herself too and couldn't have been more than seventeen. Her hair was blond and thin and stringy and hung down like a dirty wet mop and made her round face rounder and fatter. She kept her hands in her pockets.

"Is that your canoe?"

So, it wasn't so well concealed. I'd never make it as a commando. Or else she had seen me.

"Where're you going?"

"Down to New Orleans."

"Is that what you're thinking about?"

"No. I'm thinking about a place to camp."

"Why don't you just camp right here? Nobody will care."

"The police might. And who knows who else might come along to bother me. That's why I'm waiting. Until those lights all go out and everybody goes home."

"You'll be waiting a long time then. The lights don't go out and there's somebody walking around down here all the time. Poor colored people come down around here looking for stuff all night long."

"Doesn't sound good."

I picked up a hard clump of dirt and threw it toward the water. It never splashed.

"How far down before I get away from town?"

"A ways. Not too far though. But it's dark out there and you're liable to run into something and sink. And anyways, it'll be safer here than in those woods."

"No. The woods are the safest place on earth."

"Aren't you scared of all those animals and things creeping around at night?"

"Not me. And they're not nearly as dangerous as people."

"But there's light here. At least you can see."

"The dark is safer. If I can't see them, they can't see me."

"Who?"

"Whoever."

"You like camping out?"

"I'm beginning to."

"How long you been at it?"

"I started up in Minnesota."

"Wow! And you're going all the way to New Orleans. That sure is something. You must be mighty brave and real strong too. I knew me a boy who was like that. But he went off and joined the army. They sent him to someplace in Carolina—North or South I can't remember which. But he comes back once every so often to eat his momma's cooking probably, and I see him then, but mostly he's gone and I don't think about him much. Except when the other boys around here start acting like just what they are: dumb dopey country boys. Then I miss my Larry. He was older. He was a real man, you know?"

She hadn't sat down all this time, just standing in one spot or another, not really moving, just shifting her weight from one foot to the other. She wore tennis shoes, dirty and run down. Sometimes she looked at me, but mostly she just gazed out into the darkness hanging over the river.

But now she sat and she scooted right up close to me on that hill, put her knees to her chest and her arms locked around her ankles.

"I camped one night down by the river," she said. "Larry took me. It was late in the evening but before dark. Right around sunset in the summertime. It was hot and the mosquitoes were out and I hate them things so we stayed in the tent away from them and we were sweating and drinking beer to keep cool. The tent had this thing in the back that could open up but was still screened off from the bugs and we opened that to get some air. But it was still so hot. I put the cold can on my forehead to cool me off, then I put it down on my neck and on my throat. Larry was watching me and he was getting hotter and hotter, I could tell, and just sweating away but he never took his eyes off me until he took off his shirt. His chest was strong and a little hairy and he said for me to take my shirt off if I wanted to. I did. And I held the beer can all over me and I got cool a little bit. We had more beers until I was a little drunk and I laid back and Larry came over and we started kissing and stuff like that and after a spell it got dark and we did it. It was my first time. Right there by the river and all. And at the end when we were going really fast and I was all out of breath and—you know—lights started flashing all around and in my head and there was this buzzing feeling. It was great. I laid there with Larry sleeping by me and I thought it was always going to be like that, lights flashing and everything. I was so stupid. We didn't stay all night and when we got up and left I saw what the flashing light was. It was a beacon or something flashing on the side of the river and we were camped out under it. Now wasn't that stupid of me?"

I wondered why she was telling me all this.

"Yeah, I guess," I said. "Those are markers to guide the barges at might."

"I know that now. But then I thought it was something special. Down there on the river and everything. And it's never been good like that since then. How do you figure that?"

I didn't have an answer for her, but I did have an idea why we were talking about this.

"You could put your tent up right over there," she offered. "That hill could hide you a little bit and you'd be out of the light some so you could sleep. And I could help you."

I said no. The spot was grown over with weeds and discarded bottles and cans and trash and surely rats would come around later to play. I said no for that reason and for another which I never told her.

"I haven't canoed out after dark," I said. "I think I'll give it a try tonight and see what it's like."

And I did. And it was the eeriest feeling. Sight was useless; I went by sound and by feel. Big plops like the beavers of Minnesota startled me. I didn't expect beavers this far south and didn't know what other animals would splash loudly like that unless they were huge grandaddy catfish, the ones big as whales. They could flip my canoe with just a flip of their tails if they wanted to.

I flashed my bright beacon at the next splash but saw nothing but ripples. I flashed quickly along the shore and found a suitable place to pull out.

The forest was dense. Underbrush and overhanging vines and branches from the low trees. I had to clear land before I could make camp. Luckily I was expert enough to do everything in the dark. I could pitch the tent by feel alone and could see with my hands and ears.

In the morning the river was harsh. I had refused gifts, vestal virgins—almost—offered as sacrifice, and I had declined the generosity. So the river rose up in slight anger after lulling me with an early hour of calm water. Turtles on low branches and floating logs plopped into the water as I passed, no matter how silently. Here were the noises from last night. They always heard me and shunned me, dashing down to the bottom of the river until I was gone. And they were so quick that at first I could not see them but could only hear their escape.

Then the river and the wind came up to take control away

from me and as I tried to take a short cut through the chute at Island 21, the river chopped at me and warned me to get out. This time *I* said no and I pushed on. Farther on a guy on shore put his johnboat into the water and came out to me. I thought he was coming out just for me.

"You're not from around here, are you?"

"Nope."

"You out fishing?"

"No. I'm just going on down to New Orleans."

"Well you ought to know there's a dike a little ways up and you won't be able to get your canoe across it."

"I can't?"

"No you can't. It's rocks and it goes all the way across and you're just stuck."

"I can't just go over it?"

"Well the water's riz so maybe if you're real good. Otherwise you take your canoe out over there . . ." He pointed to the island. ". . . and drag it across."

I thanked him for his warning, but I couldn't be stopped. He went on across to the island to do his day's hunting or fishing, and I watched him go. I thought about going across to the island to portage the canoe. I even thought about going back the way I had come, but only briefly. The wind would never let me, neither back nor across. Besides, I didn't want to do it that way. I kept on and I came upon the dike.

The water there roared as loud as any I'd heard on this river. The rocks were boulders and the fall was steep. But I didn't hesitate. I took the ride and I made it and I shouted hurray.

The river god had been testing me, sending up offerings he did not want me to take, sending out danger that I had to ignore, giving me a warning that I had to brush off and an obstacle that I had to fight through. I did it, and the river smiled approval.

A few miles down river, the weather changed again. The day smiled on me. The sun shone through cracks in the clouds and warmed the air around me. I felt good and was cruising easily, singing songs from deep in my memory, songs about stories from the Bible. And I felt so good and so infused with God's spirit that even if I hadn't known it, I would have felt it to be Sunday.

What a remarkable feeling, to have God in your mind so happily with every move you make, to be so tuned in on Him that every word you think is inspired by Him, every thought and every action guided by Him. I haven't felt this very often, but when I have, my soul glows and I have to hang onto myself to keep from floating away. As it was I didn't do a very good job. I laughed and sang all day. And I prayed this little prayer: *I get down when the world looks like mud, but I know that this is a damn fine life and God! if you can be as good to others as you've been to me—even with all the disappointments—there will be peace on this planet.*

What greater success can a man have than days like this one, feelings like these?

And then I was plunged fiercely into crazy water.

The map calls it Barfield Revetment, which protects the shore from the river at Barfield Bend. The mouth of the River Styx (its real name) is situated right there. And the water goes wild.

The river picked up speed and moved furiously. An undercurrent close to shore hurled water violently upstream. Between the two flows the water swirled rapidly and I was caught in the crossflow. I dropped to my knees and paddled hard to stay out of the water going upstream. I got caught in the eddies, pitched and spun like a dervish. Out in the fast current logs bigger than the canoe sped by and swirled wildly. The best I could do was hang on and keep the canoe fairly straight and under control until I passed the landing.

I did it. And the river, having chewed me up once more, spat me out and into dead water crowded with sticks and logs and branches and other debris.

I first extricated myself and let out a whoop. I felt great.

Two kids on bikes had watched the whole thing from the bank and I stopped to ask them what had happened. They spoke with heavy Arkansas accents and I couldn't understand at first a word they said. But in the end I got a good laugh out of them.

"I think," the one boy said, "there's channel underground there." And the other boy added, "Yeah. I think it must be the English Channel."

I waited until they had gone before howling with laughter.

A man in a van had come down to the river to take pictures.

He was snapping me and I hoped he had not caught me looking too stupid. Another man and his family were there near him and when I stopped to take a breather, they rushed down on me like paramedics at first, but then like disciples.

Ken and Marsha Will and their two little boys. The boys wore suits from church and they looked cute in little-boy formality. This was their Sunday outing away from the air force base at Blytheville where Ken was stationed, and the boys tried hard not to be too energetic and get dirty.

Ken was overly abundant with praise. He thought he was meeting a hero. He wanted his sons to shake my hand and remember me and this day forever.

"This is a very great man," he kept saying. "He is doing something tremendous. It takes great courage and great strength to do something like this." He was as proud for me as any father could be and happy for his boys to be a part of this history as a father might be for his sons to meet the president or Babe Ruth.

I felt glorified and yet humbled by all the attention. Was it so great what I was doing, or was Ken seeing something in this journey and in my future the significance of which I couldn't grasp? Or was it that I could see all the failures and the fears that had got me here? Whatever it was, I was left in awe of the appreciation.

At the next bend in the river a towboat and barge passed going upriver. The pilot waved down. I stopped my singing to wave back. On the side of the towboat, in big dark letters, was written the boat's name: *Leviticus.*

That night on my island of sand I thought over the events of the last few days, the generosity of the river, and I wondered what I was giving in return. I had no suitable answer. Whatever it was, if anything at all, I couldn't see it. And I took a long walk across the sand of my island and I questioned, *Why me?* The river and life itself had, upon careful examination, been rather good to me. Selfishly I could have been content with that, even while wanting still more. But I was nagged. *Why me? What's in store? Something or nothing? If something, will I be worthy or will I be a zero?*

A Japanese potter once said that if his heart is not pure enough, if his thoughts are not pure enough nor his spirit, the clay can somehow tell. Perhaps the river and the people I met could see what I was too busy to look for, too preoccupied to notice, too tired to see.

I baked my ducks by wrapping them in foil and shoving them into the heart of the fire. I fried a few potatoes. The duck taste was strong and wild, the meat dark and chewy. The potatoes I had salted too much, but I ate it all and slept on the soft sand and satisfied in the night. Confused, but satisfied. My luck runs on.

27

WHEN I AWOKE, the smell of smoke and roasted ducks still filled the tent. Outside the air was thin and cold with morning, the sky pale with dawn. The river was at my door. When I had made camp last night, the water had been a safe distance from where I pitched the tent. During the night the river had risen and in the morning it was barely three feet away and if the canoe had not been overturned to protect my gear, it would have floated away. With the rising water came the wind and out on the river I was struggling too much and just didn't feel like it that morning. I was forced many times into the trees lining the bank like the bars of a cage. I was trapped in what seemed another occurrence of bad luck and I knew I wouldn't make many miles that day.

My map told me of a town nearby: Osceola, Arkansas. It lay along an estuary, but because of the rains and high water every little cove looked like the mouth of an estuary. I turned into the wrong one but it was beautiful. The water was muddy, thick and brown, and the trees that shaded the cove stood tall and no thicker that a man's thigh, with branches that reached up but not out. Light came down came in streaks of gold passing between the trees. Closer to the ground branches grew and there were vines everywhere. Trees bent, leaning on other trees and falling. Insects and birds sounding like the jungle and turtles plopping into the water. More like the bayous of Louisiana than Arkansas.

I found the estuary shortly and searched for Osceola. I thought the town would be right there but it wasn't. What I had come to was the Port of Osceola, a name which exaggerates the activity there. There is a landing and a grain elevator and when I came there several empty barges were parked off to the side of the estuary. One barge sat below the grain elevator and was being loaded, its front end riding high out of the water while the back end was weighted heavily and tilted, seeming about to sink.

The barges parked along the other side of the harbor were jammed into the shallow water and mud of the banks and tied off. A towboat was in the process of shoving them up there in the shallows when I passed.

I went to the far end of the harbor and back again looking for the town. From the water there was no way to reach the town. I came back and found a floating ladder leading to shore and I stepped off on it. When I did I sank in up to the knee. The river rushed into my boot with the sucking sound of a vacuum and soaked my sock. The water was cold and sudden and unexpected. I jumped back into the canoe.

"Hey! You in the canoe."

The voice—coming from I couldn't tell where—sounded aggressive and angry, but I paddled out to find it anyway. It came from the loudspeaker of the towboat that had been parking the barges and which now was crossing the estuary to dock. When he docked and tied off, I pulled alongside.

"What're you doing over there?" The pilot came down from the wheelhouse and leaned over the railing. He wasn't smiling. He was a big man. The ladder I had climbed on and quickly off turned out to be his and he wanted to know what I was up to.

"I was trying to find some way to get into town, but I couldn't find a good place to pull out. That ladder sure didn't help any. I stepped on it and sank right in."

"Yeah. I built that there." His attitude began to change. "When the river's not so high, it works fine."

He had a little johnboat parked there which he used for making trips faster than he could in the towboat.

"I didn't know it was private," I said. "Sorry."

He smiled all of a sudden.

"What can I do to get to town from here?"

"It's a pretty good ways from here. You need supplies?"

"Some, but mostly I need some water. I'm all out." I showed him my empty water bag. "Can I get some around here?"

"You can get some from my galley. Tie off and climb on up."

He took my line and tied off for me. He gave me his hand and pulled me aboard. He pointed to the galley and I filled the bag with water. He had to come in to show me what to do and then he left me as if he knew me and went on about his work. I finished up and waited by the rail and watched as the fuel truck backed up to the edge of the dock and lowered down a hose. Don, the pilot, stuck the nozzle into the fuel tank of the towboat and took on about seven hundred dollars worth of diesel fuel. And even at that, the tanks weren't completely full.

Don Smith introduced himself and looked me over when he shook hands. He looked deep into my eyes as though searching for something and I guess he found it. He offered me a cup of coffee and I took it and then I just hung around. Without asking and without Don saying anything, I had the feeling that it was all right. Right away Don started ignoring me as if I were an old friend and he went about his business as though I had seen it all a hundred times or more. He didn't stop to explain anything to me. There was about him, however, the air of a man doing everything in a big way and with a purpose, showing off for a friend, perhaps. He was showing Jimmy, one of Don's two deck hands, how to splice together two of those big thick heavy ropes that hold fast so many things on the boat, including tying towboat to pier. When one rope is frayed or torn, you can't just throw the thing away. They cost too much for that. So you splice it with another damaged rope, cutting out the useless parts, and it's long and useful again and stronger than before. You slice off the bad parts, unravel the woven cords and weave the two ropes together. Don did it quickly. He wanted Jimmy to watch and then to do it. Jimmy had a bit of trouble and Don did it again and again until Jimmy almost got the hang of it.

Don turned to me and said, "Simple, isn't it?"

"Sure," I said but I don't know if I could have done any better than Jimmy. "Looks easy when *you* do it."

Jimmy was new at the deck-hand business. Joe Bob was the other and he had been around a while but I heard that he and

Don had a pretty stormy time of it. Every once in a while Joe Bob needing extra time off and not getting it would simply quit, and Don would hire him back when he needed the extra man. Right now he needed Joe Bob ***and*** Jimmy but Jimmy was no deck hand. I could tell that. His heart was not in the work and he didn't like the water and probably couldn't swim. He was just a guy sent down by the employment office and Don didn't expect him to last, which was okay with Don. The problem for Don was that it took time to train a deck hand and if he didn't stay long, it was time wasted. But right now he needed the man.

Jimmy was young and black and according to Don had taken the job because if he didn't, his unemployment benefits would have been in jeopardy. You're supposed to be actively seeking work and can't go around turning down jobs.

"You know how it is," Don explained. "The difference between a black man and a nigger."

I, he could tell, was different. Not just from the local blacks, but different.

A group of noisy boaters had come down not very long ago and had come into the harbor looking for the town and supplies and without asking they tied their fancy white boats off Don's barges.

"Just like they owned the place," Don said and he didn't like it one bit. He blew a gasket, made them get away from the barges, from his property and out of the harbor altogether. They never did get their supplies.

He had expected the same with me, another goon coming in to use his property without asking, coming in like I owned the place, but I flipped him a curve. I was different, he said. Polite. So he let me take my water and he let me hang around all day long and he was happy to have me, and when he went down river a little ways, I stayed on board, drinking coffee beside him in the wheelhouse and watching the way things worked and getting the inside view of towboat life.

Don was a huge and powerful man, at first glance the type who would pick you up in a bar and hurl you through the wall if you upset him. But with me he was gentle as Androcles' lion. He let me hang around and explained the answers to my questions and when a crunching noise came from under the boat he even joked:

"Oops!" he said. "There goes your canoe."

I looked out in a panic. The canoe was still there. Don was laughing.

"That was just a log we went over," he explained. "Log, canoe, it's hard to tell."

When we got back to the dock, Don gave Joe Bob time off and told him to take me into town to the supermarket.

Joe Bob took his time. He got gas for his car and we stopped and grabbed a sixpack of beer which we drank in the car back down by the dock. On the way back we met Joe Bob's father along the road and when the old man saw a stranger in the car, Joe Bob naturally explained the situation.

"Yeah," Joe Bob's dad said. He had that look of recognition. "Didn't I see you yesterday tangled up in the logs and wood on the river?"

I remembered the tough time back in Barfield and how I'd been spun around in the crazy water and then caught up in logs and debris floating near shore. I laughed.

"You saw that?"

"Sure did."

"That was me all right."

"I couldn't figure out what you were doing out there. What did you call yourself doing?"

"Trying to get unstuck."

It was worth a good laugh and I laughed harder knowing the story would spread like fire and I'd be famous not for valor and strength and for canoeing the river to New Orleans, but for getting stuck in the debris at Barfield.

Later we passed a man sitting in a pickup truck parked by the railroad tracks. He was just sitting there, but that was his job, counting the trains.

"Just out of jail," Joe Bob told me. "He'll do this for a while before he's really free."

I didn't know whether to believe him. But it was that kind of town. A slow town where a man will use the threat of a pistol to keep another man away from his wife, and where a woman marries young before she knows what she's getting into and missing.

With Don gone home, Joe Bob working in the engine room and Jimmy hosing down and mopping up the boat, I stowed my new supplies in the canoe and took a short stroll up to the grain elevator. Once again fortune was waiting for me. The man in the office, Bill Shepherd, let me come in and sit down, have a cup of coffee and phone home. When I was through, he let me rest and we visited.

When I got back to Don's boat, Don had left again, this time in his skiff and he had motored across to the other side of the river. He had another operation on the Tennessee side and was checking on it. Even if the wind had cleared and the river calmed, I couldn't leave, I told myself, without saying thanks and goodbye to Don. So I waited, talking to Jimmy who was manning the radio for calls coming in for or from Don. Joe Bob had gone home. Jimmy was talking about his family, a tale of bleak opportunities that aimed toward jail or the dole or the army. Times maybe have changed, but not *that* much. I felt more luck and pride than pity and when I realized it I asked Jimmy for a little help. He gave it cheerfully. With me he was not the sullen loafer that Don saw. He helped me get my canoe away from the towboat and around to shore and after I had beached it and started setting up camp as evening grew dark, Jimmy shined the towboat's spotlight down on me so I could see what I was doing.

Pretty soon Don returned with another job to do. He had to go ten miles or so downstream and pick up a barge and bring it back. I asked if I could go. He seemed to expect that of course I was going along.

The barges are generally not owned by the towboats that push them up and down the river, but by barge companies and they are used and swapped on a very complicated system that seems to make practically every barge available to whoever needs it. The barges are kept track of and the leasing of space on the barges for each trip somehow gets taken care of because the system works, and Don—and others like him—see to it that the barges get where they're supposed to be in order to be picked up by the traveling towboats or filled or emptied at the elevators.

We went speedily downstream. The river was still choppy and the towboat, monster that it was, bounced around more violently than the canoe. With no heavy barges lashed to the front of the towboat to stabilize the thing, we pitched up and down and swayed side to side. But we made good speed. Once we picked up the empty barge our speed dropped to nil. If the barge had been loaded and riding low in the water, creating still more resistance, we would have gone even slower. The Mississippi is not the fastest moving river, but it's fast and strong enough to make upstream travel in a towboat and barge deadly slow. In a canoe upstream would be nearly impossible.

Along the way I watched the radar screen. It was even better than my big maps for marking out the shape of the river and the shoreline, islands, sandbars, other boats and large floating debris. Large logs and canoes appear the same on the radar screen, and towboats routinely run over the logs. Canoes too, I presumed, if they are not recognized as canoes.

The glowing line rotating on the screen swept across the terrain and all features appeared as green blips that glowed brightly for a second and then faded. The scope of the radar's range could be changed by a simple switch, and when Don broadened the field of vision, he showed me storms forming off in the distance. They were the reasons for the wind and the rough water and they would be out there tomorrow and probably the next day as well. I saw what rain looks like to radar.

I also saw what those channel markers, buoys and mile markers look like—on screen and from the wheelhouse at night. Those green or red triangles and rectangles that guided the barges day and night reflected brightly in the beams of the towboat spotlights scanning the banks. I learned what they mean. "Red—right hand—returning," Don told me, which means keep the red markers on your right hand side when returning from the direction of the sea. The rule applies no matter what river you happen to be on.

Additionally, the triangles and the rectangles signify another difference. To stay in the shipping channel, the towboat pilot aims for the one and merely passes by the other. They tell him when to go straight on, and when to flank.

I had been looking at those day markers for weeks now and never suspected what they meant. I also had no idea that when certain markers flashed in the night each marker flashes off and on in a distinct sequence, regulated intervals of so many seconds between flashes, a sort of code that is written in some book that the pilots have and that tells the pilots exactly where they are at night. Each light has its own signature.

In the daytime, of course, life is much easier. Everything is marked on those maps—the same maps that I was using. I felt like a member of the club.

When we arrived back at Osceola we had to tie off the barge we had just picked up. Don had to stay in the driver's seat and take care of the throttle. He shoved the barge up into the shallows and against the bank. It was the deck hand's task to fish out the cables permanently anchored under the water and to haul them up and run them along the side of the barge and secure them. But those cables are extremely heavy, and the deck hand that night was Jimmy. It was his first time at this and he wasn't doing it very well.

"He's got to just grab on and pull and keep on pulling until he's got the whole thing up," Don said. "If he stops to rest, he'll never get it."

So I volunteered to help. But first I would need a pair of work gloves. Don offered his. He held them up.

"These are very good gloves," he told me. "And I've never ever let anyone else use them."

I promised I wouldn't drop them overboard or ruin them, but that's not what he was saying. He was telling me he trusted me.

I ran down along the side of the barge and helped Jimmy strain. I saw why he was having so much trouble. I could not see how any one man could do this job. The cables were steel and enormously heavy. The two of us together had a world of trouble, but we finally managed to get the thing up and secure the barge and there was no worrying that this barge would go anywhere tonight.

But Don told me I was wrong.

"Those cables can break," he said. "I've seen them stretch and snap and they can lash across with enough force to slice a man's head off."

And then I heard them. They never stopped creaking and squeaking under the strain of tension. I was glad the job was over.

We docked on the other side of the estuary and Don sent Jimmy home. He wouldn't need him anymore tonight. Then the two of us—Don and I—drove into town and bought a case of beer. Back down by the towboat, we started drinking.

To my chagrin, as we drank, with each beer we finished, we tossed the empty cans into the water. Don pitched his cans in as if he did it all the time and it didn't bother him one bit. Joe Bob in the afternoon had done the same thing and I had asked him about using the river as a garbage can.

"Everybody does it," he said. "The stuff just sinks to the bottom."

I hadn't done it then in the afternoon but I found myself doing it now. I didn't much like it and wasn't very proud of myself. I was following someone else's lead and I felt also that I was defiling the river that had been so fair and honest with me. I kept on anyway.

To my great pleasure, however, as we drank, Don began to talk. It was talk of a different nature, a deeper more honest kind of talking than I have ever gotten from another man. He had shown me earlier by lending me his gloves that he trusted me. Now he was showing me how much. He told me secrets.

He spoke nervously at first, worried about how I would take what he had to say. Then he slipped into a higher gear and we talked about attitudes, about race, and of course about women. Somehow we got into inter-racial romance and he volunteered his feelings that it was one thing for a white man to be with a black woman, but another thing entirely for a black man to be with a white woman. He had no logical explanation when I asked him why, but the one was quite all right, the other utterly utterly wrong.

I began to see then that the argument had nothing to do with logic, and nothing to do with racial purity but rather with racial insecurity.

The process of selection for blacks during the slave days was even stricter than nature's process. Only the strongest had survived the horrible voyages on the slave ships, and of those that remained and of those born generations later, only the strongest of the strong were wanted. These sturdy ones bred together and created a race of great physical strength. Naturally, such strength was feared. To offset the strength and physical prowess and to dampen the fear, someone started the rumor that these blacks were inferior, animals. They had been taken from their homes and were continuously separated from family members and friends and they had no support system. "You don't even know who your mother or your father was or where you came from." The inferiority complex sets in and takes root and becomes a belief first and then a reality. And when you tell the lie long enough, you begin to believe it yourself, although somewhere deep inside resides the truth, and the insecurity and fear remain.

The fear isn't and has never been that the race will become impure, but that all the women will be snatched up and stolen by these strong and virile men.

I would have dropped that bomb on Don, but by then he had begun unloading on me the darknesses that lurked inside him and needed outlet. He told me secrets as if I were an old friend. Or better, he talked with the freedom of speaking to a stranger he never expected to see again. When I traveled on my way, I would be taking his secrets with me. I would not be around to look at him and to judge him nor for him to feel the judging. And I would not be around to tell. He was safe. And yet he knew I was a writer and would be writing. But he trusted me. He asked me please not to tell a single soul, not even in casual conversation and I promised I wouldn't and still he hesitated before speaking, but finally he let go and out poured the humor and sadness and torments of his secrets. Of course I could tell what he told—but I won't.

Later on Don told me I had set up my tent for nothing. He would not let me be plagued by southern mosquitoes tonight. I could sleep on board the towboat. There were plenty of beds and no mosquitoes. I could shower if I wanted to and while he was gone home to spend a little time with his wife before coming back to guard the boat at night which he was in the habit of doing lately, I could help myself to beer and to any food in the galley. I did just that. I ate chicken pot pies and frozen pizza heated in the oven. I drank beer and I watched part of a football game on TV. I felt civilized once more and back in the swing of what was going on in the real world. Football. The real world, actually, was too much. I didn't watch for long.

When Don came back we sat in the wheelhouse darkness and talked some more. When I couldn't keep my eyes open any longer, I went below and climbed onto a bunk and slept.

28

WHEN I WOKE UP in the morning the wind was still high and the water too rough and Don got a call on the radio saying that he needed to get downriver and drop off a barge. I prepared to say my goodbyes. Joe Bob came aboard and did a little work in the engine room. He and Don, caught up with preparations for the job ahead this morning, ignored me and seemed to have totally forgotten about me. I felt that I was in the way and so I jumped off. As I broke camp, I looked out toward the end of the estuary and toward the river. The water out there was not calm at all. I had that sinking feeling that I had as a kid when all my pals went off on summer vacation and I was stuck to stay in town. I wanted to go too.

I went about the suddenly lonely business of taking the tent down and packing my gear in the canoe. Normally I was eager to get on the river, in a hurry to get going each morning. Today I felt sluggish. But I couldn't stay. I went back to say goodbye.

"You taking off?"

"I guess," I said. "As far as I can get in this wind."

"How far you think you'll get?"

"I made ten miles yesterday. Probably the same today."

"It'll take you forever just to get to Memphis."

"If this wind keeps up."

"I'm going that way, you know. You want a ride?"

I did not have to be asked twice. I did not worry about cheating.

"You bet!" I said.

Joe Bob helped me get the canoe up onto the towboat. We laid it against a rail along the port side and stowed the gear in the bow. Then we shoved off, picked up the barge, lashed it with steel cables and those thick ropes to the front of the towboat and off we went.

In the wheelhouse I felt on top of the world. High above the river, the water shimmering silver under the bright morning sun. We pulled down transparent shades on the windows all around and saw the world in shades of green and grey.

Don handled the levers, engine speeds and steering mechanisms with practiced ease. They moved with just a touch from his big hands. He seemed to be thinking instructions to his beast and the beast responded.

Down below Joe Bob was hanging over the front edge of the towboat. He wielded a blowtorch and was welding shut a hole that gaped in the bow and took on water. The hole was well above the water line, but with the river so rough and the water sloshing so hard and so high, the gash in the hull was catching too much water to be left alone.

I helped myself to breakfast in the galley and when we arrived at Richardson's Landing, Don came below and told me to help myself to anything I wanted—cans of soup and corn and tamales and beans. I took a few to be polite.

A huge towboat and barge had been shadowing us for miles. I soon saw why. We were going to rendezvous with this beast at Richardson's Landing, do some shuffling of the barges parked there, and deliver a load to the beast behind us. There was much work to be done and it was time for me to go.

With Joe Bob's help I lowered the canoe over the side. We all shook hands and said farewell. It was almost teary, but it was too joyous for that. I was leaving two good friends, but I saw it differently this time. I saw that I had made two good friends and was happy for that. The lump in my throat wasn't so big.

"Did you get some things from the galley?"

"A few."

He took a look.

"Hey!" he said. "That's not nearly enough. Go back in there and take what you need. Take it all if you want to."

Yeah—he was my friend.

I got onto the river and paddled out quickly. It's best not to linger. It was also a good idea to get away from Don's engines, so I paddled out far and fast. I had time for one more good wave. They stood on deck. One down low, Don up high. They were waving. I wondered what they were thinking, if they would miss me too. I was sure they would. Then they got busy, and I had to fight the river.

I cruised swiftly downstream and around the bend and out of sight. The river cooperated. Once Don and Joe Bob could no longer see me, the river started acting up again. I had made sixteen miles on the towboat, not rapid miles, for towboats only run about ten miles an hour down river. Still, they were faster miles than I could have made paddling. I made only ten miles before I had to pull out.

I thought I would just sit and wait awhile. It was still early yet. I could relax and wait out the wind.

I pulled the canoe up the sandy bank, took out a book from one of the bags and lay back in the canoe to read. I was looking straight up into the branches of leafless trees, stretching across the blue of the sky like bony skeleton fingers reaching for something. I put the book down and lay there with my hands folded across my chest. I rested there thinking, wondering what I was reaching for, if I knew, and what I was finding.

I saw a bumble bee, solitary and buzzing loud. He zipped past my ear, circled and returned. He moved in super-slow motion. I could see the pattern of his wings, grey and delicate and transparent, his body the pale golden color of dead dandelions with little black stripes, the eyes tiny bumps, the antennae like little curly hairs. He was right there, close and staring me in the face. I thought he must be after something sweet in the canoe—a granola bar or something. I lightly shooed him away. He came back angry and startled me. I thought he was going for me. I ducked and dodged and jumped from the canoe and ran. I swatted the air all around, twisting and turning to get out of the way and keep the bee off me. When I went back to canoe, so did the bee. He was still buzzing all around me and I thought I was under attack. I took off my cap and swiped at the bee and got him. I thought he was dead and I put the cap back on. The bee was not dead. Not yet. He was inside the cap and—*Yeow!*—he stung my head. I swatted him hard and sure and he died.

The pain. It would have been fierce if the whole thing hadn't been so funny. I pictured myself panicked by a bee and acting a fool to escape. And then I was sorry for having killed him. It hadn't been necessary. Maybe all the bee wanted was to be my friend. I had seen his face, but I hadn't understood it. A sweet bee face.

The river was still too rough. I took a walk through the trees and into a sandy clearing. A woman and a man were there.

Shirrel and her husband Ron had been on an outing with their kids. They had driven their truck with its camper shell on the back on the soft sand and now they were stuck. The kids were running around and Shirrel was standing around and Ron was digging in the sand and laying logs and branches under the tires for some kind of traction. Nothing was working. I came to the rescue. Finally! some physical proof of my worth to strangers.

Ron and I jacked the rear of the truck as high as we could get it. The rear axle was still resting in the sand and the truck wasn't going to budge until the undercarriage was no longer jammed into the sand. We dug around it, wedged planks under it and laid wood for traction. Then at the crucial moment, Shirrel started the truck and put it in reverse. Ron, using logs as fulcrum and lever, raised the truck inches. And I pushed for all I was worth. The engine revved and the wheels spun in the sand and it was a failure. We repositioned the wood and tried again. I dug in the sand around my feet to create a brace to push against. The wheels spun but they grabbed the wood, splintered it and moved an inch or two. The jack fell over, Ron dropped his lever and ran to the front of the truck and pushed with me. Together we shoved that truck right out of the soft sand and onto firmer ground.

Now we had a chance to talk. They were from Alabama but were doing a tour of duty at a nearby air force base. Shirrel couldn't wait to get back to Alabama.

Ron was impressed with my journey and started talking about a survival course he had taken. He explained to me how to cook and eat snakes if it ever became necessary.

His young son came up and wanted to play, but it was time for them to leave. Ron wanted to repay me for the help.

"We'd have never have gotten out of there if you hadn't come along."

And so he wanted to come back later with steaks to cook on my fire. He'd bring a couple of buddies with him and we'd have a really nice dinner and sit up and talk all night and drink.

"What do you drink?"

"How about a little bourbon?"

Sounded great. His young son wanted to come back too and Ron agreed. They would camp all night.

I hadn't planned on staying. I wanted to let the wind calm and then I would move on down the river. But now I was glad I had stopped and would stay the night here. The promise of steaks and bourbon and company. I was almost as excited as Ron's son.

"My real name is George," he told me. "My nickname is Tiger. You won't forget, will ya?"

Of course not. Not even after they all failed to show up later.

The wind had started to bluster and in the evening I could feel a storm forming. The air cooled off and dampened quickly. I knew they wouldn't be back. It was understandable, but I was still disappointed. Every crackle in the woods had me up and flashing my light back toward the clearing just in case they did manage to return and needed to see where I was camped. But they never made it.

I settled in and watched the storm.

Across the river, north and west, lightning flashed fireworks of crackling light across the sky and over the treetops. Thunder followed many seconds after. The storm was far off. The lightning appeared to be moving away to the north. And when the rains finally came, they sprinkled lightly.

I waited as long as I could. Then when I was absolutely positive my friends weren't coming, I built a fire and made dinner. I could still have a few drinks if they came later. But they never did.

Instead I was treated to a calm evening watching the show in the sky. Later on the night turned violent and I'm sure Ron and Co. were happy to be home and dry. I however got drenched and during the night heard a tornado touch down nearby. At least it sounded like one. Trees fell and my tent strained at its supports. I was relieved when the rains returned. I had always heard rain signals the end of tornado threats. I managed to survive, and in the morning the trees knocked over and the wet ground were the only evidence of the hard night.

I coasted easily down to Memphis, pulled my canoe out at Mud Island and wandered around.

Mud Island holds a shiny new entertainment complex of shops and restaurants and a boat marina. To get on the island, you either have to pay or you must be a member of the marina. To pay, you have to come over on the tram from downtown Memphis. To get in where I stood, you need to be a member. Willie James Smith told me all this. He sat as sentry in the little guard house at the rear entrance. He gave me the lowdown, told me all the rules and regulations, and then he let me pass. I told him I wouldn't be long. I just wanted to see the river.

The biggest attraction on Mud Island is the scale model of the Mississippi River system. It must be half a mile long, perfectly scaled and bending the way the river does, made of brick and concrete, wide where the river is wide and narrow when the river gets skinny. It covers the whole Mississippi drainage basin and you get a feel for how the other rivers contribute to the system. Mostly what I got, however, was a feel for where I had been and where I was going. Like a giant, like Paul Bunyan, I walked the length of the river in a few minutes, looked down on towns and counted the miles remaining. I was impressed with myself for all I had done so far and could see what a thrill it would be when I arrived. I could measure time ahead now in days rather than weeks and I wanted to celebrate.

When I got my canoe around to the riverfront levee the afternoon was still early and bright. I had plenty of time to explore and then get back to the river and downstream to camp before dark. It didn't work out that way.

The levee looks remarkably like St. Louis' riverfront.

Memphis is undergoing the same kind of development to rekindle the flames of downtown. But there seems to be more to do here, more paddlewheelers and a downtown closer to more living. St. Louis' downtown is mostly for working.

I stopped at the new development called Beale Street. I had a beer. People were getting off work and coming for happy hour. Everyone was dressed for success, and so was I. A different sort of success, a success only I appreciated. No one talked to me. Even the bartender snubbed me.

I left and went searching for a really good steak. The place I found seemed happy to have me. The owner came out and showed me the steaks he had cooling on ice, but he said the restaurant wasn't open yet.

I walked around and then gave up on the steaks. I went back to the river. I wasn't so worried about losing canoe and gear, but what if someone went through the stuff and found the pistol? I didn't want some crook walking around with a new weapon—not *my* trusty gun.

By now I had piddled around too long and I lost the light. Where to go? Certainly nowhere along the wharf. It would have to be Mud Island.

At the very tip of the island there is a flat. I pulled the canoe up and turned it over there. Then I climbed the hill and the first set of steps and used the walls of the development which rose out of the grassy hill like a fortress to shield me from the wind. A row of flagpoles rimmed the very edge of the development and the flags flapped noisily in the wind. So did the tent.

I stayed in the shadows and slept early. No fire tonight and no dinner. I felt like a fugitive. It was thrilling.

To my delight and surprise no nightwatchmen stumbled across my camp, but in the morning I discovered the water rats had. The plastic bags had been gnawed through and the Malt-o-meal had been eaten. There were traces of it on the ground and a trail of discarded plastic and paper containers led down to the water. I would have been upset if it hadn't been so funny.

I set out at first light. I skimmed under the Interstate 55 Highway bridge and past the industrial waterfront. I made the bend and headed for open water. I hit another patch of crazy water that swirled like a nightmare. I went into it bravely and paddled hard. I must have hit the currents just right. They grabbed me and tried to spin me but I kept the canoe straight and the currents took hold and spat me downstream at great speed. Today would be a good day.

Today I was going to pile on the miles. I wouldn't stop for the night until I reached Helena, Arkansas.

I didn't anticipate any problems—but you never know. I also didn't have Helena as a goal at first. I just wanted to get in as many miles as I could. By the time the sun had reached its zenith in the cloud-swirled sky, I had left Memphis forty miles behind. I began to push harder. I started to think of a hundred miles in one day. I went faster and I strained to do it, but I knew I would never make it if I didn't stop for lunch. I had taken no lunch or dinner yesterday, only snacks, and my energy was low.

When I pulled out at a sandy beach just above Mhoon Bend, my back was tied in tight knots and my left shoulder burned inside. I pulled the canoe up and walked around bent over like a hunchback for five full minutes before I could straighten up. My knees ached and I could not sit down. If I had, I wouldn't have been able to get back up. I ate standing, a lunch of two cold hot dogs, a peanut butter sandwich, a couple of apples and water from my canteen. The water was cool and sweet, but mostly wet and as refreshing as ambrosia. Cool water. Absolutely nothing can take its place for goodness when you're burning inside.

I noticed here for the first time signs posted telling me and the world, except for a privileged few, to keep out. Naturally I took that as an invitation to stay and if I had not been pushing for distance that day I would have made that sandy beach my home for the night.

The map, however, told me the river would narrow around the next bend. A narrow channel flooded with rain from upriver should give me speed. I hurried to get into it. The speed was not there, however. I had to make my own.

I passed the mouth of the St. Francis River just at sunset. The sight of one more river pouring itself into the Mississippi and contributing its life to the larger life was enough to take my mind off my pain. I let myself drift and watched the two rivers blend into one.

The St. Francis is a tiny river, barely more than a large stream. If you pass by too quickly you'll miss the opening. Both sides of the mouth are hidden by tall leafy trees. The mouth looks like a small inlet, a cove flooded by the rains. But if you look farther up, you can see how it stretches far away into the distance and bends away. Just a quiet life, a ripple of water, almost unnoticeable. It surrenders itself peacefully to the big river.

I slid past and pushed on. Helena was not far away now. The light in the sky was fading and I was losing my strength, but I swore I would not fail. I could make it in ninety minutes if I gave it my all. But did I have ninety minutes of light left?

I didn't, but I couldn't stop now. The sky went from the pale blues and purple stripes of sunset to the cold grey of dusk and then no color at all. But I refused to stop.

Only one more bend in the river and I'd be there. I could see the marker light flashing in the distance. I had no other reference points in the darkness so I aimed straight for the light, and in a little while I came to Helena. There is a terminal there, I found out, with barges parked and lights on all night and the clangings of heavy work. When I came into the inlet I saw the men working—loading barges, I supposed. I paddled around silently like an Indian scout and came back out of the inlet. I was too tired to search for the town and a place to eat. Since there was no place along this developed waterfront to camp and build a fire, I went back upstream with my lantern scanning the shore. I finally found a place in the shadow of the noise and camped in the trees and weeds. It wasn't a great spot and it swarmed with mosquitoes, but right then any spot would do.

In the morning I found the town and I went for breakfast. I was starved and it was all I could think of. Some fellows down at the water's edge were working on a barge and they showed me the way to town. One of them told me where to stash the canoe. Signs all around said to keep out and warned against trespassing, but this fellow told me not to worry. He'd keep an eye out.

Up the hill I went and beyond the retaining wall and across

the railroad tracks. An old building that looked like it used to be the railroad station faced me and there were faces in the windows watching me. The building was old and seemed especially junky and beat up now that it had found a new purpose. I would have investigated a little more to see what they were doing inside there, but loitering nearby was an old black man. He looked leathery and as old as the town itself and he stood watching me carefully.

I walked right up to him and spoke. He warily nodded and turned away. I followed after him. I didn't want him to get away. He had that beat up look about him, used up and scarred around the edges and maybe a little burned out in the middle. He walked with a limp and later told me about the construction work he used to do, the accident he'd had with his back and the minuscule disability check he receives each month which barely keeps him alive. He was one of those who had fallen through the cracks and his face showed it. And yet when he spoke to me he wasn't harping on old wounds. He was just trying to make it—and determined to do so.

His name was Daniel McGee and I asked him where I could get something to eat.

"Oh just about anyplace."

"Where's there a really good place?"

"Well this place right here." He pointed to a restaurant called Casqui's Restaurant on the corner. "You can get anything you want right in there. Breakfast or lunch or anything."

"They have good steaks?"

"Steaks and everything."

So I went inside. Naturally I was the only dark face in the place, except for an old black woman in the kitchen—the cook, probably. She peered through the opening in the wall where she placed the orders to be served and she eyed me secretly. I wondered what she was thinking, if she was having any trouble dealing with the fact that I was in there waiting to be served. Maybe she thought I was out of place there. Maybe blacks in this town had their own places to eat.

No one else, however, paid me much mind. The men lingering over breakfast before going to work went back to their newspapers and their conversations. And the waitress who came to take my order reacted to my presence with the cheeriest "Good morning" ever. She was very pretty and when she smiled at me, the smile was more than friendly. It brightened the room and her face radiated warmth. In my malnourished and semi-crazed state I saw her as the most beautiful woman in the world.

I asked for steak and eggs and potatoes and, since I was in the South, grits. I'd never had them before and wanted to see what I was missing.

My friend Daniel McGee was hanging around outside and I felt bad about not passing on the generosity. I ran out and dragged him inside.

"Do you want anything?"

The beautiful waitress came back and Daniel asked for coffee.

"Anything else?" she asked.

He only wanted coffee.

"I'm buying," I said, but he still only wanted coffee.

Daniel and I talked, but he never looked at me. He wasn't looking at anything, the way New Yorkers pass you without looking at you or seeming to look at anything.

When he drank his coffee, he poured it first from the cup into the saucer—I guess to let the coffee cool—and then he drank it with noisy slurps from the saucer.

My breakfast arrived and I dug in like a released prisoner of war. The scrambled eggs were soft and creamy, the minute steak very tender with the right amount of fat throughout to make it juicy and tasty. And the grits with just a dab of sugar on top were smooth and hot, not lumpy like oatmeal and I didn't have to make a face to choke it down. I actually liked it. I loved it all. Must have been those fresh-from-the-farm ingredients.

I spent the better part of the morning walking around Helena with Daniel. I needed to buy a few things and he went with me to show me the way to the market with the best prices. Along the way he pointed out the churches and the places for drinking, all the businesses that had gone out of business, and he told me how hard it was to make a good go of it in Helena since everything was closing down. But people still hang on, he said, and he showed me the dirty run-down shotgun shacks as flimsy as cardboard, shacks hardly suitable for animal pens and that people pay for the privilege to live in. Dirt and squalor all around, it looked like Mexico. I had thought out-houses had all been replaced by indoor toilets a long time ago. I had thought even the most impoverished parts of this country were a zillion steps ahead of Third World poverty. I was wrong. This *was* the Third World. And I was wrong too when I thought that *my* luck was bad, and wrong again if I ever considered a man's fate to be entirely his own choosing and making. Wrong and naïve.

I wanted to leave. I was much more comfortable and at peace on the river, far away from the horrors man creates out of what should be beauty and plenty. Even the most ugly industrialized strips along the river were not as horrible as this.

I can't take it, I guess. I've been at it too long. The effort for so many miles has been sapping my strength, sure, but now I see that my whole constitution is affected. I'm not as tough as I thought. I can't look at people so poor, so dead-ended and not want to cry.

Daniel walked me back through town. I offered him a couple of bucks for helping me, but he wouldn't take the money. And when I got back to the site where the canoe waited, Daniel stopped. The sign told him he could go no farther and by God! he would not cross the low cable that barred his way. I bid him farewell there and stepped over the cable and walked down to the canoe. When I turned around, Daniel was gone.

It had taken me this long to figure it out, but finally I learned how to pack. At the market I had grabbed a couple of big empty boxes and bought new trash-can liners. I lined the inside of the boxes with the plastic sacks, put the food and cans in the lining, and then placed each box inside another plastic sack. The outer bags would keep the cardboard of the boxes from getting wet and falling apart. The inside bags would give an additional layer of waterproof protection to my store, and the boxes would make everything easy to carry and easy to pack and easy to place in the canoe. *Why didn't I think of this sooner?*

One more thing before I could leave Helena. I ran back to the hardware store to buy batteries for my lantern.

A guy called Harrison was filling in for the owner who was in the hospital. He sold me the batteries and then he just started talking. As if that's how it goes. You do your business, and then you stick around and visit.

"Couple of other fellows came through here doing what you're doing. Five of them, if I remember right. In two canoes tied together." He didn't say when. "They were from out east. Harvard boys on a lark. They came in here to buy something but I can't remember what, and they got interested in these new rifles I had with plastic barrels and I let them take one out back to test it out and when they left, I had sold every one I had. Harvard boys."

He went on talking while I stood there, telling me about the old days when blacks and whites didn't have much to say to each other, and then about the tensions when civil rights became the big thing, and then about how it was now, still not buddy-buddy but making strides forward.

"Sometimes," he said, "I think it's better down here because it all used to be so bad and we have to make extra effort to get along. It's all right there on the surface. We don't hide nothing."

But how many times a week do y'all invite a black man home to dinner? How many of y'all have black friends?

"Not friends, but we do have contact. Everyday."

Which I guess is something. I thought of weddings and parties that would be totally monochromatic if not for me. And again, if not for me how many people that I know could pass a lifetime without a black friend? Without close contact even?

While we were talking, a man came in with a problem. He was black and had bought something that didn't work. I don't know if Harrison knew this man, but they talked as if they had run into each other many times. Harrison set out to solve the problem.

The black man had bought some kind of cylindrical wick for a kerosene pot—the kind of thing used in orchards to keep the frost off the trees. I don't think that's what this man was using it for, but I don't know. He never said. The wick was supposed to fit into a little groove where it then could be raised and lowered by turning a lever. This man and Harrison were now trying to find the way to make it fit properly.

Harrison knew about as much about it as the other man, which was nothing. He brought out pliers and screwdrivers and after he ruined the first wick, he brought out another one. He was determined to make this thing work. And while he worked, he talked, which may have contributed to his troubles with the pot, but he talked about the days when he worked for the Grand Ole Opry in Nashville and when he worked for United Insurance Company and for Purolator Hauling and how when he moved to Helena he had to work in the same office with a black man and this black man showed him more than he could remember and he in turn taught the black man how to drive a car. Harrison at one time or another had chauffeured Howard Hughes around when he came to town.

"Howard Hughes?" I said. "The real Howard Hughes?"

He said Howard owned the insurance company and would come to town from time to time to check on things. And Howard couldn't drive.

It sounded funny to me, but I let it pass. I felt strange. Harrison started talking about black people not being able to hang on to much once they've got it and he used the story of a self-made black millionaire who amassed a fortune and a lot of land farming cotton. Eventually the man died and his land was divided among his kids.

"The one son I know," Harrison said, "drank up his share. That's what happens when you just don't know. You seem like a bright boy. Been to college?"

I told him which one but he wasn't impressed. He kept on talking.

I still had this strange feeling crawling over me. It was more than simply thinking the trip was over. There is an emotional point in every voyage where the voice inside says "Okay, that's it. We've done enough. We're done." The trip may go on farther, but the emotional climax has been reached and the rest of the way is a strain. I had reached that point but I knew something else was going to happen. I could feel it like an itch that was more than the itch from being so dirty. The crawling on my skin was more than tiny bugs. Something more was coming. I could smell it.

I tried to put that apprehension out of my mind and concentrate on the river.

The river is still frightening, half a mile wide and more in places. And those submerged features still suck at the bottom of my canoe and pull down on me. I can feel the suction when I go over those swirls in the river. They still try to spin me, but I know how to handle them now. I just paddle hard and use the swirls to give me speed. And where the swirls are most violent, most numerous, I can see the river dipping, undulating like rolling hills. I take each dip like a small roller-coaster, the initial drop with its accompanying whooshing sound creates bubbles in my stomach and my stomach rises to my throat. Once I'm into the dips and riding them like soft waves, the riding is smooth and fun. I not only can see the river as it falls nearly 1500 feet from the Minnesota highlands and plains down to sea level, but I can also feel the drop. Each rise and fall leaves me a few feet lower and closer to the sea.

The river hasn't stopped its meandering. I'm in that phase of the snaking back and forth where the river over the years has cut back on itself so close that the zig has almost touched the zag. During high water when they do actually meet, the river has abandoned the wide loops, straightens itself out and cuts off miles of its journey. The borders between the states used to follow the river. Where the river bent and looped, so did the line between the states. But that river knows no convention. He doesn't run where the path is laid, he goes where he needs to go, where he wants to go. He has forced the states to shift their lines, no longer following the flow of the river, but shifting and staying in the old flow where the river is no more. Otherwise, towns that used to be in Mississippi would now be in Arkansas.

I wasn't sure where I was anymore, Arkansas or Mississippi. Even the map called them indefinite boundaries. I didn't know where I was, and I didn't care. The river had become a sanctuary once more, tranquil, a haven far from the world of man. I wouldn't come to another town until Greenville, Mississippi, 120 miles from Helena. Two days of solitude.

When you've been alone so long, not having to answer to anyone, the solitude becomes the norm, a haven. The quiet that surrounds you opens your senses. The serenity bathes you in peace and you think this is the way it ought to be all the time. You're not fit for the company of men because they make you angry and restless. They don't understand you and you no longer understand them. Their company is required only once in a while and not because you need someone to talk to, but because every so often you need to know that you are human. Often it's not a fact that you welcome.

The river traffic seemed to have thinned out some. I could coast along after dark. I found a couple of remarkable sunsets, beautiful sandy sites for camping, and one night I even hallucinated from fatigue. I had crossed the river searching for the spot to pull out and camp for the night. The sun had gone down and dusk had slipped into its wake. Out of the darkness came a line of barges aiming straight for me. I thought I could cross the river before they reached me but no, I was too tired. I quit right in front of them. But they didn't devour me as I expected, nor did they veer away. Instead they dissolved into islands in the channel. I heaved a breath of relief and pulled alongside them. They vanished. There had been lights on them which made me think they were barges, but now there was no evidence of them at all. I knew I was seeing things and I pulled out right away. As soon as I made camp and ate, the islands returned. They were merely shadowy shapes in the night, but this time they were real and not going anyplace. I didn't know whether to be relieved or what. I could only shake my head. The river was playing games with me.

Through it all I felt safe. The river was watching me in my solitude and guarding me and I felt secure.

Late one evening the air was still, the river was calm and the sky was streaked with ribbons of fire. I stopped for the night on a sandy beach that jutted out like a peninsula. A deep ravine carved itself into the back of the beach and the edges of the clearing were protected by trees. Tall dry grass grew up along the ridge of the ravine. The wind was not blowing and the grass was silent. I stopped there in that stillness and listened to the quiet. All day long the popping explosions of deer hunters had stabbed the silence on the river from time to time. I had spoken to a trio of fat hunters waddling about in their camouflaged outfits in single file along the trail at the river's edge. They called out to me, asking if I had any beer. I mis-heard them, thought they were offering beer, and together we held out our hands waiting for gifts and refreshment. They had been equally unlucky as hunters. They did not look like hunters, but like beer-bellied men who needed to walk in the woods for exercise. They were all three panting for air and took a break from their walking. I hoped they would not give up the hunt and start shooting at anything that moved on the river. I've seen road signs shot to pieces by people with nothing better to shoot at. I hoped these men would settle for nothing but shooting at deer. They waddled off like camouflaged ducks and I flinched when they were out of sight and I once again heard those distant poppings crack the quiet.

The quiet was back now, though, and as I lay in my tent the sound of strange rustlings in the grass crept behind me. I had pitched the tent right at the edge of the tall grass and the rustling noise was right there. *What kind of animal is it this time?* Pistol in one hand and lantern in the other, I went to find out. It was an armadillo. Its armor of bony plating had been dented and chipped. Someone must have shot at it or hit it with rocks or a shovel. Poor funny looking little creature! But it went right on sniffing as if nothing could really bother it. It was a funny sight and it didn't run or even startle when I flashed the bright light on it. It kept right on with its foraging, like an ancient knight in tarnished armor on a quest. It took its time and ignored me and eventually disappeared in the grass, and I wondered what in the world an armadillo was doing in that part of the world. I thought they lived in South America and in Texas.

I stuck the pistol in my boot, as always the handle of the gun available as if from a holster.

Every once in a while, a rifle shot would go off and I'd jump and instinctively reach for the gun, but other than that I was feeling pretty good and safe and taking it easy. I was ready for dinner, and dinner tonight would be a special one. I had bought potatoes in Helena and chicken thighs. There were six thighs. I had flour to coat them and oil for frying. I was all set to make southern fried chicken and fried potatoes sliced thin and cooked with onions. I had a couple of beers left over from Osceola and Don's towboat. I drank one while I made the fire.

Of all the nights I'd camped along this river, all the wood I'd searched for and found, all the fires I'd built, this time with such big plans for such a beautiful meal, I couldn't get the fire started.

There was nothing soft about this wood I found. It wouldn't break and it wouldn't burn.

Off into the ravine I went searching for better wood, but even better wasn't so good. I got the fire started at last but had a heck of a time getting a blaze out of it high enough to heat oil and fry chicken. But I managed. Frying the chicken took longer than I'd expected.

The sweet smell of chicken frying hung on the still air and the quiet held the sizzle close all around. The sizzle and the aroma closed in around me and I was warm and cozy. I peeled potatoes under a canopy of calm and I sliced an onion.

The chicken fried up golden and crispy, tender and moist—juicy with oil dripping all over. I fried all six thighs, put them on two layers of paper towel to drain the oil, and I fried the potatoes.

I couldn't wait for the potatoes. The fire was playing hard to get and the potatoes cooked slowly. The chicken waiting to be eaten grew impatient and absolutely cried out with its aroma and the golden color of the crisp skin picking up orange hues from the firelight flashed its invitation: EAT ME! I bit into the first piece. It was too hot to taste. The oil and juices gushed out and dripped down the corners of my mouth and into my beard, all over my hand and down my arm. The skin crunched. It was very crisp and crackled when I bit into it. Just a little bit cooler and the chicken would have been perfect. The second piece was cooler, and it was delicious.

The potatoes urged me to wait, but the chicken cried out its loneliness. I wanted to wait and have a proper meal, but the chicken wanted me to eat. And so I did. I ate another piece and then another. And when the potatoes were done and tender, some of them crunchy and almost burned black, I pulled them off the fire and let them cool. I was dying to eat.

Then there came a loud crackle. Not from the fire or the food, but from the woods. The armadillo, I thought, smelling food cooking and coming back for a snack. But the rustling in the trees was loud and heavy and quickly it was on me. It was no armadillo.

I was down on one knee hunched over the fire. I had my head down and was blowing on the fire to get the flames burning high. Out of the corner of my eye I saw them. Two greasy rednecks stood over me. They were greasier than the chicken and looked like goons out of a chain saw-chop 'em up movie. They carried shotguns.

"Hey, boy! What you call yourself doing?"

"He's cooking, Virge. Can't you see that?"

"But what's he doing out here all by hisself? Don't he know it can get right scary all lone like that. And dangerous too."

"He knows that, Virge. Don't you boy?"

"Well," I said, not moving but looking up at them now. "It hasn't been too dangerous so far."

"What's that you got there? A canoe?"

Their faces flashed evil mayhem in the flickering firelight. The one poked the other in the ribs with an elbow and they read each other's minds. They were grinning but those grins spoke more of alcohol and of mischief than of merriment. This was certainly not going to be merry for me.

"I guess you ain't been out hunting for deer like us. What you going to do with a deer on a canoe?"

"I haven't been hunting. I'm just canoeing."

They weren't listening. They didn't care what I had to say.

"We've been hunting all day long, haven't we, Virge? That's awful hard work, walking around in them woods all day."

"Sure enough, and we ain't shot at nothing since early morning."

"Seems kind of a waste, don't it?"

That was enough for me to hear. When there was movement with one of the shotguns, that was more than enough.

In one deft move I leapt up, kicked over the fire and dashed away, taking a few steps and then diving. I could hear them howling with glee. Then I heard the crunch. I heard it before I felt it. When I landed from the dive, I landed on a rock. A boulder, actually, and I hit it with my chin. Luckily, at the same instant, my shoulder banged into the trunk of a small tree. The tree didn't give way and my short flight ended. If not for the tree my face would have smashed into the boulder even harder than it did.

I didn't feel the effects of the tree quite so much because of the pain radiating from my chin. I nearly blacked out but I held on. There was a new pain reigning in my mouth and it kept me conscious. My teeth had banged together on impact and it felt like I had broken one. *Damn it!* That was my first thought. Chipped and broken teeth. *Great!*

Then the danger returned. I heard them laughing and looking for me in the dark, calling out to me with hideous, taunting cries they might use for calling animals. I couldn't see them. I could only hear. They talked about the canoe and the tent and said I'd have to come out sooner or later.

I pulled the revolver from my boot. I cocked it and I aimed it at the sound of their voices.

My father taught me about guns and he told me never to use one to protect my belongings. They could be replaced. He told me to use a gun only if I were threatened and that if I wanted to scare someone, use something else. He told me to never aim a gun unless I planned to shoot, and to never shoot at a man unless I planned to kill him.

I aimed at the voices and I fired four times. The gun shots echoed off the walls of silence and out of the darkness of the night the echoes were followed by shrieks.

"God damn!"

"Yeow! Son of a bitch!"

Then there was scurrying and hustling to get out of the way.

"The son of a bitch's crazy."

They must have bumped into each other trying to get out of the way. I heard them stumbling. One of them fell. He moaned pain and I don't know if it was from the fall or from the bullets.

I sat there in the darkness for several minutes. My gun was empty and I couldn't get to more ammunition. It was in the tent. I was trapped, not knowing if the goons were out there waiting for me. I sat still until I was fairly sure, then I hurried forward toward the fire.

The fire's embers glowed. The only light came from the lantern as I searched for damage. The beautiful remaining two pieces of chicken had fallen in the sand and were coated with grit. There was sand in the potatoes too. I ate two quick forkfuls of potatoes but they were ruined. I buried them and the bones and the rest of the chicken and garbage and hustled in the lamplight to gather my gear together and take camp apart and get going. I knew my friends would be back later after they thought I had gone to sleep. Only when they returned, I'd be gone away.

I couldn't go far, not in the night on the river. That was too dangerous. But I had to get as far away as I could.

I crossed the river. I hadn't gone under any bridges lately and I hoped there wasn't one downstream anyplace soon. If not, I'd be fairly safe on the west side of the river. But even then I would make no fire. I didn't even pitch my tent. Instead I looked for shelter and got lucky. I had passed a lot of summer shacks during the last couple of days and in the night when I needed one, I found one, a little grey place perfectly square and very small, erected on stilts to keep the river away in times of flooding. I pulled my canoe up and sat against one of the stilts. I faced the gravel and mud driveway and kept vigil for headlights from cars. Autumn. I was glad I had chosen late autumn for the journey and not summer. In summer surely someone would have been home.

I waited until it was late enough to be sure that no one would be coming. I took my sleeping bag with me and jimmied open the front door. The door was flimsy and the lock not very solid. I broke in easily.

The shack was a mess, the furniture a hodgepodge of second-hand junk from a salvage shop. Most of it was dirty and falling to pieces. I didn't turn on any lights. I sprayed my lantern about the rooms to get my bearings inside, then I switched it off and kept it off. I spread my sleeping bag on a broken reclining easy chair and lay on it. I tried to sleep and finally did, but it wasn't easy. I was dead tired suddenly, and that helped. I slept, but not for long.

I was awakened by bright lights flashing all around and the scraping of tires tearing up the gravel driveway. I jumped up and dashed for the door. Outside I saw nothing but the black of night. It did not reassure me. The lights and noises could have been my dreaming but I wasn't taking any chances. I sat watching until the grey morning fog came down upon the shack and softened the night and blended it with dawn.

The fog was thick enough to taste. Thick enough to hide in. I left the shack and set out on the river. I should have left a thank-you note, but I wasn't thinking of courtesy at the time. I just wanted to get out of there and far away and off this damnable river and out of this idiot adventure.

That does it. I'll make Vicksburg and then I'm definitely through. I've had enough.

I was angry and I was fed up with the whole thing and I was damn scared. When I could see anything at all through the fog I saw snipers behind every tree. I heard strange morning noises bouncing off the fleecy walls of the fog. And out on the river I couldn't see a thing. I couldn't see where I was going. I crossed the river again anyway, mixing up my tracks. I worried about rednecks and Southern sherrifs in pursuit.

My shoulder throbbed and my chin ached and my tooth raged at me. I was so mad! Only one tooth was cracked. An incisor. At the bottom. Right in the front. I was so mad! I kept feeling the cracked tooth with my tongue. I scraped my tongue over it so often checking the extent of the damage that my tongue became raw and sore. Later on, when the pains eased and I tried to eat an apple, I bit the apple and the pain shot through my face like a nail was being driven into my mouth. I felt the tooth loosen and thought it was going to come out. I was mad enough to kill.

I was approaching Greenville, Mississippi. A long time ago the spot that is now Greenville probably sat right on the river. Now it sits on an estuary left behind when the river changed its course. To get to the harbor and town you have to get off the river and go up into the oxbow now called Lake Ferguson. I thought about going up into Greenville, giving up right there and calling it quits, but I didn't want to get that far off the river. I was overtaken by the thinking of the long distance runner who feels he can hold on for one more mile. *I can hold on until Vicksburg*. Even though Vicksburg had no special pull on me.

I slid past the estuary opening at Greenville. There was a little towboat traffic and I had to be careful crossing the mouth of the inlet. A man had brought his two kids down to the river. They were playing and he stood there drinking in the morning peace and freshness. There was a little picnic area with a tiny playground and swings for the little kids. They were swinging and never saw me. The father passively watched me. His mind was probably elsewhere and he saw me without seeing me. He had that look. He didn't wave. Neither did I. Nor did I show any sign of defeat or weakness—in case the man really was noticing. I put my back into my paddling and lengthened my strokes and moved faster along.

Later in the morning as the fatigue from so little sleep and the worrying all night sneaked into the canoe alongside me, I slowed down again. I stopped dwelling so much on how I hurt and the hurting eased. I didn't try to eat again. I stopped concentrating on my fear and just let the fog dampen my face and cool me. I settled down then. The fog was all around me, yet at the exact spots where I canoed there was a a donut hole in the cloud. And the hole moved with me. I'd tear a new gap in the front and the fog behind would seal up and close around me. I was a nut in a protective shell. I couldn't see out and no one could see in. Or so I thought.

"Hey, you in the canoe!" The fog distorted the voice and I wasn't sure if maybe he had said, "Mister Canoe!"

The voice had come from some PA system somewhere. At first I had no idea from where, but when I turned to my right I saw steaming right alongside was a Coast Guard vessel. It should have been a submarine, the way it appeared completely and suddenly out of nowhere. It hadn't made a sound nor any trace until I saw it, and it appeared like a ghost out of nothing, out of the fog which had deadened the engine's putter.

They were laying out those big red floating channel markers. The deck was lined with new ones. The voice said, "Good morning."

I answered back, not knowing if they could hear me, but I guess the PA system worked both ways.

"Is everything all right?"

"Sure is."

"Well, you'd better stay pretty close to shore. Those towboats won't be able to see you in this fog and you won't be able to see them until it's too late."

He was right about that.

"I'll be careful. Thank you."

The hands on deck waved down to me and then the boat swung around and headed back upstream. It was as if they had come down with the express purpose of warning me and, once done, they could leave and do whatever else they had to do. I appreciated it. It made me feel good and special and safe again, watched over by the river god.

Floating in my grey and white cocoon I got a handle on my emotions. The anger and fear didn't come so much out of the idiots in the night, or even danger on the water. They came from my not being in charge and able to control my environment. It's what we all want, I figured, and when we don't get it it leads to anger and doubt and frustration. The unforeseen, the unexpected leave us unnerved when they arrive.

I drifted under the Highway 82 bridge spanning the river. The bridge was merely an outline of a structure riding lightly on the fog until I came near. Then it took shape and became heavy and strong, very rural like a back-road bridge, only two lanes. A truck screamed over. He honked. I don't know how he saw me. My donut hole must have widened for him to look down into and for him to drive safely through to the other side of the river. His roar lingered in the air until he was long gone. It faded gently. When it was gone, there was silence. Not another car passed on the bridge while I could see or hear.

I stopped just after that to stretch and to pee and to try once more to eat something. Apples were out of the question. I made a peanut butter sandwich with peach jelly. I couldn't bite the way I normally bite sandwiches and I couldn't chew very well. But I found a way. I kept the food in the back of my mouth and only chewed lightly and not for long. I swallowed the thing nearly whole. I wished for a mirror so I could see how bad the tooth looked.

While I was on shore the mosquitoes swarmed all around and attacked me. The terrain was thick with greenery and the air was damp and warm and the water here was a stagnant pool. Perfect for mosquitoes. I took them as long as I could stand it. Then I pushed off and got out of there. If I couldn't control the environment, I could certainly change it. Mosquitoes never followed me out onto the water. Thirty yards from shore and I was safe from their biting.

I thought back to the day before when I had passed the mouth of the Arkansas River. So much foamy scum floated on the water I thought I would vomit. From a distance it looked like I was coming into a field of miniature icebergs. When I got closer they looked like a hundred thousand sponges floating on the river. Not moving, just staying in one place as if anchored there. When I got into the field of scum, I was surrounded by big puffs of soap-sudsy debris that were streaked with brown slime. It could have been some kind of discharge from the barges or chemical fertilizer run-off from farms but I thought it must be sewage dumped into the river. I looked up the Arkansas River and the field of pollution extended for miles. I would have gotten sick if I hadn't been so angry. I didn't even want my canoe touching this muck, or my paddles and so I drifted through very slowly so I wouldn't have to paddle.

I thought back on that because I realized now how futile it is sometimes to want to control everything. If some idiot upstream wants to dump into the river, what can you do? You scream and shout and holler, but you don't lose your mind over it. When mosquitoes attack you, you get away from them. When other pests and goons try to upset you, you do what you have to do, but you don't let any of these things ruin your life. Not even signs stuck up all over the place by Abbay and Leatherworth Inc. that say: Posted—Stay Out. You live your life the way you want to, follow the rules you make and ignore the fools. You can't control it all.

I promptly got lost. The map said the river was supposed to go one way, but the river I was on went the other way. A huge sand bar blocked the straight way through. One way was longer, the other shorter and the fog wouldn't let me see what to do. The high water had divided the sand bar up into many pieces and now it no longer resembled the island marked on the map. I didn't know where I was. I didn't really care. I paddled on and trusted in the river to carry me out. I put my mind instead on the ducks that swarmed on the island as thick as clouds of mosquitoes. I fell in love with the hills rising above the fog. They were covered with trees and rose high like the cliffs in Iowa. I thought I was dreaming. The sun appeared as a round glow in the fog, not very bright, and looked down on me and followed me like an eye in a painting.

The river divided and came together and I didn't panic. I knew I could not get lost.

I camped for the night on someone's farm. I could see the farmhouse not far away through the trees. The field between the river and the house was sprinkled with cows and they mooed all night. There was an abundance of dry wood stacked as if someone had cleared the opening for me and left the wood for my use. I built a great fire and shielded it with the tent so no one in the house would see it. I slept well, and the following afternoon I reached Vicksburg.

29

VICKSBURG, MISSISSIPPI, sits high on the hills and overlooks the river like a citadel. It is a city unattainable by direct assault. General Grant and his armies found that out during the Civil War when his Union troops could find no way to assail the city. Union gunboats were useless: the bluffs were too high. On the river side the city was easily defended and unreachable, making the city a virtual peninsula with only one side to protect. Still, it had to be taken. Because of its position, Vicksburg was of vital interest to both sides. It was the last Southern stronghold on the river. Memphis and New Orleans had already fallen and whoever controlled Vicksburg would control the lower Mississippi, and Grant had to have that control.

Failing all attempts, even an effort to dig a canal to divert the river from Vicksburg, Grant had no choice but to order a siege of the city. Two months long it lasted until the garrison at Vicksburg was outnumbered by the gathering Union troops 70,000 to 20,000. Still the townspeople resisted until finally, reduced to eating mules to fight utter starvation, they surrendered and on July 3, 1863 Vicksburg fell; starved out, but never beaten.

The sun was high in the sky and very hot as I came near the city. Vicksburg still sits high on those bluffs, still proud and important and unattainable. A good site for giving in to the siege—surrendering without feeling like a loser.

I was greeted like a conquering hero, the throng lining the route to town waved and cheered and offered tribute.

A fisherman named Butler motored to me and we talked. His boat was stocked full of catfish and buffalo fish and sucker fish that he had pulled from his nets. He had other nets to check and when he finished his work he would be on my heels and would meet up with me in town.

"You want a fish?"

"I love fish."

He looked through his catch to find just the right one. He tossed fish left and he tossed them right and finally he got the one he wanted to give me. A gasper goo, he called it. I had never heard of that kind of fish before. He threw it in my canoe and it thumped heavily against the bottom. It must have weighed a good eight pounds. The fish was a big one and it flopped noisily a few times and then was quiet. It stared up at me with eyes big and round and glazed shiny, still as death.

"That'll be some good eating," he said. "You can clean this fish right there at the foot of town, make yourself a good fire and you'll have yourself a mighty good lunch."

Another ten miles down the river and I was there. I passed two adults and a kid, all three fishing from the bank, all three squatting down like three monkeys avoiding evil, and all three wishing me a very fine day. I really felt like the conquering hero.

I turned left into the Yazoo Canal and passed the barges being loaded and the men working there. They stopped their jobs and pointed out the way past the harbor and toward the city. The gates of Vicksburg were just beyond that last barge. Another retaining wall built high to keep the river out, and I was there. Vicksburg.

I pulled the canoe up onto the grass and was ready to stop for good. But that great release of tension that I had expected to flood out of me and leave me weak and debilitated, but thoroughly satisfied, never came.

Ready to stop. Ready to stop. Who was I fooling? Who did I *think* I was fooling? *Ready to quit, you mean.* It didn't sound quite right. It definitely didn't feel right.

At the entrance to the town, just at the gate opening in the wall, there was a row of public telephones sitting like sentries, wanting from me the password, demanding to know if I was friend or foe. I wasn't sure.

A black man and his little son popped out of a black van. His wife stayed behind in the front seat while the two men of the family came up to me. They had seen me come in from the river and wanted to catch me before I got away. They wanted to buy fish. They saw my fish in the canoe and thought I was the fish man—the fisherman who had given me the goo fish. He sold his catch every day here.

"No, I'm not the fish man, but I passed him a few minutes ago. He said he'd be in shortly."

This man and his family were up from New Orleans and he started talking about all the partying that goes on in that city. He asked if I was headed that way and told me I'd absolutely love it when I got there.

"But be careful," he warned. "If you're not careful, someone's liable to cut your head off."

"If I make it that far, I'll be careful," I said. I hadn't gotten fully used to the idea of giving up yet.

"Do you know what time it is?" I asked.

"Time for me to get the hell out of this dull town," he said before he told me what his watch said. He lived with his family in New Orleans and couldn't wait to get back home for red beans and rice. He was up visiting his wife's relatives for the days surrounding Thanksgiving and already he was sick of the holidays and wanted to get home.

"Thanksgiving?"

"Yeah," he said. "Day after tomorrow. You didn't know?"

I didn't.

His son was grabbing my arm and hugging my leg. He was only about three or four years old, and maybe he thought I was an old friend of his father's—or maybe another of those relatives in Vicksburg. I was hot and sweaty and smelly, but the kid didn't mind. As long as he didn't, I didn't. I held his hand and we walked up toward the van.

"How long you been out?"

"Time blurs and loses its meaning," I said. "It seems like forever. Sometimes it feels like just a couple of weeks."

But I bet you a lot has happened, huh?"

"Just enough and too much," I said. *And still, not enough,* I added to myself.

I was happy to be in Vicksburg, but not at all happy to be quitting. I wasn't ready yet. I looked at the row of public phones, thought about calling home to get a ride out of this place, and then walked right by the phones without a second glance. I didn't know what it was, but I knew there was still something more for me to see, to find out. I would not be quitting today. Not from fatigue, not from pain, and certainly not from fear. No number of redneck crackers with shotguns or nooses in the night could scare me off that river now. After all I'd been through, all the wonder I'd seen, all the pain, that river was mine. I'd paid for it with sore shoulders and aching knees and a back that will never be right again, with smiles from strangers and good wishes too dear to waste, with two thousand miles of strain, with days of glory, with nights of peace and wonder, and with chipped teeth. This river is mine.

I strode proudly up the steep hills into the city. I wanted all the world to see what a man looks like. If anyone wanted to tell me I was crazy or simply to get the hell off the river and out of town, he could do it now and he could count on more than a polite smile as an answer.

I walked up to Washington Street where the downtown improvement seemed to have taken place, and I stood tall on the corner and looked fierce as I caught my breath from the climb. If trouble wanted a piece of me, let it come. I wouldn't budge and I wouldn't flinch.

There were no takers. The streets were quiet and the few people who were out were heading for lunch. It was that time in the day.

Even with the lunchtime activity Vicksburg seemed lazy and

slow and quiet. The sun was shining brightly. The streets sloped steeply down toward the river and just as sharply up into the rest of the city. No one climbed those hills in a hurry. And no one paid much attention to me. I guess I didn't look so strange to these people, not even with the holes in the seat of my jeans. The stripes of my long underwear could be seen easily through the ragged gaping holes in my pants. No one minded, and neither did I. I strutted up and down the block, looked into the shops and calmed down. I turned into Burger Village for lunch.

The place was clean and shiny brand new. Bobby and Eleanor Doyle had just opened the little hamburger shop and were still celebrating the grand opening. They were elated and proud and greeted each customer personally. They were not a young couple and not new to small businesses. They already owned a small dry cleaners not far away and now they were branching out, but they had not grown dull by the achievement. They were not blasé about this. They were full of joy. They beamed as broadly as if this were the first child given by fortune to an elderly couple. And they were full of energy.

I ordered french fries and a cheeseburger. I didn't want much to eat with this sore mouth and broken tooth. And a bowl of gumbo, even though I can't stand okra. It's so slimy and quick when you eat it and it has a mind of its own and is liable to come back up of its own accord and without warning—no matter how many times you chew it. But I was in the South, after all, and I had to try it. Anything Southern I was ready to eat. And in Burger Village, the prices were very cheap. All this for under four dollars, and if not for the tooth I would have eaten like a pig. Vicksburg suddenly felt homey and small-townish. I settled on my stool at the counter and drank eight glasses of cold water while I waited for my meal, and they let me go in the back to wash my hands and face.

I checked the tooth in the mirror. The tooth was loose and sensitive to the touch and it didn't look good. Not as bad as I had imagined, but teeny cracks ran through the enamel like a car window shattered. I went back to my stool and had a glass of milk.

The burger and fries arrived first. When I bit, pain exploded in my mouth. I had to bite my tongue to keep from screaming out, and a new pain developed. Now I had to bite and chew and do everything else with the back teeth and move the food around with a hurting tongue. I felt spastic, like a cripple with a sharp mind but no control over his body. I imagined how I must have appeared to anyone watching. I was the elephant man.

The gumbo came long after I had finished the burger. The gumbo had cooled off. I guess someone had forgotten I ordered it, but I didn't complain. I wasn't going to rain on this parade and when Eleanor asked how everything was, I said it was all just fine.

She hovered over me for a minute or so more, then she broke into conversation.

"You work around here?"

"I'm just passing through. Canoeing down the river to New Orleans."

"Well how's it been so far?"

And I told her.

Looking around her little cafe, the few tables in the center and along the wall, and the counter with stools on the left hand side, and seeing how spotlessly clean and bright the place was, I remarked on the lunch counters in the South's past and said things have really changed.

"On the surface," she said. "But underneath the core is still rotten. It's subtler now. You don't see the hate so much. And we black people have a new enemy. Ourselves. We're the first to complain about the lack of a good chance, and then when one of us takes advantage, other black folks resent it. They hardly don't come here to eat."

I would have thought it would make her angry and spiteful, but she kept good cheer and said:

"No. That's life and you do the best you can. Life is what you make it."

"Yeah," I said.

She was a sharp faced black woman who could easily have been my mother. She never stopped smiling. She carried on and gave me the bill. She had that twinkle in her eye that said: I like you, but this business is here to make money.

"Stop back by one of these days," she said, "and see if we're still here."

"I will," I promised, and then I was gone. Back down the steep hills and back on the river. I ran into the fisherman briefly. He was busy selling his load of fish.

"Did you cook that fish I gave you?"

"Not yet. That'll be dinner."

"Cook it right."

"Don't worry."

I was back on the water and gone. I didn't want to lose the impetus. I had strength from anger in the morning and from lunch. I carried on into the still of evening and I camped on the right side of the river. I was in Louisiana for the first time now. The end was in sight, only a few days away. Nothing could stop me now.

I built a smoky fire to keep the mosquitoes away. I took the pink fish by the head and held it firmly. I took my knife and sliced at an angle toward the fish's backbone. Then I cut along the bone right through to the tail. I had one solid piece of fish. I held it tightly and cut away the skin. I repeated the process on the other half of the fish and now had two good solid hunks of fish. No bone, no skin. I salted them down and threw on some pepper—a little too much, as it turned out—and wrapped them in foil and baked them in the fire. More beans from a can of course, and that was dinner.

The fish was juicy and sweet—despite the pepper—and hot. The beans were, well, beans. I had had enough beans. I still chewed strangely but I ate it all.

Darkness settled down around me then and brought with it a wetness in the air, a warning of rain, but very warm and the light smell in the air of drying tobacco, sweet but pungent. It was the kind of warm gentle night made for the soft music from a guitar and I wished I had one and knew how to play. I would have sat there and picked quiet cowboy songs. Music would have echoed off the walls of night moisture enveloping me and a whisper would have been loud enough.

A whippoorwill called out. I whistled back a laughable imitation. I took that laughter and that music down to the water, slapping out odd rhythms against the shore. I looked up the river and I looked down. I could barely make out where I was coming from, hardly at all where I was going. All I could see clearly was the space in the darkness close at hand.

Up river there was much reason for anger and rage. I didn't need to look especially hard to know it, only to cut through the curtain of naiveté. And downstream farther on there would probably be more. But close around me there in the envelope of damp night there was peace. That I could see clearly and plainly feel. And I could see myself. Detached from myself, as if there were two of me, one watching, the other sitting on the edge of the water.

And as I watched with my toes in the water, I could feel the cold of the water. My toes squished in the mud and silt. The texture of the sand and mud, gritty but gooey, wet and cold, the chill and wetness rising up to my ankles and knees and hips. I felt it all over. Refreshing and soothing, but more than that: awakening, rejuvenating, energizing, but without the frenzy. Under control and newly aware. All senses alive, all senses and emotions calm. And for the absolute first time since I left Minnesota, no fear. There was no room for it. It had been squeezed out. Fear could claim no more territory here.

Then I finally saw what it was all about, what it was all for.

To drive the senses alive and then to calm them. To be able to see with the eye that is the heart's eye, to see life. To become one with the river, but more to become one with life. The river, the trees, the animals, the men and women, the wind. To feel it all rushing through my veins and to love it. To know that they are me and I am them. They and their generosity and goodness and beauty are what I want to be. They and their hate and shame and evil are what I am and what I try not to see. But it's all there, the many sides. And the faces of strangers are no longer strange. I recognize and know them all. Robert and Robinovich, Emily, Don, a little boy nicknamed Tiger, two gun-toting hillbillies. I have seen them, I have known them, I am them. There is no color that separates us, no race, no issue deeper than humanity to bind us. And so the next evening when a man in Natchez said to me after I told him the wonders of the journey, "What a marvelous thing? And I bet you not everybody who helped you out was black either, was they?" I smiled and answered, "Nope. In fact none of them was." Neither black not white nor any color. He didn't know what I was talking about, and I felt no need to explain.

30

TOO MANY MARVELOUS DAYS in a row and you begin to get used to it, to think that's the way it's supposed to be. Too many good days, too many bad days—you need some break in the monotony of one to appreciate the other. If you only get sunshine, someone said, you end up in a desert.

I guess I'd had enough hard days to last me for a while, enough scary times to be able to appreciate the peaceful, easy, glorious days. On the way to Natchez, I had another one and I took full advantage of it to do absolutely nothing. No singing, no thinking, no talking to myself. Just feeling. Watching the river, noticing the changes in color, seeing the way it rises and falls depending on the wind and on what lay on the river bed. Each change had something to say, and I listened to the river. The river was talking to me, changing colors from puce to brown to thick murky green. Saying nothing. The idle chatter you get when you walk with your favorite niece or nephew going no place in particular with nothing special on your minds and the little kid just jabbers away because it's comfortable and he feels like it. The river was like that to me. A comfortable buddy sharing a lazy day.

Nothing else mattered then. Going someplace or not. Arriving in New Orleans or shooting past and landing in Brazil. I didn't care about anything. The river kept me company and kept me satisfied. Nothing else mattered.

Then the river whispered, "Get ready. Get ready."

The day turned grey and strange. Clouds rolled overhead in wild swirls like batter in a bowl. I could see the rain storm forming off in the distance but swirling rapidly toward me like a dark grey avalanche. I felt the river dip down and up—a shallow dale in the water. I passed from the cool moisture surrounding me and into a pocket of thin air hot and dry. It was as though a gap had opened in the clouds and the sun streamed through to boil the water and heat up this isolated patch of river a scant thirty yards long. My first thought was to shed a shirt and stay cool, but when I passed through the far curtain of the insulated air, I knew I had better do just the opposite. I drifted and donned my yellow rain suit and hood. The sky above grew serious and advanced in my direction with the speed of a hurricane. Looking for a place to land I scanned the shore. There was no shore. Only trees. Because of the heavy rains and the high water, the shore had disappeared and the new shoreline of solid earth had been pushed back through the trees and beyond the woods. How far beyond, I couldn't tell. I looked across to the other side of the river half a mile away. No way could I have made it over there. Halfway across and the wind would have kicked up and trapped me in the middle.

The leading edge of the storm came and the first sprinkles passed over like army scouts. The wooded area lasted only another hundred yards or so and I thought I could easily get there before the rains arrived. I could then turn left and find ground to pull out and wait out the storm. But the voice of the river came out and spoke to me teasingly but with a chill of seriousness down my spine. I could have ignored it, but as if reading my thoughts and not wanting me to fight it, the river grabbed the end of the canoe and turned me toward the trees. I thought I was looking for land. I wasn't. I was looking for shelter.

The urge to get into the trees came on me quite suddenly and really without thought or effort on my part. Almost an instinct.

No sooner had I ducked into the trees than the sky split open with a loud crash and a splintery crackle of lightning. I was not going to make it through the trees. The wind came in at hurricane strength. The tips of the trees bent way over and aimed toward the ground, like fishing rods hooked on a big one. Water flooded like the tide rushing upstream. The trees swooshed loudly as the leaves and branches brushed hard together. Branches fell. Rains came and poured down buckets-full.

The trees were tall and no more than three feet around. I maneuvered the canoe as best I could in the wind and rushing water, turned it to face upstream and kept my back to the rain which slanted in at a sharp angle. I reached out for the sturdiest tree I could get my arms around and I held on.

Water everywhere. The river sloshed over the side and into the canoe. I tried to keep the stern pointed right into the flow so the canoe could ride the waves, but it didn't work. The canoe was twisted about and water poured over the side. The rain was heavier than any I had ever been in or seen before. It really was more like a tropical storm. The heavy winds, the amount of water, the warmth of the air and the cold rain. Only my neck was exposed to the rain. When the rain hit my neck, it ran under the rain suit and very cold down my back.

The wind shifted as the storm came directly overhead. Water streamed straight down. I was drenched and the canoe was filling up quickly. Anything in the canoe that could float was floating. If the rain continued for long or if the wind kept up strong and the rain kept spilling into the canoe, I would sink. But I was not worried, hardly more than concerned. In fact I enjoyed the feeling of the water all around me and on me, enveloping me like a cocoon, and despite the drama I felt no real threat. I was more amazed than anything, trying to analyze the voice I had heard or whatever instinct or intuition it was that urged me to park in these trees. It had been something so very definite that I could feel it and yet so ethereal that I could not put my finger on it. So I stopped trying and just sat there patiently waiting and hugging my tree. I was one with this river and nothing could happen to me.

The storm slid forward and the rain slanted in on my face. Then it moved on farther up river to drench someone else. It was gone as suddenly as it had arisen. Only the trailing edge was left, a light rain that lasted almost until I reached Natchez.

The sky remained grey but lightened and I paddled from my rainforest and down river to Natchez. My little boat lumbered through the water. The canoe carried six inches of water and was heavy and I could find no speed. But I didn't need any. I was relaxed and floating in the mist as thick as the mysteries of the river. It was evening when I reached Natchez.

Natchez, Mississippi, sits high above the river. Green trees and grassy hills rise up from the river to the city. Rising out of the hills and overhanging the river, huge white antebellum mansions guard the approach to the city like statues lining the wide corridor of some great cathedral. The homes stand beautiful and proud, reminders of gentler and nobler times.

The *Delta Queen*, another reminder, was moored at the foot of the old part of town. I went right up to get a closer look. A massive paddlewheeler that takes her voyagers back in time as she carries them up and down the river, stopping for brief glimpses of history at Natchez and St. Francisville and ancient plantations along the route. The captain told me she sails as far up as St. Paul and down to New Orleans with trips up the Ohio River to Cincinnati. They were on their way shortly to New Orleans and I asked for a ride.

"You don't want a ride," the captain said. "This is something you want to do all by yourself. You'll feel better if you do and you'd hate yourself if you didn't."

No I wouldn't. If he had said okay, I would have hopped quickly on board and ridden down with him. I had already found it, whatever this trip was for; I had done it, even if I didn't understand it yet, and probably wouldn't until years from now anyway.

A few great blasts from the steam whistle and she pushed away from shore and set out, lights on the the big calliope playing merry music like a circus. It was 1836 all over again. The *Queen* paddled up river, turned around and slowly splashed south, the staterooms all lit up and gay. You couldn't see the boat at all in the darkness, only the lights. They seemed to float along with no structure holding them together. Too soon the lights were gone round the bend and the calliope faded into the night and the crowd that had gathered at the riverfront to watch as of old began to disperse.

I bailed out my canoe using a milk carton. It took a while. I had a few passing conversations and then walked up the hill. It was drizzling again and I must have looked lost.

This was the old town. A little park stretched off to the south—more a promenade than a park—and there were a few quaint shops for the tourists and a bar and a couple of nice looking restaurants. Three beautiful women were getting out of a car parked along the side of the road when I passed. The three prettiest women in Mississippi. They were going to eat in one of the cute little restaurants. They were all dressed up and hurried because of the rain. They wouldn't want to get their hair and clothes messed up. I asked them quickly if they knew the time and two of the three ignored me totally and kept walking. I felt like the invisible man. But the third woman had heard me. She looked toward her two friends. She wore a quizzical expression and it was plain that she was looking for the translation. She must have thought I was speaking a foreign language.

"I won't bite you," I said. "I just want the time."

Then she turned and the three of them walked purposefully on and I stood stunned for two seconds; I said nothing else. I chuckled to myself and silently wished for them to slip and fall in the mud. When they didn't, when they had crossed the little gravel parking lot and climbed up the three wooden steps and disappeared into the warmth and dryness of the cozy little eatery, leaving me standing out in the drizzle, I hoped they would order seafood and I hoped that each one would get a bad oyster or a tainted piece of catfish.

Two steps farther on, I passed a man sitting all alone in his pickup truck. He was killing time, watching the river and he turned to watch me walk by. When our eyes met, I tapped my wrist and gave the international symbol for what time is it. I don't know why I wanted to know; I had no place I had to be and nothing I had to do apart from finding a place to pitch my tent, which I couldn't do until all the shops had closed and everyone had gone home.

Bill invited me to warm up in his truck.

"Do you need to go to the store or anything?" He had a great Southern accent, heavy but cultured and easily understandable.

"Well, I guess I could use some milk and a few things."

He took me on a little tour of Natchez. He was proud of this little place, I could see, and he was happy to drive me around. He even tried to arrange a place for me to sleep for the night and later pointed out the Salvation Army shelter where I could at least be dry all night long. I half expected him to invite me home, put me up in the attic and then keep me over for Thanksgiving dinner tomorrow night, but that was asking too much. He already had relatives visiting for the holiday.

I told him I'd probably just pitch camp in the little park.

"I wouldn't build a fire or anything if I were you. The police will come down there and make you move. They might even want to lock you up for the night."

Then he fished in his wallet and pulled out a business card.

"If they do come along and throw you in jail, give me a call. You can sleep there for the night, and I can get you out in the morning. I'm the city attorney."

Actually, he was an attorney with a local practice and he was the acting-city attorney whenever the regular city attorney was away, like now.

I had the feeling he wasn't too thrilled to be going home to his wife and the visiting in-laws, that he would rather have stayed down on the levee watching the river and the *Queen* or talking to me or driving me around showing me the beautiful homes of Natchez. Hope Farm. Stanton Hall. Longwood. D'Evereux. Ellicott Hill. Propinquity. Montaigne. Mount Repose. Homes as beautiful and stately and elegant as the names. But Bill had to get on home.

He drove away and I hung around killing time until late in the evening. When everything had closed and everyone had gone home—about nine o'clock, I'd guess—I pulled my canoe a few yards down river and put up the tent. It was in a little gully at the edge of the water with the blunt face of a muddy hill behind me. Not one of my more picturesque campsites. A rickety rowboat full of junk was tied up not far away and later on the owner of it staggered back drunk from town, climbed into the boat and slept there. I met him in the morning and was shocked to find out who he was—shocked and pleased.

Eleven hundred miles and I don't know how many days ago, Wally at Piasa Harbor had told me about a religious zealot rowing for Jesus down the river in a rickety rowboat of homemade construction. As James White talked the following morning, pieces fell into place and it hit me.

"Hey!" I shouted out of the blue. "I know you."

"You do?"

"I don't know you, but I heard about you. Back near Alton they were talking about this nut who had taken his bicycle apart and built a contraption for pedaling a boat down the river."

"That's me all right."

How strange to have caught up with him after all this time! I hadn't thought of him once since I left Wally.

We had breakfast together in a fancy hotel restaurant and they gave us a few funny looks, but served us without complaint. Smiles and good-humored politeness instead.

We took our good sweet time and sat there like millionaires chatting away the morning, talking about the two journeys. Jim had left Idaho on a bicycle pulling a little trailer that held his belongings. He had received the call directly, he said, from Jesus who had told him to go across the country on this bicycle and spread the good word, get a feeling for this nation, and set the place right. And, I presumed, to report back.

As a man who himself had heard the voice of God, I could not brush his calling aside as fanaticism or lunacy, but I looked askance just the same. The whispers I'd heard never told me directly what to do. Not in simple English, anyway.

When Jim got to Iowa and the river, he was instructed to change his course, get a boat and go down the river until further notice. He took to rowing down the river until the his oars broke apart. He then dismantled the bicycle and set about sawing planks and hammering and putting together until finally he had constructed a paddlewheeler out of his rowboat. Now he could sit on his seat and pedal the crankset of the bicycle and the wooden planks fashioned into paddlewheels on each side of the boat would propel him.

It was slow, but a good idea, except that he got stuck in the rock dam just below Alton and Okie the salvage operator I had met had to tow him out. Then Jim had to rebuild and repair the damage.

Now, at Natchez, he actually prayed for the boat to fall apart. That would be a sign that his voyage was finished.

"I have to keep going until the voyage is done. Maybe in New Orleans, or maybe I'll have to keep going right on through to the Gulf of Mexico and South America."

"And then what?"

"I'll do whatever He tells me to do. But I'm sure sick of this river."

For a man spreading the good word, he hadn't met with much success, finding the land full of skeptics and godless people not willing to listen. So it would be disaster for them all, he said. Disaster and ruin will strike all those who refused him or who mocked him or who would not turn to God, and I made it a point not to say the wrong thing.

Jim had the look of a monk. Tall and lean, dishevelled grey hair and matching stubble on his chin, unconcerned about his appearance, a youthful face that lied about his age, and wild eyes. The eyes flared when he told me about the revolution.

"It's time," he said. "If the country won't turn to Jesus, it's up to me to make them, and if they still won't listen, I've been given the charge to destroy the country. I'm only letting them have one more chance."

When he started quoting from the Bible, I knew breakfast had lasted long enough.

"Maybe we could travel together," he offered. "Share Thanksgiving dinner, camp together, keep each other company. It gets lonely, you know."

His boat had everything in the world in it except a television. I don't know how he managed to fit inside and sleep. But he pushed junk aside and squeezed inside and showed me how he slid the plywood platform around that made his bed.

"You could ride inside with me," he said. "We could tie your canoe off and tow it and you could rest."

I declined, but did accept the offer for Thanksgiving dinner.

"You go on ahead. I need to fill up my water bag and take down my tent. I'll catch up with you."

Before he left he pulled a pair of pliers from his junk and repaired the zippers on my tent flaps. Now I wouldn't have to worry about mosquitoes sneaking into the tent at night.

"You learn to fix just about everything out here," he said.

He took off, pedaling down the river, and I watched him go. He looked very silly. Watching him, I felt the arrogance that towboat pilots feel, the contempt for lesser boats, and still the comraderie of sharers of the river—rivermen all of us.

I caught up with him after an hour or so and we built a fire on a sandbar. We boiled rice and heated a big can of beef stew and Jim prayed over it and we ate our Thanksgiving meal. It wasn't the finest holiday meal ever, but maybe this time I had so much to be thankful for and was really aware of it for once that this meal of all meals felt most like a Thanksgiving dinner.

* * *

I didn't find a place to camp until well after dark. The water had risen so high that what normally was dry land was under me now and I was canoeing right through forests with trees within easy reach on either side of me. These trees were up to their necks in the river.

I was searching for the short cuts, but there was no current and I had to work hard. The night was pleasant and I enjoyed the water rising up in mists around me, though I was startled from time to time by great plops in the water from some gigantic beast which I assumed to be granddaddy catfish, but which might have been alligators flopping in the river and snapping at passing meat. I was close enough to the Louisiana bayous and alligators were remotely possible.

In the morning the end was in sight. I came to a construction site where a dam was being built. A huge outflow canal was already there and great signs warned small boats to stay away. The heavy current would suck them into the canal like debris down a sink drain, and they'd never get out and might be chopped up by the gates of the dike there.

Near the construction site, David McKnight came down from his towboat to help me. He put me in his truck and drove me two miles to his office where I phoned home. I was preparing for arrival in New Orleans. It was Friday. I'd be there by Monday.

David, it turned out, was also from Missouri, from Hermann, the same little town where Robinovich grew up. He didn't know her, however, or her family. It didn't matter. He was still from close to home. He missed it as much as I was beginning to long for it, but he was stuck here.

Here was where the battle climaxed, the battle between the river and men. Here is where the Mississippi wants to swing west and link up with the Atchafalaya River. Here the engineers pull out all the stops to keep the river from taking its own route to the sea, the short straight route. They build outflow channels to divert the water, and dams to stop it and tame it and lessen the surge. They are winning, so far. A little farther on there is a lock and dam on the Old River which connects all these river systems, and revetments everywhere. It hardly seems a fair fight, but so far the river lets them win.

The river turns from the west, bends softly south and then makes a sharp corner to the east. Here the water slows and the river turns murky and gloomy. The water is wide and high. The trees stand waist deep in the river. The buffer of land has been swamped between the river and the Lousiana State Penitentiary. I get an eerie feeling as I pass through here. A discarded guard tower, the look of a concentration camp. Devil's Island. I wonder how many convicts try the river as an escape route and get lost in the trees or die in the swamps.

A little later on I'm called to shore by a couple of deer hunters. They have a beautiful shiny speedboat floating near their camp and a tent pitched big enough for a family. Chairs set up and a cooler full of beer and a gas stove. All the comforts. They've just finished dressing the deer they've killed and are relaxing before going out once more while they still have light. Robby Barry and Mike Hunt. Fine gentlemen from Baton Rouge. They start me off with beer and then switch to coffee.

"You ever have coon ass coffee?"

"Don't think so." I wonder if it's a brand name.

"You know what a coon ass is?"

I don't, but I could offer a few guesses.

"That's what we call Cajuns. And coon ass coffee is the best coffee there is."

"Why coon ass?"

"Cause they all talk so funny. Wait till you meet one. You won't be able to understand them."

And to demonstrate, while we talk about the river, canoe trips and fishing, the Atchafalaya flows into the conversation. But when they say it, I don't understand the word.

"Where's that?"

"What? Oh, I guess you call it the Atchafalaya." But when they say it, two or three syllables get chopped out or slurred together and the word becomes foreign.

"Did you pass the prison back up the river?"

"Is that what that was? I thought it was a death camp or something."

"Might as well be. I hear those guards like to shoot. They want you to try to escape just so they can shoot you down. I'm surprised they didn't shoot at you passing by."

The land around here belongs to hunting clubs. To shoot here you need to be a member. Unless, of course, you have a speedboat and are fairly enterprising. Mike and Robby intend to stay out until Sunday. By then, if they're lucky, they'll have enough meat to last a few months, even with deer steaks for gifts.

And so I slid out of their lives and on through Louisiana. This was the home stretch. Louisiana on both sides of the river now. Fewer than two hundred miles to New Orleans. Then I would be done. But first I had to get past St. Francisville.

31

THE NEARER THE DESTINATION, it seems, the harder it is to arrive. Deep in the heart lurks the dread of a new uncertainty: what happens next? Will everything be completely new and wonderful and foreign, which is frightening, or, which is worse, will everything be just as it was? Will nothing be different? Will none of it have mattered? To finish is to find out.

Not to finish is to remain in limbo, a baby half born.

Luckily, St. Francisville provided one night's diversion from worrying about it all.

I could have passed it by. It was early enough in the evening to go on down and find a nice site for camping. Added to that was the high water, the trees and marsh all around the landing at St. Francisville that made camping on the river here impossible. I found one spot, but nearby was a big stagnant pool of water perfect for breeding starving mosquitoes. And trash all around dumped from cars waiting to cross the river on the ferry.

St. Francisville lay two miles from the river. The road to and from the town ended here at the water. A ferry carried the cars that needed to go farther, moving out every twenty minutes or so, with a loud blast of the horn and the engine roaring like a monster.

There was really no place to camp except a gravel parking lot, just to the north of the ferry and behind it, where an inlet was formed by a derelict towboat. Not the sweetest campsite, but what the heck! I had no choice.

I pitched the tent and ignored the cars that circled through the lot and in a little while I simply left everything there and walked the two miles into town to find a good spot to eat. I couldn't very well build a fire in that parking lot. The whole world would have come down to see what I was up to.

My mind strained toward the end of the river. I was fidgety and wanted to settle down, to stay in the present. The walk would help.

The road was narrow and the night black as ink. Not a light anywhere in sight unless a car passed. And then I would stray from one side of the road to the other to keep away from the cars zooming past going ninety. Past the little shack that housed the country tavern serving ice cold beer and hot food, across the railroad tracks and the little historical marker telling all about the old railroad, down through the valley and past the dingy shacks that housed poor people, past the string of shops selling bait for the fishermen, and up the hill to a small intersection.

The main road went on straight. A dog barked viciously in the darkness. I turned right and took the long way around to town.

I made it up into the heart of town and ate in a very unlikely restaurant—the St. Francisville Inn which is really an inn for staying overnight and yes, the thought crossed my mind. It also seemed the best place in town to get a real meal and the only place open unless I wanted chicken in a basket or fried fish with fries. That wouldn't have been bad, but I craved the touch of civility offered by the inn. I only wondered how they would receive me. I wasn't dressed for caviar and champagne dinners.

For some, the color of life is red. For others, black and white. I happen to know the color of life, at least in this country, is green. If you can pay, generally you can play.

"Can I come in for dinner dressed like this?" I should have added: smelling like this.

A broad welcoming smile: "Certainly. Come on in."

I thought that maybe business was slow tonight, but the place wasn't empty. I thought she'd put me somewhere apart from the other guests, but she didn't. She put me in the far dining room with three other tables occupied. Two elderly women sat at one, a trio of tourists at the second, and opposite me, a pretty young lady suitably dressed sat with an elderly gentleman not her father. He smoked a cigar and chatted with the owner like a local bigwig. I strained to hear the conversations from their table, especially the whisperings between the man and the young lady, but I came up empty. The owner brought them gratis after-dinner drinks. I wanted one too.

I tried to be civilized. I tried to find the refinement I'd left in Minnesota. I tried not to look at prices when I ordered. But the low funds dictated and by this time I was only slightly more than savage. I tried to take my time and savor the sauce poured over my chicken (I ended up with chicken, after all) but I was too hungry and tired and thinking about the lot where I'd parked the canoe and pitched the tent. I wolfed the food down, tried to linger but asked for the check instead and left. The owner/chef did come by to chat, and just to let him know I was not totally savage and without taste, I remarked that the zucchini could have been a little crisper.

"They were prepared that way special," he told me, and I bowed out.

One of these days I'll go back there, stay the night at the inn, eat a splendid meal and have a marvelous little wine and really take the time to enjoy. But not that night.

I hurried back to camp and to bed. Sleep didn't last long.

I lay on the sleeping bag—it was too hot to lie in it—for all of ten minutes. Then the cars came. One after another. It sounded like a parade. With the yelling and screaming and tires scraping and crunching over the gravel. I had not only picked an ugly parking lot for my campsite, I had picked the local hang-out. Carloads of teenagers were invading the almost quiet to drink their beer and whatever else they had. They were too young to drink anyplace else.

They didn't notice me at first. They were too busy drinking and shouting at each other, and what they noticed first was the canoe.

"Hey! Look over there."

"Wow! Where'd that canoe come from?"

I thought I was going to have to get rough. I reached for the gun, but decided against it. I'd just go out and show myself. That ought to do it.

"Come on. Let's push this thing in the water. We can take a ride."

"Here. Help me turn this over." Then they saw the gear stowed beneath the canoe. Then they saw the tent.

"Hey, wait. There might be somebody in there."

"What're they doing camping down here?"

"Who knows?" They crunched back across the gravel to their friends and I rested easy again. They were good kids. Harmless.

Two young girls approached. I could hear them talking and giggling. They were going to be brave and take a look inside the tent.

"I'm not afraid. I don't care who's inside. I'm going to have a look."

That was it. I couldn't let them just barge in, so I would have to go out. In one swift move I unzipped the bottom of the tent flap. That was enough and the girls squealed and ran away laughing. They'd had their scare, their thrill for the week. But of course they now knew for certain that someone was inside, and to keep childish pranks to a minimum, I burst outside and into the middle of a mob of teenagers coming over to check things out.

When I emerged, their first impulse was to dash away startled, but they composed and gathered and then hit me with a barrage of questions.

"This is just so neat. Wow!"

"All by yourself?"

"Don't you get scared?"

"Can I look inside your tent? You've got everything in there, haven't you?"

We talked for a few minutes and one kid who said he worked for the newspaper wanted to interview me and get a photographer down to take pictures of everything. I felt like somebody special.

"You leaving tomorrow? What time?"

"Usually I take off at first light."

"Can't you wait a little longer? Like until ten o'clock?"

A little notoriety never hurts the ego, but I couldn't stick around that long. I knew that. New Orleans was calling for me.

"Tell you what. I'll hang around as long as I can. How about that? If I'm still here, fine. If not, well, next time."

"Are you going to do this again?"

"Never know."

And then it was my turn to fire out a couple of questions. Like what were they doing down here.

"Oh, we come down here because there's no place else for us to go. They don't let us drink in town. They don't even seem to want us in town. And we have to go somewhere. We have to do something. We can't just sit around and go crazy."

"It's really dead around here. This is the only fun we get. We come down here to drink and party and drive our four wheel drives out there across that water."

Some kid's claim to fame was the fact that he had one time made it all the way across and into the trees on the other side. They all reminisced about who got stuck when and where and how deep it was out there.

Why they found it fun and exciting, I couldn't see, but while we talked some show-off in a pickup truck with huge oversized tires roared down, went halfway out into the pool, then roared out again in reverse. Some fun!

"You want to hang out with us?"

"Sure," I said. I wouldn't get any sleep anyway. "Where's the beer?"

"Who's got any beer left?"

Apparently no one who was sharing.

"You want beer?"

"Why not," I said. "If this is a party."

"It is."

And one of my new friends went off to buy.

Friday night in a small town. The difference between being a kid in a small town and being a kid in the city is that the externals are less important. In a small town, all the kids are bored, no matter how rich or poor or young. These kids ranged in age from eleven or twelve up to seventeen. Age was no barrier. They could all hang out together. And they all did. The young and the younger. The poor kids with no cars, the middle kids with cars they bought by working weekends and after school, and the rich kids with the fancy machines daddy paid for. And you could tell the richer kids. They showed off more, drove a little faster, revved a little louder, tore up the gravel in the parking lot with their spinning wheels. And they were the ones sneered at by the others.

The beer finally came. I only got one.

The party began to break off into little groups. I watched the dynamics of the reunion of the bunch with one kid who used to live here but had moved with his dad to California and was back for a visit. He was one of them but no longer fit. An outsider they had to be polite with.

One big guy was the butt of all the jokes. They called him Dino.

"Just like a dinosaur, don't you think?"

They told me how dumb he was. Big and strong like a dinosaur, and just as stupid. He took the mocking with good humor. I liked him.

I had my own clique at this party now and when the groups began to unravel, Clint and Skeeter put me in the cramped backseat of their car and drove me through town. They talked about the girls in town and told lies. It was just like high school, only better. I only had to observe. Cruising around the town with the kids, and dozing off in the backseat like an old man.

When they finally threw me out, the party had died and everyone had cleared out. It must have been nearly two in the morning. They screeched away and tore up the parking lot. Under the orange glow of the huge powerplant lighting the sky down and across the river, I watched them leave, crawled into my tent and slept.

The kids had been a nice diversion for me, taking my mind away from heavier work. I slept well and woke up early and set out right away. I made it to Baton Rouge in time for lunch. Along the way I met a man appropriately named Rivers. He was steering a pirogue from the helm while the youngster with him shot at ducks flying overhead. When they saw me coming, they motored toward me, grabbed my arm and held onto me so we could drift together and talk.

Rivers was a Cajun and a crayfisherman, but crayfish were not yet running. He was out for some fun. He lived off on the bayous, and I could hardly understand him. His accent was thick as his mustache. But he didn't have anything to say. He just wanted to come up to me to see what I was up to, to wish me luck the same as every man along this river, and he wanted to warn me about the tankers and the tugboats.

I thought he was talking about towboats and barges. I found out later what he was talking about.

I sang around the bend and all the way in to Baton Rouge. The river makes a big dog-leg turn right at Baton Rouge and the city lies on the far side of the river. Traffic was very heavy and the river not so smooth, but I handled it deftly. I entered the city and searched for Cajun delights like red beans and rice, but had to settle for a burger and fries. The country kitchen where I stopped for lunch promised on the sign outside everything I was looking for. Inside they told me a different story. I took the burger. I moved on quickly. I didn't want to put off the end of the journey, didn't want to delay it one second. At least, not right then.

I skimmed atop the water just as light as could be, sailing on until well after dark. The next thing I knew I was sailing along in the morning sunlight, in a different world altogether, the world of supertankers and tugboats.

The realm of the barges ends at Baton Rouge. From Baton Rouge on south, the river is much deeper and the bridges across the river are higher and from now on the Mississippi can support the weight of tankers that reach out to cargo the world.

I met my first tanker in the morning. Slipping from camp early in the mist, two sharp bends in the river, and there she was.

A massive red ship riding high in the water. The *Hoegh Forum* from Oslo.

If those others were beasts, these huge things were behemoths twenty stories tall and longer from end to end than any two stacks of barges strapped together—towboats included. Bright red steel changing to a darker color below the water line, and orange rust sneaking through the paint all over. I could almost smell the salty sea mingling with the Mississippi's muddy odor.

I moved away and watched the sharp front end of the ship peel away the layers of water rushing to meet the bow. So totally unlike the river slapping at the squared off ends of barges. The river moved aside for these machines, their bows slicing right through the water and shoving aside a mountain ridge of water that rushed toward me like a tidal wave. I waited for the damage to be done and held on tight. Strange thing, though. The wake from these mammoths was high and swift, but not rough at all. Very gentle, in fact, and as long as I kept the front end of the canoe facing into the moving wall of water, I only bobbed gently up and down on the successive waves. I couldn't understand it and tried to explain it away by the depth of the river or the counter-rotation of the tanker engine's screws, or the easy way the tanker sliced through the water, but whatever it was, it felt great and a lot more fun to ride than the wake from barges.

The *South Fortune* came at me. Her name was written twice, once in English and once in Chinese characters. She could have been from almost anywhere in the Far East, but waving from her stern was that modified American flag that flies in Liberia, and her home port, in bold white letters across the stern, was Monrovia. Flying high from the bridge were two more flags, one Japanese and the other American. She was definitely owned by Japanese and registered in Liberia. Most tankers I passed had Liberian registration. All tankers flew the American flag.

When a tanker slips from the Gulf of Mexico and into one of the channels of the Mississippi down at the delta, the tanker must stop at the Passes and take on an American pilot who knows the river. The ship for as long as it rides the Mississippi is the American pilot's vessel, and he flies the US flag.

I sailed on into the valley of these tall ships: oil tankers, grain tankers, freighters. ***Exxon Baytown, Enand Hope, Alonssos,*** and some eastern vessel whose letters I couldn't read. But then came the ***Professor Kostiukov*** from Odessa. When she passed I was dead tired and my shoulder was giving me fits. But all hands on the bridge came out to look. I could see they were watching me through binoculars and maybe wondering who I was or what I was doing. Maybe they thought I was a spy. Maybe they envied the freedom. No way could they get away with this in Mother Russia. Someone would suspect them of trying to escape—which was exactly what I was doing, but of a different kind. One of them came out with a camera and took pictures. They wouldn't believe this back home in the Ukraine. I straightened up and carried on as if I were strong and fresh and just starting out. I wanted them to be jealous. And then they waved down at me. One sailor put his fingers in his mouth and pierced the air with his joyous whistle, and that gave me real strength. I raised my arms overhead and they did the same. We were brothers on the water, rivermen, seafarers, sailors all.

The stories I had heard about the tug boats were absolutely false. True, the wake from excessively loud and extremely fast boats, the actual tugs and the high powered boats that carry the crews from shore to ship and back again, create the most fearsome wakes on the water, wakes that could flip a canoe like a tiddlywink. But every one that passed cut his engines almost to nil until safely away from me. And when I was in no more danger of being swamped, they revved up again and sped on. Incredible thoughtfulness. I only hoped they could hear my whispered thanks. I'm sure they could. They often waved.

I was in heaven again. As the sun went down and the river bent to the left, I raced the wind and a tanker. The tanker won and passed us both and I rode close to it. I caught the wave of the tanker's wake and paddled hard to stay on top of it. I rode the wave like a surfer and felt exhilaration. A tug boat passed and I repeated the performance.

Later on that evening I came upon the *Delta Queen* again.

She was moored at the shore, having landed to let her passengers off for an excursion to the plantations nearby. The *Queen* had been to New Orleans already, was here for a day and would head back tonight for New Orleans again. The captain told me to find him in the city when I arrived tomorrow and he would take me aboard and show me around and buy me lunch. I told him I'd see him there.

The *Queen* passed me just as it got dark outside. She was all lit up like a party about to happen and I was feeling my way through the barges, moving and parked, and past all the industrial docks along the way. Once more I was out on the river after dark. I passed many spots that would have made suitable campsites, and certainly better than the one I finally ended up with, in the trees, on a hill, behind a parking lot of empty barges that had been loaded with some kind of grain and still smelled like it, barges that rocked back and forth all night long, clanking against one another, their ropes creaking constantly under the strain. But I could not bring myself to leave the river. I didn't care about the danger of canoeing after dark among all this crowd of rust and steel, I didn't care that I might run into something or get hit by something or fall over and drown. I wanted to stay on the river as long as I could tonight. It was going to be my last night on the river.

I wanted to stretch it out.

Tomorrow would be my last day.

32

THE LAST DAY, and the longest.

Anticipating the morrow, I have trouble sleeping. The wind rises during the night and billows the tent, pulling at it and straining the supports and stretching the tent from all sides. The poor tent takes quite a beating all night long and I sleep in fits. And yet I don't know if it ever rains during the night. My mind is filled with other thoughts and all ajumble.

Tomorrow is my last day with the river. I look forward to tomorrow, to the victory and the celebration and to what comes after. At the same time my mind reaches backwards to caress the memories of this journey. Wetted by the waters, dried golden by the sun, cooled by breezes, tended by all my new friends and now harvested by me. Food stored for my old age.

It has been a pretty remarkable voyage, hasn't it? I can't say I enjoyed every minute of it, and yet I loved every minute of it. Throughout the journey I lived my life in the present, in now, not dreaming about what had already happened and not worrying about or planning for tomorrow.

Until now.

Now the heart soars over days past and I try to sort them out. I want to remember faces and events and places, but already I can't even remember all the names.

How soon before the trip becomes glorified and I remember not as the journey was, but as it should or could have been? Instead of a few wild dogs, they turn into a pack of angry wolves clawing at the tent. Instead of a couple of rednecks, I'm fighting off a dozen camouflaged survivalists—hand to hand, and winning.

How soon before I forget all the fear and all the pain and turn myself into a larger-than-life-sized hero? How soon before I become the provider of help and blessings along the river, and not the needy? Then I will become more than I am and the river and the journey less.

I write this all down so that I don't forget, so that I don't twist what was real and true. I don't want to forget how my heart sang at the beauty of Lake Itasca or banged out panicky rhythms when barges passed or when the river swirled too much.

Oh what a voyage this has been! I want to remember because I don't want it to end.

For a moment I consider carrying on past New Orleans, taking this canoe down through the delta, down to the Passes and the very end of the river—it's only another two days—getting out and shoving the canoe out to sea. A fitting way to end it all.

Alas! The canoe is not mine. And how would I get back with all my gear? And how would I find the strength?

I wouldn't want to do it anyway. I have been with this river a long long time. I knew his mother. I watched him being born. I don't want to see him die. I watched him meandering playfully in youth and running joyfully. I don't want to see him wandering lost in the delta, searching for his way among the bayous weak and aimless like an old man. I'll get out at New Orleans.

But rivers don't really die, do they? They don't end. They become the ocean, and the ocean becomes rivers, in a great cycle. And so there is only one river. It flows endlessly, spreading out across the world, multiplying, becoming other rivers, separating, rejoining, always going and never ending, always one with the other rivers. There is strength in the unity of rivers.

I think back to the parts of the river I missed, the rides I took, the nights I spent comfortable. Did I cheat? Or did the river give me what I needed when I needed it? I can live with it either way, but I'll never really know.

Should I go back and do the whole river again, vowing not to take any short-cuts or any easy ways out? No. Of course not. I'd only be trying to recapture golden moments already lived through. Nothing would be the same, nothing would be as I remembered it and I would want it to be. It would be a disappointment.

Not that the river hasn't given me a dose of disappointment from time to time, but nothing I couldn't handle. I know that now. And so if I did cheat, at least I know it wasn't because I wasn't equal to the task. I could handle it if I needed to. A few extra miles of river, a few more days would be easy compared with some of the difficult and scary times I've already faced. I'm not afraid of hard times. The river has taught me how to stick it out and endure. Surviving the hard times makes me a stronger man able to better appreciate the good times, which makes me a better man. The river has helped me to improve my soul, and that is everything to me.

But first I have to get to New Orleans. This trip isn't over yet.

And as if to let me know it, to slap me out of my reverie and back into the present, as if to remind me that he is not old and feeble and foundering lost in old age, the river rages wildly at me all day long.

The night wind dies finally and I break camp. The sun is high already and morning is well underway. I have over forty miles to make, but that's no problem if the river is fast and calm. I should be there by one o'clock.

But the river is not going to cooperate. I eat and hurry onto the water and as soon as I am on the river and comfortable and getting into the greased groove, the wind kicks up the river and buffets me all around.

I've been knocked around plenty by the river and the wind up until now, but this is like nothing I've been in before. It's so violent and so confounding, I can't figure out how to attack it. I'm going to stop, get my bearings.

The river runs a gradual slant slightly north. After completing a little S-turn the river flattens out and runs down a perfect straightaway five miles long. A dogleg bends the river south for another five miles, then it turns and runs generally east with a couple of soft curves swinging the river into New Orleans. It looks so easy on the map. On the water, it's impossible.

I realize that my arms are shaking. I have to get out to catch my breath. And now my legs feel weak. This is really getting to me. It must be dangerous. Too bad I've made arrangements to get picked up today. Otherwise I could wait until the wind dies down. Even if I don't get to New Orleans until tomorrow or the next day. No problem! But I can't. If I don't come in today, they'll think I drowned or something. Especially when they see how crazy this water is today. They'll worry and panic and go nuts. I have to get there. So let's give it another try.

I'm going to try the tricks I've learned along the way to deal with feisty water. Keep the bow right into the wind if I can, and when I can't, I'll let the wind push me one way and I'll paddle hard the opposite way to keep the canoe straight. More or less.

But today the wind is not so easily manipulated. Today the wind is so much stronger. It's coming out of the north and no matter what I do or how hard I try, the wind knocks me into the shallow water and grinds me against the rocks.

If I can only make it to the dogleg bend. I'll be going south then and the wind will be at my back. The going will be easier, if not smoother, and I'll make better time. Already I've wasted hours and the effort is tearing my shoulder to pieces.

I've got to straighten up now, though. Can't let the pain show. I'm being watched and I can't let them see me hurting. And I don't want them to see this river kicking the life out of me.

The pilot of the *Jim Ludwig* comes out on the deck and he's calling down to me. "Good morning, sir." I can't wave at him. If I stop stroking at all I'll be immediately tossed into shore. I shout back instead and I hope he realizes how busy I am. I hope he knows I'm friendly.

Later the *Terri Lynn* greets me with a couple of horn blasts. The greetings are enough to spark a little life in me and I'm going to need it now.

The going has been slow all morning and it's taken me almost forever to get here, but I've finally reached the dogleg bend. But I think I want to change my mind. I think I'll do better if I can cross the river, get into the shade of the trees on the other side. The trees should help shelter me from the wind.

Just beyond the bend I start the crossing to the other side. I don't want to go too far down before I cross over. There are barges parked right out in the middle of the river. If I go downstream before crossing, I'll have to go around the barges and I can't see what's beyond them. They are pretty far away and look about twelve of fifteen barges across and I don't know how many deep. There are three towboats behind them. Thank God they're not moving. Three towboats at the same time. Their wakes on this wild water would kill me.

If I cross now, however, I can use the wind. All I have to do is make steady progress across the river. I don't even need to aim downstream. The water and the strong wind out of the north will carry me south.

But as I'm crossing, the wind pushes faster down river than I can push myself across. I'm going to have trouble with those barges after all. If I'm not careful, I'll hit them broadside. I guess that won't be too bad.

But wait a minute! One of those towboats just puffed out a dark cloud of exhaust from the smokestack. Those things aren't parked after all. They're actually moving, all those barges going so slowly against all this water that movement is imperceptible.

I've made a major mistake. I shouldn't have stopped my paddling to examine the movement. Now I'm almost certain to run into them. I have to make a big decision. To go on across or to quit that effort and just go on downstream to cross over later—or not at all. If I just go on down, I'll still have the wind at my back until the next bend to the east.

No. I'm going ahead and making the crossing. Ego, I guess. I want to be stronger than the wind. But right now I see for sure that the barges are moving and closing in on me. The water rushing by and the slowness of the barges make it hard to tell, but they are definitely moving and if I don't get a fast move on, I'll meet them head on and get eaten up.

The waves are getting bigger. The sun angles down on them and they sparkle. So dangerous, but so beautiful. The river gleams in bright stripes.

No time to look and admire. I'm not making as much progress as I need to and now I've gone too far. I can't stop now. If I stop or if I go, the river is pushing me so hard that I'll surely get caught under the barges. I can jump overboard. I'll have an easier time if I swim.

No. That's a stupid thought. I've just got to go hard for it. Now!

Harder and harder I push myself. Closer and closer the barges come to me. They look ugly like death, big and monstrous, and with the smell of rust and diesel fuel and smoke, it's the way death smells.

No. I'll not give in.

The barges are no more than three yards away when I finally slip under their raked fronts and past them all. Close. Too close. But I made it.

It's not over yet. The worst is still to come.

The river is extremely wide now. Out in the middle are these gigantic concrete things with steel rings embedded in them and they're used for mooring those big tankers out in the river. It's like a mine field.

After the next bend to the left, the trees on my side of the river disappear and I'm totally exposed to the wind. Lake Pontchartrain is up there somewhere and this wind must be coming off that lake which is really a salt water lagoon, an arm of the sea with tides that rise and fall. The winds that ruffle those waters must be powerful sea winds. I'm getting knocked around by sea breezes and I'm a hundred miles from the ocean.

The wind wants to slide me over to the opposite side. It's wanted to do that to me all day, to control me, to humble me maybe, and I don't want to go over there. I can't go over. It took me too long and too much effort to get here and if I end up on the other side, the wind will keep me pinned against the shore.

You crusty old river, crafty dog. You're tough, but I'm

tougher. I'm not going to let you beat me. Not after all this, all we've been through together. You've taught me too much. Now I'm going to show you just how much.

But the river persists and slides me out to the middle and I've had it. I give up completely. I'm just too tired and soon I find myself banging into the barges moored on this side of the river.

I can stay over here for awhile. It won't be so bad. I'll just go slow and take it easy. Why do I want to be on the other side anyway?

Because. That's why. Simply because.

And I find the fight again.

It's a struggle just to make it to the middle of the river. If I can stay there a little longer and keep going straight, the river will curve back toward me soon and I'll be closer to the left bank again.

The river wants no part of my plan and is trying to move me out. I'm staying, though, and I'm fighting and winning. Soon I can take a breather. The wind quits and must be doing the same, gearing up for another assault. I'll be ready for it.

In the meantime, the river itself is turning busy. Barges, tankers, tugboats. Here is where the barges from the north have brought the grain, where the tankers take on grain to be shipped around the world. One task done and now transferred, and another soon to begin.

Tankers lie at anchor on the edges of the channel. An oriental vessel is getting scrubbed and scraped and painted by crews of men hanging over the sides on scaffolding. They are waving at me and shouting down, but I don't speak Japanese or Chinese or whatever it is. I can't understand the words, but I can guess at what they're saying. I wave back.

Other ships, other crews are watching me. A tugboat roars by, its engine louder than anything else on this river. The engine dies and idles until the tug is well past me. The same courtesy as always. The captain waves. When he passes the waves he creates rock me back and forth violently, but even after he has gone, the waves don't quit. The river is ready for the next assault.

Oh, why can't you leave me alone? Why can't you make this easy for me? You could if you wanted to. You would if you really loved me. I thought we were friends.

I dig in hard but it's no use. Since I made that last bend, the river has changed. It's no longer a swirling crazy river flexing muscles and toying with me. It's the ocean and these are waves breaking six feet from top to bottom. Water sloshes into the canoe and the wind is shoving me all over the place. I'd be a fool to fight this. I'm going to let the river carry me wherever it wants me to go. To do otherwise would be suicide in this rough water.

Right away the river bangs me into the shallow water at the shore. And right away I see what a mistake I've made. I'm grinding on the rocks and stuck in the branches of a skinny sapling that bends every time I try to make a move. It's got hold of me and won't let go and I can't free myself even by going backwards. No matter what I do I'm stuck until I get out and get wet and free myself. But even then I can't make any forward progress because the wind and the river won't let me. I'm clawing and scraping for five yards at a time.

I break for lunch, although lunchtime has passed. Peanut butter sandwiches and a good dose of thinking.

What to do. At this rate I'll never reach New Orleans by dark. If I could find a phone I could phone someone just to let them know I won't arrive until tomorrow. That's what I ought to do.

A flock of white egrets looking strangely out of place among the industrial litter and development prances around on shore. In the sky gulls are hovering. I haven't seen any birds like these since I left Minneapolis, though why they should have been up there I don't know.

But then again, why am I here, stuck in this wind and unable to get free. Free like those birds.

That's it. Big waves or not, the threat of death even, I've got to go. I've got to make it. I've got to get back to the other side of the river or there's no chance of making New Orleans, and as long as I'm making some progress, however slight, there is a chance. It's only another nine or ten miles to the Huey Long Bridge. To hell with death.

And there death is, staring me right in the face, splashing its slime on me, trying to disgust me and make me quit. But not this time. Sink me and drown me, but you'll not scare me.

And then I know what it is, what it has been, what it will be forever. If I want to live, if I want to live free and soar high in search of the glory, I have to be ready to die.

So it's back out to the center of the river and I've got to keep the bow of the canoe into the crashing waves. If I let the wind or the river turn me, the waves will splosh over the side of the canoe, fill it up and sink me. But it's not easy. The shoulder. The wind. And all this water. I want to give up. I'm already out of breath. My back is soaked with sweat. And the canoe is leaping on the waves and crashing down like an ice-breaker.

I've got to time each leap into the air perfectly. And I do, going up over the crest of the waves and coming down not in a trough but on a flat strip of water. I'm lucky so far.

Too quickly I tire. I stop for just an instant, but that is an eternity. The water turns the canoe and the fight is no longer to cross the river but to get this canoe back into the waves. Water is flooding over the side. I can't worry about that now. I can't worry about anything. I just have to do it.

Come on now. Push it. Dig in it. Get mad at this damned river. Go go go! If you stop now you can just forget it. You're dead.

But somebody will see me. That big tanker there. They must be watching me now.

The shoulder burns. The waves are not letting up. But neither am I. I'm going to do it.

Seventy yards more. Fifty. Twenty.

Why am I being pushed upstream? What's going on here?

Can't think about that now. Just dig in and go. Stroke! Stroke! Stroke!

The last twenty yards are as hard as the first twenty. I'm not completely there until I'm beside the tanker from Panama and beyond it. And then I'm there. I did it. The tankers parked here block the river and the water is calm. I can rest. I can breathe. Oh God!

What an ordeal. What a triumph.

The chill of late afternoon is coming on, and now I'm alongside the New Orleans Airport. Planes flying overhead hang low in the sky, close enough to touch. I'm almost there, but I'll never get there before dark. And in this rough water I'd be a bigger fool if I stayed out after dark. It's time to quit.

And there it is. The Huey P. Long Bridge. To me it's the border of New Orleans. I'm close enough.

Once again this river that has aided me and guided me and

tested me every step of the way and all day today has fought me tooth and claw, this river sends me salvation. A funny looking aluminum boat, flat on top with a little compartment walled in for the driver, passes by. It sits high on the water and when I stick my hitchhiker's thumb out, I have to stick high in the air so this guy can see me. At first I'm only kidding, but when he cuts his engine and swings around, I figure what the hell. I crawl aboard and Steve Salles helps me pull up the canoe. Off we go, bouncing up and down on those big waves down to New Orleans.

33

I HATED ENDING the journey this way, but in another sense I didn't mind it so much at all. It was the voice of the river saying to me: "Eddy, you're all right. You've done a good thing and come a long way. But don't forget that it was me who brought you here, me who helped you, me who allowed you to do this thing. I'm stopping you here so you'll always know that."

I won't forget.

It was late when I arrived and the dusk was fading into darkness. The harbor police had been sent out to look for me and they sent me to the right landing spot. There was no cheering crowd, no celebration. It was cold out and I felt strange to be finally done with the river. No longer a riverman, and not yet fit for humans.

A cold beer, a bath, a Dominican cigar and dinner. I was still not human yet, still angry and wild. Something was not quite right, not completely finished. Not until I ordered two brandies in styrofoam cups that I could take along with me. I went down to the river, drank one, and poured the other one in.

CPSIA information can be obtained
at www.ICGtesting.com
Printed in the USA
LVHW030010280421
685732LV00007B/446

9 780805 059038